Gender and the English Revolution

In this fascinating and unique study, Ann Hughes examines how the experience of civil war in seventeenth-century England affected the roles of women and men in politics and society; and how conventional concepts of masculinity and femininity were called into question by the war and the trial and execution of an anointed king. Ann Hughes combines discussion of the activities of women in the religious and political upheavals of the revolution, with a pioneering analysis of how male political identities were fractured by civil war. Traditional parallels and analogies between marriage, the family and the state were shaken, and rival understandings of sexuality, manliness, effeminacy and womanliness were deployed in political debate.

In a historiography dominated by military or political approaches, *Gender and the English Revolution* reveals the importance of gender in understanding the events in England during the 1640s and 1650s. It will be an essential resource for anyone interested in women's history, feminism, gender or British history.

Ann Hughes is Professor of Early Modern History at Keele University; she has published widely on mid-seventeenth-century English history and is particularly interested in gender, print culture and religion. Her publications include *Gangraena and the Struggle for the English Revolution* (2004) and *The Causes of the English Civil War* (1998).

Gender and the English Revolution

Ann Hughes

Routledge
Taylor & Francis Group

LONDON AND NEW YORK

First published 2012
by Routledge
2 Park Square, Milton Park, Abingdon, Oxon OX14 4RN

Simultaneously published in the USA and Canada
by Routledge
711 Third Avenue, New York, NY 10017

Routledge is an imprint of the Taylor & Francis Group, an informa business

British Library Cataloguing in Publication Data
A catalogue record for this book is available from the British Library

Library of Congress Cataloging in Publication Data
Hughes, Ann, 1951-
Gender and the English revolution / Ann Hughes.
p. cm.
Includes index.
1. Women--Great Britain--Social conditions. 2. Sex role--Great Britain--
History--17th century. 3. Great Britain--History--Civil War, 1642-1649.
I. Title.
HQ1593.H84 2012
305.420941--dc22
2011008783

ISBN: 978-0-415-21490-2 (hbk)
ISBN: 978-0-415-21491-9 (pbk)
ISBN: 978-0-203-80470-4 (ebk)

Typeset in Bembo
by Taylor & Francis Books

Printed and bound in Great Britain by
TJ International Ltd, Padstow, Cornwall

Contents

Acknowledgements

This book was planned long ago, but many distractions delayed its completion. My most heartfelt thanks are to successive editors at Routledge, and especially to Eve Setch and Laura Mothersole, for patience and support over many years. I have learned a great deal from friends and colleagues working on gender in the early modern period. Anne Laurence was most generous with references and I would also like to thank Sue Wiseman, Rachel Weil, Mary Fissell and Mandy Capern. I could not have finished this book without successive periods of study leave granted by Keele University and I have benefited greatly from teaching a special subject on early modern women to Keele students since 1995. As always I would achieve nothing without Richard, Alice and David.

Ann Hughes
Lichfield
February 2011

1

INTRODUCTION

On 30 January 1649, Charles I, the anointed king of England, having been condemned 'in the behalf of the people of England' for treason and 'other high crimes', was publicly executed. The actions of women, and troubling disruptions of conventional assumptions about gender were alike prominent in this most traumatic drama of the English revolution. This was a political culture where all relationships of authority were seen as connected and mutually reinforcing. The 'Homily' on Disobedience, read often in parish churches, taught the conventional position: 'Take away kings, princes, rulers ... no man shall keep his wife, children or possessions in quietness'. Armed resistance of a monarch, followed by regicide, was thus bound to raise questions about family structures and the proper relationships between men and women. Charles's father, James VI of Scotland and I of England, had often stressed that kings were like gods, or fathers, or husbands, 'a King is truly Parens patriae, the politique father of his people', while Charles himself, in the *Eikon Basilike*, a revised version of his own meditations and justifications, issued in a startlingly effective propaganda move in the wake of the regicide, was presented both as a 'politic parent' to his people, and as a good husband and father to his queen and children. The republican poet John Milton retorted with an extensive exploration of the political damage done by 'effeminate and uxorious magistrates'.

Many women were political actors during the crisis. As the General Council of Officers of the Army debated what to do with the king in late December and early January 1648–49, one Elizabeth Poole, an Abingdon woman close to radical religious groups, was admitted to their debates. She urged them to draw back from regicide in conventional, gendered language: 'You never heard that a wife might put away her husband as he is the head of her body'. A wife might defend herself against a violent husband but she could not take his life; by analogy the parliament might defend itself against an aggressive monarch, and perhaps put him on trial, but neither regicide nor murder of a husband could be legitimate. Although Poole's message was ultimately unwelcome, it is remarkable that the army officers, the dominant political force in England following their forced purge of the Long Parliament, broke off their debates to listen to her. Poole was not the only woman to oppose the regicide; as is well known, Anne Fairfax, the formidable wife of the army's commander Sir Thomas, made two brave public interventions at the trial itself. When the roll-call of commissioners appointed to try the king was read out at the start of proceedings, and Fairfax was found to be absent, she cried out 'he has more wit than to be here'; then when the sentence was read out 'in the name of the people', she retorted, 'no, not a half, not a quarter of them! Oliver Cromwell is a traitor.'[1] A more obscure woman, Mary Pope, issued a brave pamphlet in January 1649 condemning outright the proceedings against the king.[2] Some radical parliamentarians also opposed the new commonwealth regime; the London democratic movement known as the Levellers argued that a mere 'change of bondage' had occurred with the king replaced by an authoritarian oligarchy. When the Leveller leaders were accused of treason and imprisoned in the Tower of London for publishing a tactless pamphlet called *Englands New Chains Discovered*, a petitioning campaign for their release mobilised many women who claimed 'an equal share and interest with men in the Commonwealth', and 'an interest in Christ, equal unto men' to justify their activism.[3]

Women petitioners and prophets, defiant women among royalists and parliamentarians alike feature in later chapters, along with quarrels over the proper manliness of the king and other political leaders, discussions of family structures and gendered political metaphors. These examples are introduced in order to indicate the range of this book, which is intended as a contribution to both women's history and the history of gender. Since the 1960s, women's history, encouraged by developments within the discipline such as a stress on family and social history, and also inspired by the modern women's movement, has immensely enriched historical scholarship. Women's history has been part of the women's movement's concern for identity, both personal and collective; it has underpinned quests to explain women's subordination, and has provided legitimation and inspiration. While 'present-centredness' can lead to some over-simplification, the general effects of feminist concerns have been overwhelmingly positive. Feminist commitment has ensured that most historians of women are self-conscious and reflective about their own purposes and methods. Certainly, the wealth of material now available on seventeenth-century women, from prophetesses to royalist conspirators, rioters to ministers' wives, would not have been discovered without the prompting of feminist politics. Historians of women have always aimed at the transformation of the discipline of history as a whole; a history of women which ignored their relationships with men would be trivial indeed. More recently, however, it has become common to stress a history of gender as an enterprise distinct from women's history. Where women's history focuses on the nature, roles and experiences of women in the past, gender history attempts to make gendered definitions of identity and gender hierarchies central elements in all historical problems and periods. This approach is summed up in the title of Joan Scott's classic article, 'Gender: a useful category of historical analysis'. Scott's work suggests three ways in which gendered analysis can illuminate our understanding of the English civil war. In the first place, relationships between men and women are a central aspect of social organisation in all periods, and a full understanding of any historical process involves consideration of how such relationships are involved in, or affected by, it. Second, gender is socially and culturally constructed, so that what it means to be a man or a woman changes over time, albeit in slow and complex fashion. In Joan Scott's phrase, gender is 'the multiple and contradictory meanings attributed to sexual difference', while, of course, how societies understand sexual difference itself varies.[4] It is important to discuss, then, how (if at all) a major political conflict affects gender identities. Finally, gendered contrasts are a major element in the cultural frameworks within which people understand their societies or imagine their potential development. Again, we need to ask how gendered understandings are implicated in political crisis; how political divisions might be seen in gendered terms, and how political crisis might transform these gendered cultural frameworks. In all three aspects of gender history, the specific experiences of men and understandings of manliness have to be considered as well as women and femaleness.

In some discussions women's history and gender history are seen as opposed. It has been argued that a focus on women risks assuming that women share a single identity and have a unitary female history; women's history may become a sort of ghetto with little effect on general historical scholarship. On the other hand, gender history has been accused of effacing women's agency, underplaying the degree to which women in the past, despite subordination and oppression, have been able to influence the conditions of their own existence and their broader societies. It can be seen as a way of restoring the masculinity of history, of using 'the category of "woman"' merely 'as a metaphor for the insecurities of a patriarchal order'.[5] This book, however, is based on the conviction that, in the words of a recent commentator, women's history and gender history are 'best seen as complementary, interacting and overlapping approaches'. It deliberately offers a broad and eclectic approach, inspired by the increasingly rich literature on both the experiences of women and the meanings of gender in early modern England produced by literary scholars as well as historians. It will thus explore the experiences and activities of women during the 1640s and 1650s, contrasting implications for male roles, and the ways in which notions of gender were invoked and transformed by these upheavals.[6] It seeks to demonstrate that attention to gender can enrich our understanding of much studied political developments. Until relatively recently political history 'has been the stronghold of resistance to the inclusion of material or even questions about women and gender'. The rich rewards of integrating both women's history and gender history with analysis of major political upheavals is amply shown in recent studies of the French revolution, many prompted by the bicentenary of 1989. These include accounts of how some women supported the revolution in Paris clubs, while others rallied to the outlawed Catholic church and many simply tried to survive; discussions of the emergence of feminist ideas and their complicated relationship with revolution; analyses of how the overthrow of monarchy and the proclamation of the ideals of 'liberty, equality and fraternity' affected relationships between men and men (as brothers) and between women and men, as well as family ideals and structures; and explorations of the importance of gendered imagery in constructing new forms of political association.[7] This book thus hopes to participate in the current welcome move in studies of the English revolution to overcome the unhelpful divisions between social, cultural and political history, and to draw on the inspiration of gendered studies of the French revolution to approach the English case in a comparably fruitful fashion.[8]

Most participants in the English revolution did not self-consciously hail its novelty, unlike the French revolutionaries who believed they were witnessing the birth of a new age, but many, like Oliver Cromwell, did feel that they lived in unprecedentedly exciting and disturbing times: 'the nation rent and torn in spirit and principle from one end to another ... family against family, husband against wife, parents against children, and nothing in the hearts of men but overturning, overturning, over-turning'.[9] The very label 'revolution' is controversial in current historiography, with the 'Great Rebellion', 'war in the three kingdoms', 'fall of the British monarchies' and the more neutral English civil war among the alternative designations.[10] One major initial justification for this book, however, is the conviction that it was a sub-stantial conflict in its practical impact and its ideological implications, amply meriting the label 'revolution'.[11] The English civil war, and still more the violent struggles in Ireland and Scotland with which I am only tangentially concerned, affected all of the population, if not directly through the fighting then through heavy taxation, plunder, free-quarter, trade disruption, troop movements and disease. At the battle of Marston Moor in June 1644, a royalist army of about 18,000 men was defeated by 28,000 parliamentarians, both English and Scottish. Thousands served in royalist and parlia-mentary armies, some in part-time attendance on garrisons near their homes, but many in dislocating service away from families in the marching armies on both sides. One historian has estimated that one in five English men fought in the civil war; this is probably too high, but an estimate of one in ten is entirely plausible.[12] It has been suggested that loss of life was as great, proportionately, in these wars, as in the first world war. Perhaps 85,000 people (almost all men) died in combat, and perhaps 127,000 men and women, soldiers and civilians, perished as an indirect result of war, especially through the infectious diseases spread by troop movements. There was plague in Oxford, Chester, Stafford and many other towns, while 'camp fever' came to Devon in 1644 with parliament's army and spread from the troops to this civilian population.[13] The figures are estimates, and open to debate, but all commentators now stress the scale of mobilisation. Any war blurs gender divisions in some ways, intensifies them in others. Insofar as the civil war involved minor skirmishes and sieges of local strongholds, distinctions between civilian and military, or between male and female experiences were relatively limited. Elite women often organised the defences of their family homes, while women as well as men helped fortify towns threatened by the enemy. But where men left home on military service, women were left behind to maintain their households in very difficult circumstances. Women's burdens continued if men returned crippled, or not at all.

Besides the direct military impact of the war, Englishmen and women faced significant economic and social dislocation. Taxation rose to unprecedented levels, perhaps to ten times pre-war rates, and affected more of the population than ever before. Whereas in the 1620s, direct national taxation was paid only by a very small minority of the landed classes, and then at easy rates, in the 1640s the weekly tax, parliament's main levy, fell on anyone with any property. And taxation was often the least of the burdens of civil war. Many villages lost almost as much in money or in kind, in informal or illegal exactions which fell on anyone with anything that could be requisitioned or stolen by force. Inhabitants were liable to forced labour to fortify local garrisons, to provision of compulsory board and lodgings for soldiers and their horses (the inappropriately named free-quarter) and to outright plunder by unruly troops.[14] Troop movements and a divided country led to disease, as we have seen, and to significant disruption of trading networks.

The heavy loss of life, along with the other burdens of war, contributed to a second crucial context within which gendered analysis must be placed – the rich variety of political and religious theorising and agitation that developed through the 1640s and 1650s. The increasingly radical demands and daring intellectual speculation that emerged on the parliament's side were driven by a passionate insistence that the sacrifices of ordinary people required some transformation in their lives rather than a simple 'change in bondage'. The soldiers who had fought for parliament were predictably inspired, declaring when they faced a humiliating disbandment once the war was over, that they 'were not a mere mercenary army, hired to serve any arbitrary power of a state, but called forth and conjured, by the several declarations of parliament, to the defence of our own and the people's just rights and liberties'. The conviction that the war was fought for 'just rights and liberties' and a bitter sense that they were to be cheated of any reward, shine through radical contributions to the famous debates on political settlement within the Council of the Army at Putney in October 1647. Captain Edward Sexby declared, 'We have engaged in this kingdom and ventured our lives, and it was all for this: to recover our birthrights and privileges as Englishmen; and by the arguments urged there are none', while Colonel Thomas Rainsborough demanded, 'I would fain know what the soldier has fought for all this while? He has fought to enslave himself, to give power to men of riches, men of estates, to make him a perpetual slave?'[15] Civilians too stressed that the sufferings of war called out for recompense. The 'Digger' or communist Gerrard Winstanley appealed to an Old Testament precedent he called 'David's law'; the principle established by David after his defeat of the Amalekites, that the spoil should be shared between those who had fought, and those who had stayed at home, not given to the fighters only as 'the wicked men and men of Belial' desired.[16] When Leveller women petitioned parliament for the release of the movement's leaders, they stressed the sacrifices of blood and treasure including 'plate, jewels, rings, bodkins' that demanded redress, while the prophetess, Anna Trapnel, justified her public interventions with reference to her contribution to the parliament's cause: 'I lived with my Mother till she died, which was about twenty years, then I kept house with the means my Mother left me, and paid taxes towards maintaining of the army then in the field; and this I did not grudgingly, but freely and willingly; I sold my plate and rings, and gave the money to the public use.'[17]

The army's claim that they had been 'called forth' by parliament's own declarations, the choice of petitioning as a mode of political action, the way in which a Stepney shipwright's daughter could identify with the 'public', all suggest the complexities and rich possibilities of parliamentarian allegiance in particular. Parliamentarianism was from the start a lively and contradictory amalgam of moderate and more distinctively zealous themes; the potential for reflection, disagreement, fragmentation and radicalisation within parliamentarianism facilitated much activism by women, as well as prompting difficult contentions over the proper manliness of politics, and urgent debate on the myriad ways in which gendered contrasts were implicated in relations of power and authority. At one level the civil war was a struggle among (largely male) elites, who differed over the ways in which monarchs should take advice from their leading subjects, and over the degree to which the English church was sufficiently reformed. Parliament thus denounced religious innovation and vowed to save a king 'seduced by evil counsellors'. But parliament from the early 1640s also claimed to be fighting the Lord's battles, for true religion against the malignant followers of Antichrist. Furthermore, parliament, or more precisely the House of Commons, presented itself as the 'representative of the people', and consciously, although not without anxiety and opposition, appealed to a broad range of the population to identify with its resistance to personal monarchy, mobilising them through a range of media and events – oaths and processions, petitions and declarations. In May 1641, all adult males were required to take the 'Protestation', an oath to:

> maintain and defend, as far as lawfully I may with my life, power and estate, the true reformed Protestant religion expressed in the doctrine of the Church of England, against all Popery and popish innovations … His Majesty's royal person and estate, as also the power and privilege of Parliaments, the lawful rights and liberties of the subjects, and every person that shall make this Protestation.

This was not an oath of loyalty to the king, but a collective commitment to defend English religion, liberties and government against popish plots. The order was widely enforced in 1641–42, and although only men were required to sign, women attended the rousing sermons that often accompanied the signing ceremonies, and women certainly signed the Solemn League and Covenant, a 1643 parliamentarian oath that marked the alliance with the Scots.[18] The people represented by the House of Commons, the people who were declared to be the source of all just power in January 1649, were rarely defined precisely but were usually, silently, assumed to be male householders; women, however, could not remain unaffected by such dramatic processes. The rich variety of recent work on women's activities during the 1640s will be deployed in this book, but it is also important not to take for granted the political participation of men. It was a commonplace of early modern politics that men, or more precisely men of some property, held public or political authority, but civil war fragmented this comfortable assumption. Which men were to hold office? Which side represented valid public authority? Consequently we will see in chapter three that civil war and unsettling political change prompted much heart-searching about proper characteristics of manliness.

Oath-taking required men and sometimes women to reflect on and then to take action on behalf of a cause; the outbreak of iconoclasm in the early 1640s when villagers destroyed altar rails and other relics of popery was in part inspired by the Protestation and the declarations of the parliament against idolatry. In the early 1640s, too, rival petitioning over religion – for and against the government of the church by bishops, or the use of the liturgy of the Book of Common Prayer – engaged many who would not normally expect to be consulted over national developments. Both sides in debates on the church sought to mobilise broad support, and of course where a polity was so divided, with two sides organising for war, both royalists and parliamentarians had perforce to appeal beyond elite opinion. Debate and broad engagement were not confined to those caught up in radical currents. Predictably, the trauma of civil war encouraged a desperate nostalgic yearning for normality, more often than a commitment to radical change. We shall see that royalist politics and ceremonial religion offered opportunities for female activism as much as parliamentarianism. Indeed the defeated royalist cause offered particular avenues for women's agency.

For both royalists and parliamentarians, cheap and timely printed declarations, resolutions, petitions, newsbooks, sermons and orders were a central means through which their cause was communicated and their opponents denounced. Print was central to the nature of the English revolution, vital to both sides, but most strikingly associated with the capacity for fragmentation and radicalisation on the parliament's side. In 1641 the parliament made momentous, contested decisions to print declarations such as the Protestation or the Grand Remonstrance, an extended polemical denunciation of Charles I's personal rule. Throughout the 1640s all 'parties' addressed 'the people' through printed orders, declarations, oaths and remonstrances. As parliamentarians divided and regrouped, they developed their positions in large part through reflection and dispute over the nature of the parliament's cause, as revealed in its printed records. The spread of literacy before 1640 made print central to the English revolution. Literacy was more characteristic of men, town-dwellers and the rich, than women, the poor or country people so that only (or as many) as 30% of men, and no more than 10% of women, could sign their names in the mid-seventeenth century. But many more people could read, and in any case non-readers might have access to printed material. In every village there were people who could read aloud to neighbours or discuss the information and issues that were found in pamphlets, books and broadsides. In London, a parliamentarian stronghold, most men and a bare majority of women could probably read. A well-documented London artisan, the woodturner Nehemiah Wallington, was exceptional in his mania for collecting printed material, but his technical skills were not so unusual. In the 1640s and 1650s Wallington quoted from or referred to more than 300 tracts in his own obsessive writings and reflections, complaining of the 'little pamphlets of weekly news about my home' as thieves of his money.[19] Print was still an exciting novelty in the 1640s; men and women were more literate than their parents (Wallington's mother was illiterate and relied on oral skills to recount to her children biblical stories or the travails of Protestant martyrs). Cheap pamphlets and 'small' books had recently become widely available; the production of devotional tracts, sensationalist news, romances, adventure stories and practical handbooks expanded significantly in the 1590s and the 1620s, but there was a decisive change in the early 1640s. In 1641 over 2,000 items were published and production virtually doubled the following year to more than 4,000; some six or seven times the average for each year in the 1630s. This was not based on an overall expansion in printing capacity, but on a momentous shift to smaller, topical works of one or two sheets (8–16 quarto pages): newsbooks, sermons, declarations and other pamphlet genres.[20] Women contributed to these genres, and were active as printers, booksellers and distributors of pamphlets, while gendered images, tensions and arguments were a prominent theme in this burgeoning print culture.[21]

It is artificial, but necessary for the sake of clarity, to separate religion from politics in seventeenth-century England. Religious and political cleavages were inextricably linked and mutually reinforcing in a culture where God was generally believed to be acting directly in this world, and where religious imperatives underlay all social and political relationships and obligations. Parliamentarians claimed to be fighting for true religion against popery and the innovations of Charles I's reign which they argued were returning the reformed English church to Catholicism. So one fundamental aim of the parliament was to complete, at long last, the reformation of the English church in a fully Protestant direction – in doctrine, worship, 'discipline' and government. This would entail a fully Calvinist theology centred on the predestination of a minority of elect saints to salvation, and by implication at least, the damnation of the majority; a purified liturgy focused on the preaching of the word and avoiding the set forms and rituals of the Book of Common Prayer; a 'discipline' that would effectively improve the religious understanding and behaviour of the population; and a church where the rule of bishops was at least qualified and preferably replaced by Presbyterian government, a more participatory structure organised through local, regional and national committees. In other words, parliament was expected to establish a reformed national church in place of the Episcopal Church and Common Prayer Book that became a potent rallying call for royalists. However, as in politics so in religion, throughout the 1640s and 1650s there was increasing fragmentation and radicalisation on the parliament's side. Opposition to a Presbyterian church as an over-rigid vehicle for clerical domination developed within parliament itself, and especially within the New Model Army. Groups emerged in London and elsewhere, campaigning for liberty of conscience outside the national church. It was argued that the true church in this world was not an inclusive national body of saints and sinners, saved and damned, but a voluntary gathered community of those, men and women, who felt they had a true faith. All sought guidance from the scriptures, but drew very diverse conclusions. Some separatist groups shunned any connection with a corrupt world; some denied the validity of infant baptism, arguing that only adults with a real assurance of God's calling should undergo the rite. Some modified or denied predestinarian ideas in favour of beliefs in freewill or general redemption; many questioned whether it was only learned men, with university degrees, who should be ministers, some denying the need for a separate 'caste' of clergy; some based their conduct on literalist interpretations of the Bible, while others stressed a more immediate mystical identification with Christ. Religious division had major implications for gender relations because a stress on the individual conscience and the imperative to obey God before human authority might lead women and children to dissent from the religious choices of husbands and fathers. Furthermore, in such times of dramatic upheaval, where armies clashed and kings were humbled, millenarian expectations were heightened. The notion grew that these might be the last days when normal worldly hierarchies were decisively reversed, foreshadowing the second coming of Christ to rule with his Saints. In such days, God's messages might be transmitted through women, the 'weaker vessels'. One suggestive text was Joel 2.28: 'I will pour out my spirit upon all flesh, and your sons and your daughters shall prophesy, your old men shall dream dreams, your young men shall see visions.' Many gathered congregations were dominated, numerically, by women – a matter that more orthodox commentators used to discredit them, and it is sectarian women who have attracted the most attention from scholars in recent years. But many women preserved in their households the liturgy of the Anglican church, while the wives of dispossessed royalist clergy were most determined in their resistance of Puritan reform; these women also have a part in our discussion.

The rich variety of speculation, mobilisation and engagement in the 1640s and 1650s is thus the second framework within which this focus on gender is located. The third context is the profound importance of gendered parallels or contrasts in early modern political thinking. The ways in which people understand the societies they live in, how they come to see authority as natural, inevitable and legitimate, are not always based on abstract general principles or rational assessments of individual or group interest. Less coherent, more emotionally telling assumptions are also crucial. The suggestive concept, 'political imaginary' suggests the force of gendered narratives and metaphors. In Diane Purkiss's terms, 'new visions of the world ... are not always created via political theory'; stories of 'family conflict, domestic drama', ideals of maleness and femaleness, understandings of the human body as exemplary or monstrous all contribute to this rich notion. Although notions of gender change over time, relations between men and women are usually seen as part of the natural order, and associating relations of obedience and power with gender or family structures is a most effective means by which a range of worldly hierarchies are made acceptable. One of the most basic ways through which people order and comprehend their worlds is through the construction of 'binary' contrasts, and the female/male contrast is the most enduring of all binaries, with the male pole almost always seen as the more valuable or positive. Consequently, as Joan Scott has insisted, 'gender is a primary way of signifying relations of power'. Accusations of effeminacy, sexual inadequacy or other 'unmanly' slurs were recurrent elements in the language of political debate and conflict, before and during the civil war.[22] The role of gendered parallels in early modern culture is especially important, for two main reasons. In the first place processes of consent and legitimation were particularly crucial where the technological capacity of governments to police their subjects and enforce their orders was much more limited than in modern states.[23] Second, arguments through analogy and comparison were characteristic of early modern political discussion, and two, interrelated, potent comparisons, between the family and political authority, or between the human body and politics, had obvious gender implications. The authority of kings was compared with that of fathers of families; the stability of families and kingdoms depended on fathers and kings being properly in control as the head directed a properly ordered body. How were such metaphors and comparisons disrupted when the king's head was struck from his physical body?

In this book, then, I will try to discuss all the ways in which the political upheavals of the mid-seventeenth century interacted with, were affected by and had an impact on gendered roles and relationships. The next chapter will explore the practical impact of war and political division on households, rich and poor alike; and the parts played by women in the war, in political mobilisations and in the complex religious divisions of the revolution. The third chapter on male political activities will discuss the contrasting modes of political manliness that emerged during civil war and revolution, and the ways in which particular visions of manhood were connected to claims for new political rights. Both this chapter and the next will be concerned with the variety of ways in which gendered contrasts and sexual slander – of cuckoldry, effeminacy or immorality – served to establish loyal political commitment in a divided polity. Chapter four also deals directly with gendered political imaginaries. How did civil war and regicide affect the parallels drawn between the body politic and the human body, or between the commonwealth and the household? Did political upheaval affect basic understandings of the body or the family? Did the non-monarchical regimes of the 1650s seek to transform sexual behaviour and gender relationships? Was there a distinct shift in how the contrasts and links between the 'public' and the 'private' were conceptualised, and what implications did this have for gender? But first we need to sketch out the multitude of ways in which gender was at the heart of political understandings and political practices before 1640.

Gender, power and politics in early modern England

The god-given and natural inferiority of women, and the necessity of their consequent subordination, were basic assumptions of early modern society. This stark statement is easy to make, but all attempts to elaborate it involve many qualifications and complications. This is not simply a matter of contrasts between theory and practice or ideals and reality. Prescriptive or normative writings on the proper rela-tionships between men and women and the correct ordering of family life – such as the guidance in the advice or conduct books produced particularly by Puritan clerics – were once seen as straightforward guides to experience, but they have been more recently contrasted with a more positive, or more complicated reality.[24] The ideals or 'norms' of male and female identity and family life promulgated in early modern England were themselves varied and often contradictory; this is itself evidence for the tensions and anxieties surrounding the social experience of gender. Furthermore, the dichotomy between ideals and reality is misleading, most obviously because those preaching or writing to promote particular visions of family life wanted and expected to influence how people actually behaved. And, second, dominant norms and prescriptions do influence behaviour through the expectations or limitations they impose.[25] In what follows, then, I try to evoke both the complexity of assumptions about gender and politics, and the even more complex ways in which these assumptions worked in practice.

The Christian religion – disseminated through preaching, Bible reading, catechising and conduct books – was fundamental to understandings of gender difference in early modern England. The precedence of Adam in the Creation story was a model for patriarchal order in families, kingdoms and the universe as a whole:

> Adam first priest, first prophet and first king,
> Great Lord of every vegetable thing.[26]

Eve was created by God for the use of Adam, out of his rib, and perhaps as an afterthought. Eve's disobedience in succumbing to temptation in the garden of Eden had prompted God to expel humanity from Paradise into a world of sin and sorrow. God had told Eve, 'I will greatly multiply thy sorrow and thy conception: in sorrow thou shalt bring forth children; and thy desire shall be to thy husband, and he shall rule over thee'. The Pauline teachings of the New Testament, an important resource in Reformation debates on the nature of the early church, were also deployed to explain and justify women's subjection:

> Let the woman learn in silence with all subjection.
> But I suffer not a woman to teach, nor to usurp authority over the man, but to be in silence.
> For Adam was first formed, then Eve.
> And Adam was not deceived, but the woman being deceived was in the transgression.[27]

The Table of Contents of one of the best known conduct books, William Gouge's *Domesticall Duties* (1622), drew on this text in listing women's responsibilities under 'Subjection, the general head of all wives duties'. A woman should be 'sober, meek, humble, honest' while the husband 'by virtue of his place carrieth the very image of Christ, even as Christ is head of the church'. Consequently a woman should acknowledge her husband to be her superior and respect him as such. Such a sweeping version of household authority did not go unchallenged, as Gouge himself admitted:

> I remember that when these domestical duties were first uttered out of the pulpit, much exception was taken against the application of a wives subjection to the restraining of her from disposing of the common goods of the family without, or against her husband's consent.

The women who objected would have been the wives of solid London citizens, used to a substantial role in their households' economies. So Gouge backtracked, acknowledging that a wife might retain control of property she had brought to the marriage and manage the household in her husband's absence. More broadly, like many writers of advice manuals, Gouge distinguished between the theoretical power of husbands and its exercise in practice. A good husband would not wish or need to enforce the 'uttermost extent', allowing his wife much leeway without surrendering his ultimate control.[28]

In any case, Gouge's deductions were not the only ones that could be drawn from the Christian scriptures. Some women founded more positive or critical versions of male–female relationships on the creation story. Rachel Speght in print, and Anne Southwell in manuscript verse that was preserved within family circles, noted the creation of Eve from man's side, rather than from the dust. Southwell denied that the succession from Adam granted an unchallenged authority to all men:

> All married men desire to have good wives
> But few give good example by their lives
> They are our head they would have us their heels
> This makes the good wife kick the good man reels
> When God brought Eve to Adam for a bride
> The text says she was taken from out mans side
> A symbol of that side, whose sacred blood
> Flowed for his spouse, the Church's saving good
> This is a mystery, perhaps too deep
> For blockish Adam that was fallen asleep.

Where Gouge argued that the parallel between the marital relationship, and Christ's headship of the Church justified female subjection, Speght and Southwell deduced the need for affection and respect. Speght, replying to a misogynist tract by Joseph Swetnam, quoted Ephesians 5.23: 'For he is her Head, as Christ is the head of the Church … this precedent passeth all other patterns, it requireth great benignity, and enjoyneth an extraordinary affection, For men must love their wives, even as Christ loved his Church'. Southwell elaborated similar arguments in verse:

> Christ is the Church's powerful head you know,
> Like title hath the man over his wife
> You find what love Christ to his spouse did show
> That gave for her his precious blood and life
> Would you command, then learn for to obey
> Would you be paid your debt, your own debt pay,
> ...
> Christ doth not curse, swear, rail at spouse's error
> But with soft voice, with humble words and tears
> And his good life, becomes her gracious mirror
> His love and patience with her weakness bears.[29]

The predominant message from Christian teachings was that women were the weaker sex, and medical ideas reinforced this view, holding that women were inferior by nature. Modern scholars have suggested that a 'one-sex model' held sway in early modern England based ultimately on Aristotle's contention that women were imperfect men: 'women are but men turned outside in' as popular wisdom had it.[30] The predominant medical theories held that the balance of fluids or 'humours' in the body determined a person's physical and temperamental characteristics. The four humours were linked to the four elements: blood (associated with air) was hot and wet; choler or yellow bile, the 'fire' humour, was hot and dry; melancholy or black bile (associated with the earth) was cold and dry; while phlegm (associated with water) was cold and wet.[31] Men tended to be dominated by hot and dry humours, which had forced their sexual organs outside the body, women by wet and cold humours which rendered them weaker, liable to lose control of their bodies, slippery, prone to deceit. In this framework, however, men's and women's bodies were not clearly distinct because both were part of 'a common corporeal economy' based on the humours. It has been argued that from the later seventeenth century there was a transformation to our more familiar two-sex model where male and female bodies were seen as distinct or incommensurable, but this linear account of change is too simple. As a number of scholars including Mary Fissell, Laura Gowing and Alexandra Shepard have stressed, there was a medical pluralism in early modern England, where a multitude of medical practitioners deployed a variety of medical theories. As Fissell explains, the narrative of bodily understandings is 'messier' than the shift from a one-sex to a two-sex model suggests. Classical and medieval teachings on male and female bodies were themselves complex while astrological or magical ideas, and a rich store of local or traditional teachings, were also important. There was a common contrast, for example, between a porous, leaky, unreliable female body, and a rational, self-contained male one, while the respective parts played by men and women in reproduction were widely debated. Were women or men the more lustful sex? Did both women and men produce seed essential to conception? Did the womb have a vital generative or nurturing role, or was it a simple receptacle for powerful male seed? As we shall see in chapter four, Mary Fissell argues that changing emphases in theories about sex and reproduction were closely connected with the political crisis of the 1640s and 1650s.[32] It remains probable that the early modern concern with properly gendered male and female behaviour, and the use of male–female contrasts for a variety of symbolic purposes, were particularly telling because medical or scientific knowledge did not reassure most early modern people that men and women were clearly distinct. The balance of humours in any individual body shifted with circumstance, with age, climate, individual excess. A woman might be too masculine, and, more worryingly, male identity might decline or dissolve into effeminacy.[33] A focus on the problems with female bodies should not lead us to believe that men's bodies were regarded as perfect. The dominance of hot and dry humours might cause disorder – an excessively angry or choleric man might be as disruptive as a milksop. Anxieties over the use of violence reveal the complex balancing acts surrounding male as well as female identities in early modern society. Violence, as Shepard explains, was a 'very powerful patriarchal resource' but it had to be deployed carefully. In some situations – in war, as a response to insult, to assert authority in household and community – male violence was approved. Yet excessive violence, whether brutal wife-beating, or disorderly street brawls, was frequently disciplined within communities or punished by courts of law, as threats to social and patriarchal order.[34]

The decrees of God and nature on gender order were thus more complex than they first appeared, and while early modern women clearly faced a number of inter-connected practical disabilities, it is important not to under-estimate either the capacity of women for effective and autonomous activity, or the barriers some men faced in establishing their authority. Nonetheless the educational, legal and economic structures and practices ensuring female subordination are clear. As the figures on literacy given above suggest, education of boys was the priority for all social groups. Elite women might be given a broad education by tutors at home, although a full classical or humanist training was more characteristic of the sixteenth than the seventeenth century, and the daughters of ministers seem to have been more highly educated than most girls. Poorer girls and boys might have a few years' training in a local, informal school at best. Advanced education in grammar schools including the Latin skills that were still an essential means of comprehending European culture, inns of court (for legal training) and universities was, of course, a male preserve.[35] Women's exclusion from formal training in rhetoric did not prevent some of them deploying effective persuasive strategies on occasion (notably in petitioning), and a silent woman was not much use to her family or community, but for the most part rhetorical training underscored the male monopoly of formal public office.[36] Women's property, their business activities and their waged work made a vital contribution to the financial strategies of households at all social levels, but their legal rights and economic capacities were inferior to those of men of parallel social status. Women worked in low-status, low-waged areas such as food preparation or general agricultural tasks; they rarely achieved a skilled work identity and their wages were usually a third to a half of men's. The latest detailed work suggests that their situation had declined relative to the century after the Black Death when labour was at a premium.[37] In most of England landed estates were passed to the eldest son through the practice of primogeniture; the very richest families might be able to grant land to younger sons also but daughters usually inherited land only in the absence of male heirs. More commonly they would be granted temporary receipts from family property to provide maintenance or marriage portions. Under the English common law, a woman was assumed to be under her father's and then her husband's control; under the concept of 'coverture', a man and wife were regarded as one person with the wife thus under the 'cover' of the husband.[38]

In theory, then, the property a woman brought to her marriage was her husband's, and she could not go to law on her own account. However, the common law was only one of the systems operative in England alongside customary law and the practices of the church and equity courts. As Amy Erickson has shown, customary provisions for widows, daughters and younger sons, as well as family settlements ratified under church court probate jurisdiction or enforced by equity courts, were more generous than the assumptions of primogeniture would imply. Women were energetic litigators in local church courts, especially in defence of their sexual reputations, and women, on their own or with others, made up a quarter of all plaintiffs in the main equity court of Chancery in the seventeenth century; women were much less likely than men to act alone however.[39] A much quoted guide to the legal status of women held, 'Women have no voice in Parliament, they make no laws, they consent to none, they abrogate none. All of them are understood either married or to be married and their desires subject to their husband.' But it continued, 'I know no remedy though some women can shift it well enough', and research on women's participation in the law underlines this qualification. A modern scholar makes a similarly nuanced judgement, outlining the legal discrimination against women, but also showing how many women 'refused to be passive victims of a restrictive legal system and became active plaintiffs or vociferous defendants in a clutch of different law courts'.[40] There were some very specific discriminations against women enshrined in legal convention – the (rare) murder of a husband by a wife was regarded as petty treason and treated more seriously than the considerably more common murder of a wife by a husband. No-one approved of husbands who murdered their wives but they did not transgress all the assumptions of good order as murderous wives' crimes did. Similarly, a sexual double standard operated whereby women's chastity was seen as more crucial and thus its absence treated more harshly than men's. The mother of an illegitimate child was usually whipped and sent to a House of Correction for a year; the father, if he could be identified, was required to provide for the child. Social as well as gender privileges were at work here, especially where the man was of higher status than the woman (as in the common situation where a master had seduced his servant). This is not to say that men's sexual reputation was unimportant, as we shall see, and it is clear that women's superior knowledge and experience of conception and pregnancy might offer some precarious room for manoeuvre, in accusing men of seduction.[41]

Of course, in early modern England, not all men were powerful and not all women were subordinate; a propertied woman, especially if she were a widow, had more freedom of action than a labouring man. The control of women by men was much more precarious than it first appeared, and manhood, itself, was a complex status or aspiration, riven by distinctions of age and social and marital status. The assumption that it was necessary to teach women to 'live under obedience' suggests some of the difficulties, while the contradictions in ideas about gender hierarchy, along with the many exceptions and qualifications in practice, also explain why the subordination of women was at the same time seen as natural and fundamental, yet a matter for lively debate and profound controversy. Debates about the nature of women were a staple of Renaissance culture; the most dynamic and wide-ranging polemic before the civil war was prompted by Joseph Swetnam's *The Arraignment of Lewd, Idle, Forward and Unconstant Women* in 1615. In lively, and perhaps not entirely serious, prose, Swetnam condemned women for their frivolity and excess: 'Eagles eat not men till they are dead but women devour them alive; for a woman will pick thy pocket and empty thy purse, laugh in thy face and cut thy throat. They are ungrateful, perjured, full of fraud, flouting and deceit, unconstant, waspish, toyish, light, sullen, proud, discourteous and cruel.' Swetnam's pamphlet was a great success, going through ten reprints in twenty years, and prompting a play, *Swetnam the Women Hater*, in 1620. Although he was an inveterate opponent of play-going, William Gouge was presumably citing this when he claimed in *Domesticall Duties* that he did not want to be considered a woman hater. Swetnam was clearly seeking responses which were duly produced. One was certainly by a woman, the young and godly Rachel Speght, while two others purported to be, although their pseudonyms invite skepticism, the 'Esther Sowernam' who produced *Ester hath hang'd Haman* claimed to be 'neither Maid, Wife, nor Widow, yet really all, and therefore experienced to defend all'. Other publishers took up the issues; in 1620 a pair of pamphlets *Hic Mulier* and *Haec Vir* attacked overly masculine women and effeminate men – as revealed especially in inappropriate and extravagant dress. One newsletter writer declared:

> Our pulpits ring continually of the insolence and impudence of women, and to help the matter forward, the players have likewise taken them to task, and so too the ballads and ballad singers, so that they can come nowhere but their ears tingle; and if all this will not serve, the king threatens to fall upon their husbands, parents or friends that have or should have power over them, and make them pay for it.

The controversy should perhaps not be taken too seriously; it was to some extent a profitable literary game, directed as much against the serious conduct book accounts of family life produced by men like Gouge as against actual women. The ubiquity of such debates in the early seventeenth century must nonetheless indicate widespread genuine anxieties about gender hierarchy and order, anxieties displayed in the royal court as well as in every English village.[42]

Early modern women were thus expected to be subordinate, but they were also necessary to the functioning of households and communities so that the men who were supposed to exercise authority over them were also dependent. Women were inferior but their unreliable bodies, their mysterious powers of reproduction, and their tendencies to sin and disobedience meant that they were always on the verge of escaping control; the authority of men was both essential and difficult to achieve. Gendered relations were expressed most characteristically in the household where husband and wife, children and servants lived together. The household was the crucial social institution and it is also central to any discussion of gender and politics. It was, as Gouge put it, 'a little Church and a little commonwealth'. Households are of course political units if we define politics broadly as concerned with the exercise of power and the distribution of resources; furthermore as commonwealths in miniature, it was predictable that the right ordering of households under the authority of rational men was seen as fundamental to general stability. Hence the parallel or close association between a father's authority in the family and the king's authority in the state was a prevalent (although not unchallenged) way of understanding politics. Finally the household was the arena in which men, or more precisely some men, demonstrated their self-mastery and their authority over others, and so displayed their fitness to serve in the wider polity: 'commonly we do not call any a yeoman till he be married, and have children, and as it were have some authority among his neighbours'.[43]

As well as conduct books like Gouge's, normative accounts of households were based on classical models, notably Xenophon's *Oeconomicus*, transmitted through humanist translations by Vives and others. Xenophon offered an account of a household where the woman had an important role under the instruction of an affectionate and conscientious husband. The other major classical source – Aristotle – offered a bleaker vision with a sharp division of labour based on his understanding of the natural characteristics of the sexes.[44] Classical teachings on the household were based on a distinction between the man who was out in the world, gaining a living, while his wife preserved the family substance. In Puritan conduct books and sermons, similarly, the ideal woman kept to her house. William Gouge praised Margaret Ducke in the sermon preached at her funeral for being 'so far from the gadding disposition of other talking, walking women, that she was as the most part as a snail, Domi-porta, within her own shell and family'; and the comparison to a snail as a compliment to women was repeated elsewhere.[45] But this is one sphere where the realities of social experience differed very greatly from the theory. The household was embedded in economic structures; for the propertied it was the basis for local influence and, in the case of aristocratic and royal households, of extensive political power; it was where children and apprentices were trained and religious ideas inculcated. It was not a private realm cut off from a public sphere. As already implied, the proper functioning of households depended on the active participation of competent women, educating children, supervising servants, providing medical care, and in many cases making a direct economic contribution through participation in farming or a business, marketing or waged work. It was generally agreed that a woman could exercise authority over young children, apprentices and servants, and in any case at any one time as many as a fifth of all households might be headed by women, mostly widows, but some independent single women.[46] Women could not operate as snails, although, as we shall see on many occasions in this book, prevailing assumptions that the world beyond the home was not for them rendered them vulnerable to criticism and contempt in 'public'.

For the vast majority of men and women, marriage and the establishing of an independent household was the crucial step to full adulthood and full participation in their community, as well as a means to a more comfortable life than was possible alone. A popular ballad offered an idealised but compelling narrative. Part One describes the indulgences of the single life:

> Much company I used to keep,
> Before I had a wife.
> The memory doth make me weep,
> For 'twas a wicked life:
> Such comfort now at home I find,
> From marriage to arise,
> I wish all men were in my mind,
> Then 'tis not otherwise.

Unthrifty games I now have left
As Tables, Cards and Dice,
That oft hath me of wealth bereft,
I curse no Ace, nor Sice: [six]
I do not now the cards bid burn,
That made my anger rise,
A wife hath caused me to turn,
Then 'tis not otherwise.

So civil I am grown of late
Since that I made my choice,
I hate each swearing swaggering mate,
Which makes me to rejoice:
The company I now do keep
Are honest men and wise,
That not with drink, but sense do sleep,
Then 'tis not otherwise.

In Part Two the mature pleasures of marriage and the respect of neighbours are presented:

Against I from my labour come,
My wife provides me meat:
When I was single none at home,
Found I, or what to eat.
At sight of me she lays the cloth,
And then for meat she hies,
Which makes me to forget all sloth,
Then 'tis not otherwise …

When that she doth in child-bed lie,
The neighbours in their love,
Will with her sit, and pleasantly
To mirth they do her move:
By christening of my little lad
I did in credit rise:
All this by my good wife I had,
Then 'tis not otherwise …

All bachelors I wish you wed,
If merry you would live,
A single man is oft misled,
And seldom doth he thrive:
I lived before, but better now,
My joy and wealth arise,

To live well I have shown you how,
Then 'tis not otherwise.[47]

Marriage is here a means by which men became civilised and respected members of society; to be a full member of a craft guild or a trading company, or to hold office in parish or ward a man had to be a householder, which usually entailed marriage. We need to stress again the mutual dependence of men and women and the potential tensions this might involve. Wives were also necessary partners in a joint enterprise which was as essential for men's standing in the world as it was for women's. Early modern England is sometimes described, in short-hand form, as a patriarchal society, where patriarchy is understood as the domination of men over women. Patriarchy should, however, be defined more specifically as a form of power based on father-hood, giving some men authority over children, younger and poorer men, as well as over women. It was by no means a system that benefited all men. As Alexandra Shepard has elucidated in a path-breaking study, 'patriarchal authority itself was contradictory and inherently problematic'. We have touched on the ambiguities surrounding male exercise of violence, but there were similar problems with the affection and love that, as all agreed, husbands owed to wives. Love, in moderation, was a good thing, but it could become an over-fondness that disempowered, or unmanned. Male authority in the household was not automatic, hence the combi-nation of 'both assurance and anxiety' in advice literature.[48] But many men at many times did not exercise even this precarious patriarchal authority as heads of households. This dominant version of manhood was usually deemed an 'estate', a privilege to be acquired, not automatically given. It was accepted, sometimes grudgingly, that young men might exhibit different styles of manliness, as in the more aggressive, improvident, collective behaviour described in the first half of ''Tis Not Otherwise'; the young would settle down in time. But processes of social change through the sixteenth and seventeenth centuries made the achievement of 'self-sufficient mastery' through householder status very problematic for many poorer men. As many as a fifth of people in the seventeenth century never married, and so never attained the full adult mem-bership of the community or polity that marriage brought. Such men spent their lives in dependency on others, lacking the self-sufficiency seen as crucial to manhood. Similarly, an increasing dependence on wage labour in this period (for married men as well as bachelors) sabotaged the autonomy also seen as central to dominant notions of manliness. The political implications of these issues will be discussed in chapter three.[49]

The men and women who wielded influence in their communities, then, were marked out by age, marital status and economic self-sufficiency. Local office as con-stables, churchwardens, jurors or overseers of the poor was the preserve of respectable male householders, although where office depended on property – as in villages where the duty to serve as a constable moved yearly from house to house – widows or other female householders might be eligible to serve. However, they appointed male deputies who actually undertook the office.[50] This is not to say that women wielded no influence. Female expertise was frequently called upon by courts and other public authorities to examine the bodies of other women for signs of pregnancy or the marks of witchcraft, or to interrogate pregnant single women over the paternity of their children. In small, face-to-face communities, reputation was crucial; what your neighbours thought and said about you established your place in society. The evidence of 'defamation' or slander cases in church and secular courts suggests that women's standing depended primarily on their sexual honour, although it was also important that they were regarded as prudent, conscientious housewives. Men also went to court to defend themselves against accusations of sexual immorality, but they were as likely to be affronted by slurs of cuckoldry, of deception by adulterous wives, and by insults that impugned their social standing (such as rogue or knave). Shepard suggests therefore that men policed social boundaries, women moral ones.[51]

Women were the moral arbiters of their communities through the power of their tongues. Social historians and anthropologists have rescued female speech from the condescending label of 'gossip'. Talking about disruptive behaviour, discussing your neighbours' misdeeds and passing judgement on them, are vital means by which social norms are defined and community identity constructed. In their everyday lives at church, at work and in the market place or on the special but frequent occasions of female sociability, notably in the rituals surrounding childbirth (as suggested in the ballad), women met to discuss and moderate female, and, more riskily, male behaviour. The limits of female influence have been carefully established. Laura Gowing's work on defamation, for example, shows that a common insult reaching the church courts was 'thou art my husband's whore'; women argued with other women, rather than criticising husbands directly. Gossip within female networks might be a defence against marital violence or sexual harassment if it prompted community disapproval and disciplinary action. As ever, status and wealth interacted with gender to make this a very risky business. In Nantwich, Cheshire in the 1620s, a poor married servant, Margaret Knowsley, complained to mostly female neighbours of sexual harassment and attempted rape by her employer, the local Puritan minister Stephen Jerome. In the subsequent legal proceedings, almost sixty local conversations about the matter were called in evidence. Two of these discussions only involved men; twenty-nine took place among women only; while twenty-eight were mixed. The predominantly female mutterings of complaint ultimately exploded into open and divisive scandal in the town, and prompted the harsh punishment – not of Jerome, whose sexual reputation was very dubious – but of Knowsley, who was convicted of slander and sowing sedition.[52]

Female speech might be very powerful, but it was also very dangerous. Assumptions that respectable women kept silent in public could produce community hostility and sometimes recourse to the law. A woman regarded as overly aggressive in the use of her tongue might well be defined as a scold, and punished in humiliating physical ways, including ducking in ponds, and the wearing of a bridle that prevented speech. Even witchcraft, often rightly seen as an exceptional crime, can be connected to the informal influence women wielded in their communities through speech. Vulnerable, troubled women, who lacked any material influence in their communities, might develop an imagined, but temporarily effective power to overawe their neighbours with curses and spells. Ultimately this risked terrible punishment. The stress on women's silence in the normative literature was thus all the greater because female speech was actually a powerful and disruptive presence in communities.[53]

Women might act in more overt fashion; they were often prominent in food riots, particularly when harvest failure and high prices sabotaged their capacity to provide for their families. In 1629, Ann Carter was executed for her part in struggles to prevent scarce grain being exported from Essex to continental Europe.[54] Rich and complex attitudes and expectations surrounded the notion of the disorderly woman. On the one hand, disorder in households concerned neighbours because of the practical impact disharmony had on the wider community and also because of the belief that order in the microcosm of the household was crucial to order in the macrocosm of the kingdom or commonwealth. Male behaviour – excessive violence against wives, servants or children – was subject to discipline, as we have seen, but women's conduct was more commonly blamed. Women who were unfaithful, or who ruled the roost at home, were the main targets of the ritual community punishments known as ridings or 'skimmingtons'. The name probably comes from the ladle used by women working in west-country dairying. A skimmington was a ritual shaming of a household, intended to bring it to its senses – to restore appropriate patriarchal authority. It involved discordant 'rough' music, insulting and aggressive processions through a village, humiliating representations of the offending couple and, often, men dressed as women to indicate the transgressions of gender order.[55] Cross-dressing was a potent symbol of unruliness in general. Enclosure riots and other popular protests often involved men dressed as women; the forest riots of the 1630s in the West Country were led by an aptly named 'Lady Skimmington'. It was popularly held that women were 'lawless'; that they could escape punishment in the courts because, under coverture, they were not fully legal persons. As the example of Ann Carter starkly shows, this was not true, and it was perhaps not believed to be true. Rather, the notion of the disorderly woman, often indicated by a cross-dressing male, was a broader imaginative or cultural resource that made gender inversion a sign of a world awry. Most often, as with the village ridings, gender inversion served as a means of bringing life back to normal, but as with other forms of 'carnivalesque' disruption, it might also help people to imagine how their worlds might be different. At a local and particular level, as well as in the high political world, gender was a way of signifying power.[56]

At a higher social and political level, too, the parallels between the household and the broader polity meant that criticism might focus on a man's sexual conduct or family life as much as on his conduct of 'public' affairs. The Earl of Huntingdon, in early seventeenth-century advice to his son, explained that 'public governments' in the commonwealth were to be compared to 'private government' of the household. He also produced elaborate regulations for the well-ordering of his household: 'My house doth nearest resemble the government in public office which men of my rank are very often called unto ... if I fail in the lesser, than the which there can be no greater dishonour, it followeth of necessity I shall never be capable of the greater.'[57] A man's own sexual behaviour might be attacked, but so might his inability to control an unfaithful wife, which indicated a broader incapacity in the exercise of authority. Thus gentlemen resorted to the courts to defend themselves against insults relating to their 'private' as well as to their public or official lives. In the early seventeenth century, a Leicestershire gentleman, Sir Thomas Beaumont, brought a Star Chamber suit against his neighbour Sir Henry Hastings (a kinsman of Huntingdon) and a former servant, John Coleman, alleging they had spread scandal about the sexual behaviour of his daughters and wife, including the allegation that Lady Beaumont had committed adultery with Coleman, a slur that breached social as well as sexual norms. Further similarities with village conflicts are that the women from gentry and aristocratic families who gave evidence in a largely male dispute were particularly knowledgeable about the alleged sexual misdeeds. We should not exaggerate the practical political results of such disputes: parliament's first military commander in the civil war, the Earl of Essex, had probably suffered more public sexual humiliation than any other prominent man, and there is no evidence that a wife's adultery ever led to a man's dismissal from office although it may have undermined his authority. There are some, rare, examples of men being dismissed for their own adultery; one Christopher Smith was dismissed as an Alderman of Stratford upon Avon in 1625 because he 'hath much wronged this company and disgraced them ... by his heinous offence in committing adultery'. Even here, however, the corporation was also affronted that Smith had refused to be censured by their local ecclesiastical court, 'thereby weakening our liberties of this borough'.[58]

Besides the conflicts that arose from sexual transgression, actual or alleged, a more general language of male and female contrast, and of sexual insult, might be found at all social levels, in disputes that might in origin have nothing to do with sex or gender. Because male superiority was seen as god-given and natural, for a man or a cause to be smeared as womanish was an effective insult, while masculine bravery or rationality might be applied as compliments to exceptional women or approved stances. Religious polemic, particularly directed against Catholics, 'papists' as Protestants deemed them, deployed gendered religious language where the true church, the bride of Christ, opposed the great whore headed by the papal Antichrist.[59] In religious and political conflict accusations of whoredom, cuckoldry, effeminacy and sodomy were useful weapons. Both gendered language and attention to household authority connected local societies to the workings of politics and religion at the highest level.

At this level, the 'political imaginary' of the family or household worked to legitimate personal monarchy: the household 'at once illustrated and legitimated the benefits of monarchy', in the words of Cynthia Herrup. King James VI and I, an intellectually sophisticated monarch, frequently emphasised the natural or inevitable authority of monarchy through comparisons with the body, or the family.[60] He presented these arguments in his treatise on kingship, *The Trew Law of Free Monarchies* (1598), and delivered a particularly elaborate version in a parliamentary speech of 1610:

> There be three principal similitudes that illustrate the state of monarchy: one taken out of the word of God, and the two other out of the grounds of policy and philosophy. In the scriptures, kings are called Gods, and so their power after a certain relation compared to the divine power. Kings are also compared to fathers of families: for a King is truly *Parens patriae*, the politic father of his

people. And lastly, Kings are compared to the head of this microcosm of the body of man.

James spelled out the implications: 'A father may dispose of his inheritance to his children at his pleasure … make them beggars or rich at his pleasure … so may the king deal with his subjects.' Rebellion by subjects was as unthinkable as a child's challenge to a father.[61] Parallels with fatherhood did not simply imply monarchical government but also suggested that monarchy could not be limited by external authorities. Sir Robert Filmer (1588–1653) provided the most developed patriarchal theories of politics, arguing for absolutist rather than limited or constitutional monarchy. His most famous treatise, *Patriarcha*, was not published until 1680, as an intervention in the Exclusion Crisis, but it had been circulating in manuscript since the 1620s, and similar arguments were contained in tracts published in the late 1640s. Filmer attacked the 'resistance' theorists of the sixteenth century who argued that power came from the people and could thus be recalled by them. He justified absolute power on the basis of the Book of Genesis, arguing that what was there described was a developed polity, not just a family.[62] In *Patriarcha* he claimed, 'If we compare the natural duties of a father with those of a king we find them to be all one, without any difference at all but only in the latitude or extent of them.'[63]

In *The Anarchy of a Limited or Mixed Monarchy*, first published in 1648 during anti-parliamentarian agitation in his native county of Kent, Filmer retorted to advocates of constitutional monarchy:

> Neither Eve nor her children could either limit Adam's power or join others with him in the government. And what was given unto Adam, was given in his person to his posterity. This paternal power continued monarchical to the Flood, and after the Flood to the confusion of Babel … It was God's ordinance, that supremacy should be unlimited to Adam, and as large as all the acts of his will; and, as in him, so in all others that have supreme power, as appears by the judgment and speech of the people to Joshua.[64]

Patriarchal arguments for monarchical authority were never uncontested, and were shaken during the revolution, as we shall see, but Filmer remained relevant into the 1680s.

A different but equally telling political metaphor for monarchy was the comparison with marriage. The marital relationship, ideally, was both hierarchical and harmonious, suggesting that contented subjects owed an unproblematic obedience to benevolent monarchs. It was another metaphor mobilised (along with his other favourite arguments) by James VI and I, especially in connection with his attempt to unite his two kingdoms of England and Scotland:

> I am the husband, and all the whole Isle is my lawful wife; I am the head, and it is my body; I am the shepherd, and it is my flock: I hope therefore no man will be so unreasonable as to think that I that am a Christian King under the

Gospel, should be a polygamist and husband to two wives; that I being the head, should have a divided and monstrous body; or that being the shepherd to so fair a flock (whose fold hath no wall to hedge it but the four seas) should have my flock parted in two.[65]

In England, as Anne McLaren has explained, marriage was particularly indissoluble, unlike in other Protestant states where divorce was possible. James's speech thus caused intense alarm among elites in both nations who feared a perpetual union.[66] Throughout the 1630s, through drama, poetry and portraits, the actual marriage of Charles I to his French Catholic queen was presented as a model for harmony and good government in the kingdom as a whole. French cultural influences – Catholic and neo-platonic – stressed the importance of love and female influence as a force for civility. Charles and Henrietta Maria's growing brood of healthy children seemed evidence of divine favour as well as human happiness. After the trauma of Buckingham's assassination in 1628, Henrietta Maria and Charles became increasingly close but the queen's political influence in the 1630s seems to have been limited. She tried to moderate Charles's pro-Spanish foreign policy in the interests of her French allies, but with little success. It was only with the crisis of Charles's monarchy from 1638 that she came into her own, and played an important role in the 1640s, as we will see in chapter two. In the 1640s, Charles's uxoriousness was attacked by parliamentarians as emasculating, and the Catholicism of his wife attracted criticism from the start, but in the 1630s there was also a welcome contrast between his decorous household and his father's more dissolute and scandal-ridden court.[67]

Early modern monarchy was a hybrid form of rule in which public authority was derived from personal inheritance, and in which power was exercised partly through institutional means (councils and parliaments) but partly through personal relationships whereby proximity and friendship with the monarch might bring more influence than holding high office. These personal ties were played out within the court, which was, among other things, a household, where women as well as men might be important channels of patronage and influence. Lucy Harrington Russell, for example, protected advanced Protestant preachers, and supported an active Protestant foreign policy.[68] Dancing in court masques, which unlike the public drama allowed female performance, could be a means of demonstrating patronage connections or advancing particular political stances. Alliances were mostly founded on family connections defined by men's priorities, but there were opportunities for female solidarity. Anne Clifford, daughter of the Earl of Cumberland, and successively Countess of Dorset and Countess of Montgomery and Pembroke, was to an extent the victim of the patriarchal priorities of her class when her male uncle and cousin received the bulk of the land, as well as the title passed down from her father; and her husbands were unsympathetic to her obstinate pursuit of her rights. Nonetheless she found support from other women within the royal household. In January 1617, she:

went presently after dinner to the queen, to the drawing Chamber, where my Lady Derby told the queen how my business stood, and that I was to go to the king; so she promised me she would do all the good in it she could … the queen gave me warning not to trust my matters absolutely to the king, lest he should deceive me.

Clifford was emboldened into refusing to agree to a settlement promoted by James: 'I beseeched his Majesty to pardon me for that I would never part with Westmoreland while I lived upon any condition whatsoever.'[69]

The maintenance of gender order and propriety within the royal household was an important register of royal authority; so the widespread discussions of the scandals in James's court were not mere voyeurism but serious political concerns. The most serious court scandal before the civil war was the Essex Divorce and the associated Overbury murder; it was minutely dissected within a lively news culture (of cheap print and circulated manuscripts) and provoked many verse libels not so different in style from those that might comment on village scandals.[70] It concerned Frances Howard, the daughter of Thomas, Earl of Suffolk, who was very unhappily married to Robert Devereux, third Earl of Essex, and fell in love with James's Scottish favourite, Robert Carr. This connection was of course very attractive for political reasons to the Howard 'faction'. The stumbling block was Essex but in May 1613 a 'Nullity Commission' was established to assess the truth of Frances Howard's claims that her marriage had never been consummated because of Essex's impotence; she was still a virgin and the marriage should be annulled. After months of salacious testimony, her account was confirmed and she married Carr, by now Earl of Somerset, in December 1613. By this time, another barrier to their marriage had disappeared in mysterious circumstances. Carr's close companion, Sir Thomas Overbury, who knew all their secrets, had fallen foul of factional conflict at court and had been confined to the Tower in April 1613, dying there in September. Suspicions festered that he had been murdered because he knew too much about the Carr–Howard liaison, and the rise of a new favourite, George Villiers (later Duke of Buckingham), gave the Somersets' opponents their opportunity. In October 1615 they were arrested, and in May 1616 convicted of Overbury's murder and condemned to death, although the ultimate penalty was respited by James. The Earl and Countess did spend six years in the Tower, but their subordinates were unluckier; Overbury's keeper in the Tower and Howard's confidante and servant, Anne Turner, were executed in November 1615.[71] Around the impotence of Essex and the poisoning of Overbury hung the 'scent of maleficent witchcraft', and a widely circulated libel denounced Frances Howard as 'a wife, a witch, a murderer and a whore'. As in disorderly households in English villages, women were given most of the blame for sexual transgressions with Howard, and particularly Turner, receiving most of the opprobrium. Turner's aggressively luxurious dress as well as her devilish skill with poison were thoroughly rehearsed in print and manuscript; she was blamed, among other crimes, for the masculine fashions satirised in *Hic Mulier*. To some extent James's authority was damaged by his failure to maintain patriarchal order in his own court and he was criticised particularly for backing the nullity proceedings, but the subsequent trial of the Somersets and their accomplices enabled him also to represent justice and divine vengeance.[72]

Rude poems attended the dominance of Buckingham, James's Ganymede, who managed the transition to become Charles's favourite also, but Buckingham's faults were financial corruption and military incompetence as much as sexual transgression.[73] Charles I consciously cleaned up the court, regarding its good order as the foundation of sound government. In an early proclamation attacking the 'much disorder in and about' his father's household, he declared he had 'resolved the reformation thereof' and established more restrained and more formal procedures, influenced by the stately self-enclosed Spanish court, rather than the more relaxed French styles preferred by his father.[74] After early estrangements over the influence of Henrietta Maria's French attendants, Charles's own marriage was loving and exemplary and he encouraged chaste, affectionate marriages between his closest advisors. He would not confirm the appointment of James, Marquis of Hamilton as Master of the Horse until the Marquis promised to consummate his troubled marriage to a niece of his dead favourite Buckingham.[75] In the major aristocratic scandal of his reign, which combined popery, sexual deviation and horrifying social disorder, when the Catholic Earl of Castlehaven was condemned for abetting his servant in the sodomitical rape of his own wife, Charles I acted as the agent of justice and order.[76] Despite Puritan hostility to the papist queen, the verses circulated about Charles's court before the civil war were gentler than those surrounding the Howard scandal, and directed against courtiers rather than the king and the queen.

> See what a love there is between
> The King and his endeared Queen,
> And all their subjects love and care
> Is fixed on this royal pair …
> But did their Majesties select
> Deserving persons to affect
> Like to themselves and not love all
> The court would soon be very small[77]

Parallels between familial and monarchical power was a profound way of conceptualising and justifying political authority, but it was not the only way. This is not to say that rival groups of people were committed to one approach or the other, but that formally contradictory frameworks were combined within the same person's world view.

Although the theories that drew parallels between fatherly and monarchical power are commonly described as 'patriarchal', the fifth commandment, which was often cited in support of authority in general, exhorted people to 'Honour thy father *and thy mother*', and women did have influence in households, as we have seen. In a system of hereditary monarchy the contingencies of inheritance might and did, in the sixteenth century, produce the troubling anomaly of female rule within a culture that stressed female inferiority. The reaction of the radical Protestant John Knox, although untypically extreme, suggests the terrors aroused by female rule through vivid evocations of the monstrous body. His targets were Mary Tudor and Mary of Guise in Scotland, whose Catholicism compounded the outrage offered by their sex:

For who would not judge that body to be a monster where there was no head eminent among the rest, but that the eyes were in the hands, the tongue and mouth beneath in the belly and the ears in the feet? Men, I say, should not only pronounce this body to be a monster, but assuredly they might conclude that such a body could not long endure. And no less monstrous is the body of that commonwealth where a woman beareth empire.[78]

A more measured comment from the humanist Sir Thomas Smith, an Elizabethan public servant, reveals a different set of assumptions about politics. Rather than drawing a parallel with the family or the household, Smith's comment is based on the view that politics, normally, is a distinct and a male preserve.

We do reject women, as those whom nature hath made to keep house, and to nourish their family and children, and not to meddle with matters abroad, nor to bear office in a city or commonwealth, no more than children and infants: except it be in such cases as the authority is annexed to the blood and progeny, as the crown, a duchy, or an earldom … For the right and honour of the blood, and the quietness and surety of the realm is more to be considered, than either the tender age … or the sex not accustomed (otherwise) to intermeddle with public affairs, being by common intendment understood, that such personages never do lack the counsel of such grave and discreet men as be able to supply all other defects.[79]

Neither social nor political historians have emphasised sufficiently the fact that early modern politics was seen, ideally, as a male activity, or highlighted the importance of politics to male identity. Most political history has taken for granted the maleness of high politics, or indeed the largely male monopoly of local office exercised by humbler householders. On the other hand, the pioneering social history of masculinity, for good reasons, has focused on male sexuality and male household authority. Formal political or public office was, however, a central element in male identity – at least for independent male householders.[80] Along with ideas of lineage, service in the public good was an essential element in elite honour codes, and local office was a crucial marker of a parish 'notable'. In one recent formulation: 'Classical definitions of active political virtue and its discharge in the service of the general welfare were very often mixed and merged with Puritan or hot Protestant notions of the godly magistrate to form an ideal of the Commonwealthsman, or Patriot.'[81] This was a male ideal, founded on a rhetorical contrast between the public and the private, a contrast that was of long standing, being indeed one of the most 'influential, structuring myths of western culture'.[82] It derived ultimately from classical, Aristotelian ideas which stressed that men were dominant in both the household and the state. As the public world of the state was, ideally, a male world, it was among male office holders in early modern England that contrasts between public and private realms had most relevance, as the remarks of the Earl of Huntingdon suggest.[83] Anne McLaren has argued effectively that the anxieties aroused by female rule under Elizabeth led to a greater emphasis on the maleness of the broader polity, that, ideally, constrained the powers of personal, female monarchy.[84] Smith's 'grave and discreet men' were the active citizens in whom true political virtue and authority lay. As the example of Elizabeth I herself suggested, women were not completely excluded from humanist learning, but in the main a classical training for public life was confined to men who had access to grammar schools and universities.

In contrast to a classically derived understanding of a distinctly male political realm of politics, patriarchal thinkers who connected the family and the state had more muddled views on women and political power. James VI, the son of a female ruler and the successor of another, did not deduce from his family analogies the logical conclusion that women might exercise authority effectively. In advice to his son, James emphasised:

> keep specially three rules with your wife: first suffer her never to meddle with the politic government of the commonweal, but hold her at the oeconomic rule of the household, and yet all to be subject to your direction; keep carefully good and chaste company about her, for women are the frailest sex; and be never both angry at once.[85]

Filmer, on the other hand, had a more relaxed view of female rule. He acknowledged that 'of late years Queen Mary and Queen Elizabeth, by reason of their sex, being not so fit for public assemblies' had not exercised all the powers of the monarchy (in attending parliament for example), but there is no sense here that their authority was illegitimate, and there was praise for queens in his more private or domestic writings: 'war and government of kingdoms have been often times well handled by women, Queen Dido may be example for all, or rather Queen Elizabeth in whose time these things flourished'.[86] Filmer's own wife was a formidable woman, given wide authority over household affairs.[87]

The preceding discussion on the nature of the household or of monarchy affords ample evidence that there was no clear-cut division, in theory or in practice, between public and private spheres; the boundaries between the two are always permeable, 'ragged' and contested.[88] A public–private split does not apply in a society in which households have public functions and are subject to all kinds of public scrutiny. Neither was there any necessarily evaluative distinction between public and private, with one preferred to the other. Private most commonly and simply meant the individual or the particular as opposed to the common or collective; it might have more pejorative connotations with the selfish or the conspiratorial, and these certainly became more prominent in civil war disputes, but they were by no means always present. Often private and public were part of a continuum, as with private prayer and public worship, where both were valued and necessary.[89] The rhetoric of public and private did not describe reality, but it had some impact on it. The assumption that public life was a male preserve did not prevent women being active in their communities or having political influence, as we have seen, but it did mean that their activities were 'freighted with suspicion' and made them vulnerable to criticism and punishment as

Margaret Knowsley and Frances Howard learned to their cost. The boundaries between public and private were supposed to exist, as again Huntingdon's advice to his son suggests, and contrasts between them were an important theme in political discussions. Civil war dilemmas intensified anxiety about what was public, and what was properly private, as we shall see in chapter four. Notions of public service and the public good – often valorised as male – were subject to intense scrutiny and debate, contrasted with a feminised notion of privacy.

Ensuing chapters will demonstrate that the upheavals of the 1640s provoked all kinds of 'gender trouble' – in Mary Fissell's suggestive phrase (taken from the pioneering work of Judith Butler). The connections are not always straightforward. Assumptions about the nature of men and women, or the proper relationships between them, are much more impervious to short-term change than arguments about the powers of parliament and kings, or even ideas about the nature of the true church. Equally, it is important to note that concepts of radicalism, moderation or conservatism – already very slippery terms that always need to be contextualised – do not map easily from politics to attitudes to women, or the family. The 'Digger' Gerrard Winstanley is an obvious but instructive example, as imperturbably patriarchal as he was socially egalitarian. In his utopian tract, *The Law of Freedom in a Platform*, 'true Common-wealths freedom lie[s] in the free enjoyment of the earth', but political power was derived from 'Adam … the first governor or officer in the earth, because he was the first father', and political authority was based on a kind of natural patriarchy where older men had control over younger men, and all women and children.[90] Finally, of course, neither women nor men form a homogeneous category, and in this book their experiences during the English revolution are structured by age, social and marital status, religious and political allegiance, and sometimes by national or ethnic identity, as well as by gender.

2

WOMEN AND WAR

Some contexts

The narrow royalist victory in October 1642 at Kineton fight (better known to us as the battle of Edgehill) introduced the English population to the full horrors and burdens of civil war. *Strange Newes from Warwicke*, an aptly titled pamphlet, claimed that a wounded parliamentarian Corporal, Jeremiah Stone, came to the Anchor Inn in the town, and gave the hostess 'a bag of money' pillaged from the bodies of the dead to keep until he recovered. Two weeks later, Stone asked for it back, but 'it grieved his unhonest hostess to part from so great a prize'. She and her husband debated 'what shift they might find to detain the said bag of money', and so they denied ever receiving the bag and dared the soldier to challenge them: 'Mark the boldness of the wicked woman.' A bitter quarrel ensued in which 'the soldier bold in war, at home thought in a good quarrel, he might be more bolder, and ... stoutly drew his sword'. At this the landlord called in his neighbours and had the soldier carried off to gaol. So far – so predictable; the tensions arising from the presence of strangers quartered in private houses or inns can be illustrated from a variety of sources. Such intrusions bore particularly on women. At the end of the war, again in Warwick, a servant Elizabeth Wright had been struck by a soldier quartered in her household in a quarrel over lost keys, and her husband subsequently prosecuted the soldier for assault. This case came before the Indemnity Committee which sought to preserve parliament's agents from prosecution for actions undertaken in the course of the war.[1] The real if understated hostility of a maid-servant in the house of the Warwickshire royalist Thomas Holte is revealed in complaints against the parliament's own soldiers. The men had taken all the plate, jewels, furniture and household goods, leaving 'nothing left standing. Tables and stools and chairs were all broken into pieces.'[2] The Buckinghamshire gentlewoman, Mary Verney, returning from exile in France was outraged at the insolence of the troops in 1647: 'I protest not which way we shall live if the country may always quarter soldiers ... I vow I had much rather live with bread and water than to be amongst them.'[3]

But a bizarre turn in the 1642 narrative suggests that deeper anxieties were provoked by household intrusions. As Jeremiah Stone languished in prison, the devil came and promised to deliver him from his trials in exchange, of course, for his soul. The soldier refused but the devil generously offered to help such a just cause, and agreed to act as the soldier's attorney. In that capacity, dressed in a red cap with a white feather, the devil urged the court to search the inn for the bag of money. The host with 'many blasphemous oaths' denied any knowledge of it: 'I would, quoth he, the Devil would fetch me away now presently body and soul before you all, if I swear unjustly.' Consequently the 'devilish lawyer, or this lawful devil, left the court and snatched his body according to the vengeance he desired'; the host was carried 'visibly over the market place' leaving nothing behind in the court but 'a terrible stink'.[4] The devil was very busy in Warwickshire in the winter of 1642. The same pamphlet also offered 'Strange and Miraculous News' from Coventry, again combining dark fantasy with commonplace personal dilemmas. The young Richard Bond was betrothed to Anne Kirk, a mercer's daughter. When he was called to the war, she vowed and protested she would never marry any man but him: 'this on her knees did swear in private', calling God to witness that if she married another, 'the same day she was married, that the Devil might fetch her'. Richard did survive Kineton fight and was given leave to visit his betrothed, only to discover her about to marry another. He accused her of breaking her vow and when she retorted, 'where is your witness?', two sinister men in black carried her off, never to be seen again, only her clothes left behind.[5]

Amanda Capern has commented that 'the study of women during the English Civil War encompasses the fake woman as much as the real woman', and indeed the two are difficult to disentangle. Propagandist reflections and self-serving interpretations provided frameworks within which female experiences were understood, and helped to structure the ways in which conceptions of gender were inflected by civil war upheavals.[6]

Printed reports — sometimes banal, sometimes fantastic — are a central element in the gendered imaginings prompted by the intimate traumas of war. Such stories were not to be taken seriously, then or now, but the mixture of providential judgements and satanic punishments, with precise detail of person and place, and all-too-plausible dangers, hints at real anxieties. Civil war did bring armed aggressive strangers into people's households with particular difficulties for mistresses and maidservants alike; absence, death and disability did sabotage or delay marriage plans. Wives and widows were left to shoulder increased burdens and sometimes to take up new opportunities. Women were often particularly vulnerable to aggressive soldiers in an increasingly militarised society, but they usually managed to defend their households, preserve family fortunes and protect their children, despite the absence of men. Few women were merely passive victims, although it was sometimes politic for them to present themselves as such. Many participated actively in the military events of the 1640s, as spies and intermediaries, maintaining garrisons, enduring sieges and following field armies. They wielded political influence for both parliament and the king, most often through their families but also in broader initiatives, and, above all, they influenced, took advantage of and opposed the dramatic religious fragmentation that was one of the most significant aspects of the English revolution.

Summing up the complex variety of women's experiences during the civil war requires a difficult balance between synthesis and anecdote, as well as the interweaving of reality and representation, especially in print. What are we to make, for example, of the circumstances that led the royalist newspaper *Mercurius Aulicus* to print what it claimed was an intercepted letter from a London wife to her husband on campaign with the London-trained bands? She complained at his continued absence, now that all his married neighbours had returned home: 'I am like never to see thee more … either I am afraid the Cavaliers will kill thee, or death will deprive thee of me, being full of grief for you.' Dark hints were dropped that desperation might drive her to infidelity: 'I am afraid if you do not come home, I shall much dishonour God, more than you can honour him, therefore if I do miscarry, you shall answer for it. Pity me for God's sake and come home.' The parliamentarian response denied the story but implied that Susan was a real person: 'He jeers us with an intercepted letter of Mistress Susan's the citizen's wife, complaining for her husband's company, which she utterly disavows.' It was clearly important to counteract this story for a London readership.[7] It is not fictitious, as the devil's temptation of Anne Kirk presumably was, but both printed accounts drew on and reinforced troubling anticipations about the impact of male absence on marital fidelity, given men's assumptions about female inconstancy.

Civil war had a profound impact on the fundamental social and economic structures within which women lived. The poet Anne Bradstreet had no illusions about the impact of war:

> My plundred towns, my houses' devastation,
> My weeping virgins and my young men slain;
> My wealthy trading fall'n, my dearth of grain.[8]

Demographic trends are difficult to connect precisely to the war, not least because religious divisions affected parish record-keeping, but the marked rise in the English population during the sixteenth century, already slowing down in the early seventeenth century, went into reverse after 1650. The population went from about five and a quarter million mid-century to just over five in 1701; English fertility, in Keith Wrightson's words, was at its 'early modern nadir' between 1650 and 1675, 10% lower in the 1650s than in the 1630s.[9] The high death rates among English men in the 1640s must be important here, and another factor may be lower rates of marriage in the 1650s when the republican state imposed a civil marriage law which seems to have been widely resented. Economic conditions in the late 1640s and early 1650s prevented many young people from establishing independent households.[10] A civil war where troops quartered in civilian households, and the ability of men serving in rival armies to escape responsibilities, might well have led to increased illegitimacy rates but patchy sources have prevented systematic analysis. Anecdotal evidence reinforces common-sense assumptions, as in the royalist garrison of Chepstow where four bastard children were baptised in February 1645 including Anne, the daughter of 'a soldier, his fathers name unknown who was quartered in the widow Lewis house in Welsh street'.[11]

Heavy taxation everywhere, with free-quarter and unauthorised but endemic plunder in regions affected by war, caused widespread economic hardship. In an 'antemasque' or prologue to a 'pastoral' written by Jane Cavendish and her sister Elizabeth, Lady Brackley, a group of 'rustics' are portrayed lamenting the losses of civil war:

> I have lost my milk cow
> And I have lost my sow
> And for my corn I cannot keep
> Neither can I my pretty sheep
> And I have lost four dozen of eggs
> My pigs are gone and all their heads
> Come let us wish for health
> For we can have no wealth.[12]

Royalist landowners, rich and poor, had their property confiscated. Most had their lands restored on the payment of a 'composition' fine, but the property of the most prominent or irreconcilable royalists was put up for sale. Women bore the brunt of these difficulties, and often played a major role in mitigating them. They might well have been better placed to lobby parliamentarian authorities, precisely because they were less likely to be seen as political agents. There is scattered evidence that entrepreneurial women managed to carry on their activities despite the depredations of war. In June 1644 Margery Davies, a haberdasher of Dudley (a royalist stronghold), was granted a warrant to sell her hats in parliamentarian Coventry as she had done before the war, provided she 'carries nothing with her prejudicial to the state, or doth not convey any of her hats to the enemy's garrisons'.[13] Like many other widows and spinsters, Joyce Jefferies, a Herefordshire gentlewoman who had never married, provided a vital function as a money lender in her neighbourhood and beyond. She suffered threats and plunder from soldiers, even after she bribed them to stay away, and had to leave her home in the royalist garrison of Hereford, but she was still lending substantial sums throughout the war years, albeit the money lent (some £333 pa) was but 60% of 1630s levels. Jefferies continued to charge relatively modest rates of interest, with particularly generous terms for widows and other women among her creditors.[14] England experienced a very serious economic depression in the aftermath of war as military dislocation of farming and internal trade was compounded by a series of poor harvests. In 1647–50 conditions for the labouring poor, male and female, were worse than at any other period in the seventeenth century.[15] Moreover, war had also disrupted local administration, particularly affecting the poor relief. In Warwickshire, Quarter sessions, the main organ of county government, could not meet between summer 1642 and autumn 1645, and in the later 1640s the Justices of the Peace spent much time sorting out poor relief arrears and disputes.[16] The broad outlines of this are clear, but the specific personal impact on women can only be illustrated in a rather piecemeal way through cases such as that of Margaret Doughty, an elderly Warwickshire widow. Doughty petitioned the justices at Easter 1646 that she was owed more than 30 shillings from a pension of 6d per week formerly granted her by the parish of Salford Priors. Two years later, aged seventy-six, she complained again that the arrears had not been paid and that she 'is now by reason of the present scarcity in extreme want', but eighteen months later she was still owed money.[17]

Women's domestic responsibilities meant they were badly affected by the excise, a novel tax on consumption, particularly on food and drink, paid at the point of sale. Women were prominent in its evasion and resistance. In Scarborough they avoided the tax on fish (and normal market regulations) by selling their wares directly on the shore; while the role of women in anti-excise protests in Derby is vividly demonstrated in the complaints of the excise official. The excise had been collected for some days without any trouble until market day, 23 May 1645, when 'two women of the town went up and down the town beating drums and making proclamation ... that such of the town as were not willing to pay excise should join with them and they would beat the commissioners out of town'. When the excisemen asked the Mayor for help he retorted that they 'brought the trouble on themselves' and when they consulted Thomas Gell, the Recorder of the town and Lieutenant Colonel of the local regiment, he:

> answered that one of the women that did beat up the drums was wife to a soldier, and they durst not meddle with them for fear of putting the soldiers into a mutiny. The mayor said he would not believe there were any such women beating drums but presently one of them did beat her drum upon the market cross before the Mayor's window.

On this day the women were pacified when the Mayor promised that the excise would not be imposed without further instructions from parliament, but six weeks later the excise officials tried again, meeting with similar defiance by local women, and similarly unhelpful responses from local authorities. The women again 'beat up the drum and made proclamation to the same purpose as before' and when the excisemen asked Sir John Gell, the parliamentary commander, for assistance, 'he refused either to punish those women or secure the women but told us that he did not use to meddle with women unless they were handsome'.[18]

The women of Derby benefitted from their connections to the troops, and from the undisguised sympathy of local notables equally hostile to a novel and unpopular tax. Relationships between women and soldiers were rarely so harmonious. The most terrible way in which men's power over women is exercised in wartime is through sexual assault and rape, too often a means through which armed men terrorise women and humiliate their male enemies. Sensationalist print early in the war again drew on these dark threats. According to *A Blazing Starre Seene in the West* 'Master Ralph

Ashley, a debauched Cavalier, attempted to ravish a young Virgin' of Totnes, or as he had it a 'Round-headed-whore'. But 'as he was going to lay hands of her entranced body' he was providentially struck by a comet streaming fire, and 'so he died raving and blaspheming to the terror and amazement of the beholders'.[19] The notion that debauched Cavaliers threatened parliamentarian virgins had wide currency. A troop of horse recruited in Norwich with money donated by women became known as the 'Maiden troop'; according to the London Puritan wood-turner Nehemiah Wallington, an inveterate collector of news and portents, the women were inspired by the need to protect their virtue from royalist assault.[20] The use of sensationalised stories of abuse to smear and discredit opponents, and the difficulties women face in bringing accusations against men, are familiar in many periods. So when the royalist Bruno Ryves described parliamentarian troops assaulting young maidservants in Northamptonshire, or the parliamentarian Sir Samuel Luke denounced the debaucheries of Sir Marmaduke Langdale's soldiers – apparently running amok in the same county later in the war – we should not take the accounts at face value; but equally we may be sceptical about the conclusions to be drawn from Ian Gentles's remarks that no accusations of rape were made against Cromwell's or Fairfax's soldiers. It is impossible to assess how common rape was given patchy and often dubious evidence. Rape was forbidden and condemned in all the articles of war issued to discipline soldiers' behaviour although royalist articles were less concerned than parliament's with broader sexual offences. Parliamentary soldiers were punished for fornication, although the harshest punishments were imposed on the 'whores' who were whipped and expelled from the army.[21] There is no record of official punishments for rape in royalist armies, but when it was, rarely, discovered in parliament's forces, the penalties were severe. None of the thirty-seven soldiers court-martialled in Sir William Waller's army between April and December 1644 had been accused of rape but six of the fifty-five cases in Cromwell's army in Scotland in 1651–52 were sexual crimes, with one case of rape, and five of fornication.[22] The worst single atrocities against women were committed by parliamentarian soldiers, as we shall see below.

Women at war

Women's opportunities for active involvement in the war, and male responses to their actions, were structured by underlying assumptions about women's nature and appropriate roles. Women were less likely to be regarded as independent political actors; their relative immunity from suspicion enabled them to travel or lobby in arenas barred to more exposed men. Women were crucial to the running of households, subordinate to their husbands to be sure, but expected to step in if men were absent or dead; male absence was, of course, a commonplace during civil war. Honourable men were expected to show proper respect to women and children, so consequently accusations of brutality were common currency in propaganda wars between royalists and parliamentarians. On the other hand, women whose behaviour, ethnicity or religious background transgressed conventional assumptions about feminine behaviour were treated without mercy.

Women made good spies and intermediaries, in war and peace. In Cornwall as the royalist cause faltered, Philippa Coryton, the daughter of a leading royalist, went in disguise to Plymouth to coordinate the surrender of her father and other royalists to Sir Thomas Fairfax.[23] In the midst of the war, the parliamentary commander Sir William Brereton sent a woman to royalist Worcester to gather intelligence; she survived a grilling from the royalist leader Prince Maurice and reported back. As he besieged royalist Chester, however, Brereton was himself a victim of female invisibility when the Mayor's maid passed unchallenged through his lines to gain information for the beleaguered city. Sometimes we know a little more about the women involved: Elizabeth Alkin, also known as 'Parliament Joan', spied for the armies of the Earl of Essex, Sir William Waller and Sir Thomas Fairfax; after the war she turned to news-book production.[24] Women detected in spying or conspiracy were not protected by their sex. Parliamentary troops captured a suspected royalist spy as the king's army approached London after the battle of Edgehill. They threw her in the river, as if ducking a scold or investigating witchcraft (a true witch would not sink). At this the woman confessed that 'she had been often of late in the city of London to hear how and which way the people stood affected both to the king and parliament'. In further dark echoes of witchcraft she claimed that Rupert had been killed in the battle: 'an Irish commander very like him, led the army in his shape and arms'. Finally she was killed and thrown back in the river. A threatening woman, discovered out of her normal place, was thus associated with other alarming women, scolds, or even more ominously, witches.[25]

The most notorious royalist female conspirator was Katherine Stuart, Lady Aubigny, who in May 1643 was granted leave by parliament to travel to London to deal with the affairs of her husband who had been killed at Edgehill. She came instead with a royal commission to raise supporters in the city, prompting an abortive plot named after one of its likely leaders, the poet Edmund Waller. The enterprise was betrayed and Aubigny was imprisoned for several months. Her notoriety as a plotter was magnified in parliamentarian propaganda: in a print of 1646 a full-length portrait of Aubigny clutching the offensive commission was surrounded by smaller pictures of the Earl of Strafford, Prince Rupert, Montrose, Newcastle, Laud and other prominent royalists. Released and undaunted, Aubigny maintained her taste for intrigue. With her second husband, the Scots peer Viscount Newburgh, she made an attempt – again abortive – to rescue Charles I as he was brought to London for his trial and execution. In exile she worked hard as an intermediary between quarrelling Scots and English royalists and on her premature death she was remembered affec-tionately by Edward Hyde: 'a woman of a very great wit, and most trusted and conversant in those intrigues which at that time could be best managed and carried on by ladies'. Thus for friends as well as foes she had become a type of the busy public woman, so that in discussing her own decision to leave political matters entirely to her husband, another royalist Lady Ann Fanshawe drew an explicit contrast with Aubigny.[26]

Civil war garrisons were often family affairs, and women played a full part in organising the defences of besieged towns. Female assertiveness unsettled gendered relationships, and became a target for enemy contempt. The Yorkshire gentleman Sir Hugh Cholmley had at first sided with the parliament, but then declared for the king at Scarborough: 'My wife was at London ... and they being nettled that they had lost a person so useful to them as I had been, did not only pass some sharp votes in the House of Commons against my person, but plundered my wife of her coach horses and used coarsely, yet she procured a pass to come to me, and with her my two girls, the elder then not above eight years of age.' Lady Elizabeth remained with Sir Hugh at Scarborough during his command, both before and during the siege, despite many hardships, catching a 'touch of scurvy' and 'being forced to lie in a little cabin on the ground' after the keep was destroyed by parliamentarian guns.[27] In Hereford, according to a parliamentarian account, a 'papist commander' was almost surprised by the enemy 'being with his wife and some other popish friends, met at his inn ... with dalliance, drinking and music and sport'. Many royalists came and went from Hereford to Gloucester when it was besieged by parliament, 'some with wives, children and servants, all to get plunder'.[28] In isolated but well-known instances, romance blossomed amid the fighting. When a royalist garrison was established in Hillesden House, the seat of Sir Alexander Denton in Buckinghamshire, his daughter Margaret fell in love with the commander of the garrison, while his sister Susan married a parliamentary captain who had escorted the women and children from the captured house.[29]

In parliamentarian Hull, Bristol and Coventry, as in royalist Hereford, Worcester or Chester, women helped to strengthen the city defences and sometimes joined in the fighting. At Bristol Dorothy Hazzard who, as we shall see, founded a gathered church, was prominent in work to fortify the city and went to London after the city's surrender to denounce as a coward the commander who had delivered up the city.[30] As the king's army marched towards London after Edgehill, women and girls marched two by two with baskets of earth and stones to bolster the city fortifications.[31] In Portsmouth, according to a derisive royalist account Lady Norton, mother of the parliamentarian commander, was in effect 'Governess for the present ... for the Committee dare do nothing without her advice'. She oversaw the construction of the defences, and, as in London, thirty or forty women and maids came each day to work with the men digging the trenches.[32] At Chester one witness claimed the women were most staunch:

> By this time, our women are all on fire, striving through a gallant emulation to outdo our men and will make good our yielding walls or lose their lives. Seven are shot and three slain, yet they scorn to leave their undertaking and thus they continue for 10 days space. Our ladies likewise like so many exemplary goddesses create a matchless forwardness in the meantime by their dirty undertakings.[33]

Soldiers' wives helped with civil war administration, as they organised households in normal times. The wives of some of the captains serving in Coventry garrison kept the troops' account while the wife of Humphrey Mackworth, a Shropshire gentleman in the service of the Earl of Denbigh in the west Midlands, received fifty muskets on his behalf for the supply of his new regiment in January 1644.[34] Sir William Brereton's wife lent £50 for the pay of her husband's forces besieging Lichfield in 1646; it was rapidly repaid.[35] Forcible women might attract envious notice. The wife of parliament's commander at Warwick Castle, Colonel John Bridges, was, according to hostile (parliamentarian) witnesses, put in charge of the 'pillage cellar' and persuaded her husband to embezzle many of the king's goods which had been seized at Edgehill. Bridges's wife and daughter carried out plate and jewels 'by the apronful' and wore 'very rich jewels ... beyond the usual wearing of such persons'. It was alleged that the Colonel himself had confessed that any misdeeds had been 'his Mistress's doings who was a very hard woman'.[36] The accusations may be doubted, but the ways in which normal family life and conventional household responsibilities might be reconstructed in abnormal militarised contexts is revealed.

Some aristocratic women took responsibility for their households in the most extreme circumstances. At Corfe Castle in Dorset, Lady Mary Bankes, with five men and the help of her daughters and servants, repelled initial parliamentarian assaults in the summer of 1643, giving time for a garrison to be established which held out until the later stages of the war. Parliament then had the castle demolished. Lady Brilliana Harley was left behind at Brampton Bryan, an isolated parliamentarian stronghold in royalist Herefordshire, while her husband Sir Robert was a busy Puritan MP at Westminster, and her sons fought in parliament's armies. She longed to escape to London, but her duty to her husband, and to the cause, kept her there: 'It is the Lord's cause we have stood for', she insisted to her son. Harley clients and tenants were threatened from the summer of 1642 and the house was besieged from July to September 1643. Lady Brilliana refused demands for her surrender, appealing variously to parliamentarian principles that 'the laws and liberties of this kingdom' protected her property, and to her obedience as a wife: 'my dear husband hath entrusted me with his house and children, and therefore I cannot dispose of his house but according to his pleasure'. She encouraged the garrison 'with such a masculine bravery, both for religion, resolution, wisdom and warlike policy, that her equal I never yet saw', and died a few weeks after the siege was raised.[37] As the grand-daughter of William the Silent, Charlotte de la Tremouille, Countess of Derby, was part of an international Calvinist elite, but she was a staunch royalist, and held off parliamentarian troops besieging her family home at Lathom House in Lancashire from February to May 1644: 'though a woman and a stranger, divorced from her friends, and robbed of her state, she was ready to receive their utmost violence, trusting in God both for her protection and deliverance'. Her determination helped sustain a royalist presence in a hostile area, as Prince Rupert marched north. When offered terms allowing her to depart with her household and the garrison in March she declared she preferred to 'preserve her liberty by arms than to buy a peace with slavery', and although she claimed to be acting on her husband's behalf, he was clearly more cautious. In March he had written to Fairfax asking for 'an honourable and free passage' for his family so that 'hardy soldiers' would continue the defence.[38]

Masculine bravery by women on your own side might be praised but royalist and parliamentarian propaganda alike debated the nature and meaning of women's activism, while parliamentarians in particular used women (and children) as pawns in ritualised blackmail during bitter sieges. The royalist newsbook *Mercurius Aulicus* denounced the zeal of the women of parliamentarian Coventry, who allegedly forced the parliamentary committee there to rescind an order allowing a royalist clergyman to leave the city with a 'small remnant of his goods'. 'Mistress Mayoress and some nine more blue stomachers so full of zeal that they dare commit anything' argued that 'they were as much concerned in the cause as their husbands, or any other man'. After much argument 'among whom Master Robert Phipps that learned physician (knowing the insolency of a domineering wife at home) grew most hot ... against the women', the 'good wives' got their way.[39] But the contempt of *Mercurius Aulicus* for assertive parliamentarian women did not extend to noble and royalist 'ladies': the women shut up in Eccleshall Castle, Staffordshire, and under siege from Sir William Brereton, were apparently:

> Ladies and Gentlewomen of that county, who purposely came thither to secure themselves in these times of danger. And that they are so gallantly resolved upon it, that though their victuals do begin to fail already, they mean to stand upon their guard and defend the place (in hope his Majesty will relieve them ere it come to that).

The contrast and the moral was drawn: 'Which as it shows the bravery and courage of those noble ladies, so is it an infallible argument of the incivility and rudeness of those barbarous rebels who regard neither sex nor quality of persons.'[40]

Although parliament's forces at Corfe or Lathom wished to encourage the surrender of embarrassingly determined noble ladies, as the war went on they were increasingly unwilling to allow women to leave embattled garrisons. Fairfax, as commander of the New Model Army, refused safe passage to women, hoping the extra mouths to feed would force a prompt surrender. Thus when Lady Grace Campion, the heavily pregnant wife of the commander of the garrison at Boarstall House near Oxford, tried to leave she was summarily sent back by Fairfax.[41] A grotesque charade was enacted during the dying weeks of the royalist garrison in Lichfield cathedral close. Parliamentarians held the city itself, and Sir William Brereton, commander of the besiegers, feared that the wives remaining in the city were giving intelligence to their husbands in the close, 'to the great prejudice' of his forces. In May 1646 he ordered that the wives of royalists in the close 'be speedily sent into the Close to their husbands' and 'if any shall dare to come out of the Close the officers of that guard are required to shoot them or otherwise to be answerable for the same'. In an enterprising example of 'psychological warfare', Brereton composed a letter, purporting to be from the 'women of Lichfield' to Lady Dyott, the wife of a prominent Staffordshire royalist, who had joined her husband in the close. Brereton had a good grasp of the idiom of feminine appeal. He asked Dyott 'to take a view of our many miseries being deprived of the fruition of our husbands, the only stay and comfort of us and of our families, and having our houses filled with soldiers, our land untilled that should maintain our families for future, and paying weekly so great assessments … as we are not able long to subsist'. 'We acknowledge it presumption in us to take upon us to give counsel to men of wisdom in times of war, though that wise and valiant warrior of God the prophet David both accepted and pronounced a blessing upon a woman's counsel at such a time.' This ventriloquised 'women's' counsel urged surrender, pointing out the many garrisons already surrendered, the hopeless plight of Oxford and Worcester, and that 'the King himself for safety has cast himself upon the affection of his native people'.

'Sundry poor women and their innocent children', as the royalist commanders termed them, were forced from the city, but denied entrance to the close by the royalists, and in their own words, were 'enforced to lodge in the cold open air and there likely to perish for want of relief'. Eight local women, not simply pawns in a male drama, petitioned Brereton for mercy, only to meet with a contemptuous reply:

> If your husbands and their commanders-in-chief will not show you mercy, you must know the greatest mercy that can be showed from us is to execute justice upon you. Only this for your comfort, that the Lady Bagot, Mrs Sneyd, Mrs Skrimshawe and Mrs Archbold [wives of royalist leaders] with many more of your sex and opinion, so soon as they can be apprehended, shall be sent unto you for your comforts.

Lady Bagot then tried to broker a settlement, which only provoked more recriminations. The royalist commanders, including her own husband, Colonel Harvey Bagot, insisted Brereton's 'uncivil act' would not induce them to surrender – 'we are resolved to defend this place like men, and shall be ready to encounter those attempts that you shall make upon us in a manlike way'. They had no 'entertainment' fit for the women and 'if we should receive them to a diet so unnatural to their weak bodies, we should expose them to a destruction as inevitable as by famine'. Brereton was unrepentant: he was only sending the women to their husbands 'whom the laws of God and man have joined together', while some of the women 'were never ceasing to petition for admission to them'. He had not ejected any children – these had simply followed of their own accord; and he claimed that the royalists were detaining some women in the garrison against their will, even as they barred the way to new-comers. Finally, of course, Brereton insisted that parliamentarians would be 'as man-like and soldierlike' as any. The outcome of this stalemate is unclear but there were many 'ladies, gentlewomen and all other women' in the garrison on its surrender some six weeks later. Parliament could now afford to be more gracious: all the women were allowed to go where they wished 'with all their wearing apparel whatsoever, and two suits of bed-linen apiece; and there to remain and be protected from violence or plunder of soldiers, doing nothing prejudicial to the parliament'.[42]

Women and children were used as pawns in the terrible siege of Colchester in 1648, where parliamentary commanders, outraged by the renewal of war by a capricious king, showed no mercy to women or men. A woman who tried to escape the town with five children, including a baby at her breast, was brutally sent back by parliamentarian soldiers. To save resources the royalist commander, the Earl of Norwich, sent out 500 women and children; they were met by warning shots from parliamentarian soldiers, but tried to carry on; the soldiers then began to strip them. The desperate women ran back to Colchester, but Norwich had barred the gates. Only when it became clear that the parliamentarian attackers were implacable did he relent. Parliament also tried to use the sickly young son of one of the royalist leaders, Lord Capel, as a hostage to force the release of the parliamentarian committeemen trapped in Colchester. Even when he was paraded round the walls his father refused to succumb to the 'inhuman act' – and it was only through the lobbying of his female relatives, and of Lady Fairfax, that young Capel was allowed home. According to one female diarist, 'his mother was brought to bed of a son the night before with the grief of it'.[43]

If women perceived as vulnerable non-combatants could be brutally treated, women who directly challenged feminine norms risked terrible revenge. Some royalist articles of war qualified the condemnation of violence against women with the proviso that protection did not apply to women who assaulted soldiers.[44] After the battle of Naseby in June 1645, the parliamentarian cavalry fell on royalist women camp followers. At least one hundred were killed and many more were mutilated, especially by slitting their noses, a standard punishment for a whore. This was, writes Mark Stoyle, the 'single worst atrocity' of the civil war in England; it came not as a bolt from the blue, but as a catastrophe with long-standing roots in gendered, cultural hostilities.[45] We have already described the drowning of a royalist spy in 1642, while at the siege of Lyme in 1644 a parliamentarian mob killed an elderly camp follower, slashed her face, and threw her into the sea in further echoes of community punishment of whores or witches. Parliamentarian sources described the peace petitioners of 1643 as lewd whores, who deserved punishment:

> The lewd women about London petition for a peace, who came in an abusive way to the House of Parliament, affronting them with ill language, swearing that they would have a peace, there was amongst them 500 whores as its conceived, but some of the women came short home, and some disfigured, one of them without a nose.[46]

Parliament's army too prided itself on its contempt for 'whores', but there were specific assumptions that the women at Naseby were Welsh or Irish, with the further conclusion that Welsh and Irish women were only too likely to be throat-cutting whores or even witches who would slaughter men with their long knives or 'skeins' as Irish men and women had massacred honest Protestants in 1641. When Sir William Brereton defeated the royalist troops lately arrived from Ireland at Nantwich in January 1644 his prisoners were reported to include 120 'women with long knives' besides 1,700 common soldiers. Newsbooks described these women as Irish. Many were probably nothing of the sort, but newsbook accounts stuck and were repeated, for example by the London artisan Nehemiah Wallington in one of his notebooks.

There were elements also at Naseby of revenge for the mistreatment of Essex's troops in 1644, when women as well as men assaulted the defeated, retreating parliamentarian army in Cornwall, another trauma which combined ethnic and political hostilities. Thus the parliamentarian chronicler John Vicars rejoiced that women at Naseby had been given no quarter: they were 'many Irish women, inhuman whores, with skeins or long Irish knives about them to cut the throats of our wounded men'.[47]

Dark fantasies about witchcraft surfaced on several occasions. War rendered men vulnerable to dissolution even as it highlighted their capacities for violent mastery, and civil war, where men fought neighbours and former friends, intensified such basic anxieties. Where men and women were fighting, in part, for rival visions of true religion, fears that women might use supernatural powers against the enemy, or even against men in general, could escalate into an inchoate horror of 'feminized chaos' in Diane Purkiss's terms. Male vulnerability in war could be projected onto female deviance explained as witchcraft. Parliamentarian soldiers were all too conscious that they were fighting God's war, so unnatural female opponents might well be the devil's creatures. Three women who had, allegedly, cut the throats of parliamentary soldiers after the battle of Brentford in December 1642 were seized and thrown in the river in the traditional 'swimming' test for witchcraft; two drowned but the other, horrifyingly, would not sink and was battered to death. Other royalist women were lynched as witches in Wiltshire and at Newbury. Conversely, it was logical that women accused of witchcraft were also suspected of royalism. Newsbooks claimed that some of the witches tried in Suffolk had confessed they had been in the king's army, and concluded that the king's forces were 'beholding to the Devil' (another story picked up by Wallington). During 'witch-hunts' in East Anglia which led to more than a hundred witches (mostly women) being executed, people felt it was a time 'wherein the Devil reigns'. First in Essex, and then in most of East Anglia, long suppressed suspicions were thrust into the open, exacerbated by the traumas of civil war, and prompted by the troubled Puritan 'witch-hunter', Matthew Hopkins, in a context where conventional legal caution had been thrown to the winds. Thus occurred England's 'worst-ever witchcraft persecution' with many more prosecutions and many more executions than before the war. In Chelmsford in July 1645, twenty-eight out of twenty-nine accused were executed whereas even in Essex, there had been many fewer prosecutions, and acquittals had been much more common in the 1630s. The East Anglian trials are the most well known, but in many parts of England more witches were prosecuted in the 1640s and 1650s than in any other period. The civil war years saw exceptional peaks in witchcraft cases, interrupting a general declining trend.[48]

A 'soliciting temper': women and survival strategies

When men were killed, or had office and property confiscated because they were on the losing side, the energy and adroit lobbying of women were essential to family survival. As many as 80,000 men may have been killed in the war, many leaving dependants, while in other homes men returned from war crippled and unable to provide for their families. The effects on the humbler women and children left to cope are usually hidden from us, until they were driven to apply to the authorities for relief. Petitioning for pensions by the dependants of parliamentarian soldiers (royalists had to wait until after 1660) was carefully organised; successful claims depended on community support and the help of skilled and experienced scribes. In Essex, women made up a third of those who petitioned the Justices of the Peace for aid; they often approached the magistrates in groups and their petitions were often more detailed and more assertive than those of the maimed soldiers who claimed on their own account. Widows were strategic in their self-presentations, stressing the sufferings of their families: 'five small children in a very sad and deplorable condition'; and the loyalty of their husbands: who 'did voluntarily at his own charge furnish himself with a horse and arms'. In effect they were not asking for charity but for their rights, as when Margaret Beavis asked for a pension 'according to the act of Parliament as to other widows in the like case hath been granted'.[49]

We know more about the defiance of clerical families. A clergyman ejected by the parliamentarian authorities, for royalism or unacceptable religious views, was turned out of his house as well as his office, rendering wife and children homeless along with himself. Many women did not take this lightly. Mrs Rawson, the wife of a Leicestershire clergyman, was forcibly ejected from the family home by soldiers, and then had to take refuge with her children, firstly in the church porch and later in the belfry. Robert Lovell was removed as rector of St Peter's church, Sandwich and imprisoned, but his wife resisted eviction for more than two months. When the order for her removal was first delivered in early September 1643 'no answer at all was given unto us notwithstanding it was apparent that there was somebody in the house'. She told the churchwardens in October that she 'utterly refused to deliver up the same averring that her husband was put in by the king and themselves, [and] could not be put out without the king's writ', and when the town authorities tried again, she again 'kept her doors close up, and by her kinswoman absolutely denied obedience to the order till those who kept her husband sent him unto her'. By 14 November her tactics had shifted: Mrs Lovell 'seeming to be somewhat distracted did upon her knees beseech me to spare her till Friday next and then she would quietly surrender'. But on Friday next the Mayor 'found the doors fast barred and locked up', and – finally losing patience – broke down the doors and established the successor in possession.[50] Many wives obstructed the payment of tithes to their husbands' successors. An enterprising Yorkshire woman, Mrs Manby, along with her sister, circulated a forged paper purporting to be an order from the royalist army forbidding the payment of tithes to the newcomer. Where forgery or outright defiance failed, more conciliatory petitioning might mitigate a family's situation. Mary Cosin, the daughter of the eminent Anglican John Cosin, petitioned on behalf of herself and five siblings that Cosin's books in Peterhouse, Cambridge Library might be sold for their maintenance. This request was refused but the young people were granted some small alternative maintenance by the Council of State.[51]

Propertied royalists had their estates sequestered (confiscated) during the war in areas controlled by the parliament, although as parliamentarians gained the upper hand, most royalists were allowed to 'compound' for their estates, regaining them on the payment of a fine and a formal submission to the victors. After 1649, royalists who were particularly offensive to the parliament were not allowed to compound and their estates were put up for sale. In all these processes women's lobbying was vital to the preservation of family property. By the time royalist lands were put up for sale, it was worth printing a generic petition from women asking for allowances from the estates: 'Whereas by the wisdom and piety of this honourable parliament, especial care and regard hath been always formerly had, that the wives and children of such as have not compounded, should, and hath been allowed the fifth part of said delinquents' estates. For which goodness we bless God.' The petitioners then asked that 'such pious provision' be taken to continue fifth parts before the lands were sold.[52]

Parliamentarians rarely wished to ruin their opponents, or to shake the social order. They were usually willing to grant allowances to women and children, while renting sequestered estates back to women regarded as less culpable provided a steady revenue for parliament and minimised disruption to local relationships. Anne Filmer, wife of the patriarchal theorist Robert, ran the estates during the civil war, while Margery Dugdale, wife of the royalist herald William, rented the family's confiscated Warwickshire property for £10 pa between March 1644 and June 1646, when the estates were restored on the payment of a 'composition' fine.[53] The parliamentarian committee in Staffordshire was willing to rent sequestered estates back to the wives of very prominent royalists. Lady Bagot, whose husband commanded Lichfield garrison, was on her own 'motion and request' granted a lease of her husband's lands, while even the wife of Thomas Leveson, the very unpleasant commander of Dudley garrison, was allowed her house and lands in Staffordshire, although she needed the intervention of the Earl of Denbigh, the highest-ranking parliamentarian commander in the west Midlands, before the lease was granted.[54] Ralph Sneyd was imprisoned as a royalist and his main residence at Keele threatened with demolition, but Mrs Jane Sneyd was granted all her husband's clothes and trunks (apart from some things picked over and purchased by the wife of a parliamentarian committeeman) and allowed to live unmolested with her mother-in-law, 'she behaving herself as she ought to do'. In March 1644 Jane was granted all her husband's estates at a rent of £400 pa and over the next year she frequently lobbied the local committee, for reductions in tax, for the return of stolen oxen and to ensure that local people ground their corn at the Sneyd mills in Newcastle under Lyme.[55] Margaret, wife of Captain Francis Biddulph (also in prison), was granted her husband's lands including mills, coal-pits and a smithy for £20 pa, and like Mrs Sneyd she ensured that the parliamentarian authorities supported her efforts to exploit them. When she reported that she 'suspecteth that the tenants which now hold the same may do her wrong in the working of the said pits', she was advised to get 'three or four honest skilful men to view the same' to ensure there was no damage at the end of the year and the tenants were ordered to 'work it workmanlike and so leave the same'. The committee also disciplined soldiers who seized her cattle.[56] With their husbands in prison, Jane Sneyd and Margaret Biddulph no doubt still had effective legal and financial advisers, but they were clearly confident and capable in their dealings with potentially hostile authorities.

A familiar example is both instructive and moving. Mary Verney was the wife of Sir Ralph Verney MP. Unlike his father and brother, Sir Ralph had never been an active royalist, but he had refused to take the Covenant in 1643 and fled into exile in despair at the bitter English conflicts that had torn his own family apart. The confiscation of his property was ordered in 1644 but only implemented in autumn 1646 at which point it was decided that his young pregnant wife should return and seek to get the sequestration lifted. Sir Ralph risked arrest if he returned and a woman had many advantages as a humble petitioner. As one friend advised Sir Ralph, 'women were never so useful as now … instruct your wife and leave her to act it with committees, their sex entitles them to many privileges, and we find the comfort of them more than ever'. Another suggested: 'it would not do amiss if she can bring her spirit to a soliciting temper and can tell how to use the juice of an onion sometimes to soften hard hearts'. Sir Ralph retorted that an onion was superfluous: 'it is not hard for a wife to dissemble, but there is like to be no need of that for where necessities are so great, the juice of an onion will be useless'.[57] Mary's letters to her husband in France recount an exhausting and expensive round of lobbying and consultation. She was always short of money for coaches, food and official fees, scrabbling for suitable lodgings in London and sorrowful at the desolation of her abandoned house in Claydon, Buckinghamshire: 'I am at a very great charge here, for I pay twelve shillings a week for a chamber for myself and another for my maid two pairs of stairs high, fire, candles, washing, breakfast and diet besides'. She had to deal with parliament's committee in Buckinghamshire which was 'very malicious and extremely insolent' as well as the Committee for Compounding at Goldsmiths Hall, London, 'where we must expect nothing but cruelty'.[58] A family friend, the Dowager Countess of Sussex, had recently remarried the Earl of Warwick, an influential parliamentarian, and the Verneys hoped to mobilise these contacts on their behalf, despite the ungallant nickname, 'old men's wife', given her in their letters. This proved difficult: although Mary 'told her very many times that it was friends which did all', she was reluctant to engage herself or her husband. Mary could 'never find her alone for her house is always like a court' and her husband 'that vinegar-faced fellow' too often 'sat like a clown and said nothing' although his brother, the Earl of Holland, offered his services.[59]

In June 1647, Mary gave birth to a son. She put him to a wet nurse at three weeks, and within five weeks resumed her lobbying. She missed the two children who remained in France, even as she was reunited with a son left behind in 1643: 'truly 'tis time you had him with you for he learns nothing here' she wrote to her husband:

> he is a very ready witted child, and is very good of company, and is so fond of the name of his father and mother, he is always with me from the first hour that I came, and tells me that he would very fain go into France to his father.

Loneliness and personal tragedy were accompanied by success in her practical affairs. Her daughter in France died, although for weeks her husband did not dare to tell her, and the new baby also sickened and died from convulsions. But through systematic exploitation of all her influential friends, and lavish dinners for sympathetic MPs, Mary obtained a favourable hearing in the House of Commons and the sequestration was finally removed in January 1648.[60] Lady Warwick had 'at last in some measure played her part, but I put her soundly to it, for I have been 4 or 5 times with her this week; her husband was there and brought others with him whose presence did much good'. Mary was careful to thank her, and Lady Warwick in turn assured Ralph that 'your good wife solicited your business with all the care that possibly might be'. Mary was now free to return to France with her son John in April 1648, but her lonely efforts had broken her health and she too died some two years later.[61]

The Verneys made strategic use of female vulnerability as a lobbying tactic on behalf of a loving and united family, but other contests over confiscated property exacerbated family tensions. Eyton Crompton, a Shropshire gentleman, sought to use political divisions to further his conflict with his royalist step-mother, who he claimed had swindled him out of his inheritance. His step-mother had turned the family's home into a royalist garrison when his father died while Eyton had served in the parliamentary forces that recaptured it. We may be a little sceptical of this version as despite a powerful intervention from Major General Thomas Harrison urging a speedy hearing for Eyton 'who has had some hard measure from a very wicked woman', his claims were not upheld and allowances for his half-brothers were instead confirmed.[62]

Complicated relationships might be exposed even where a family was in theory politically united, and agreed on family strategies to minimise civil war losses. It was inevitable that the estate of William Cavendish, Earl of Newcastle, was put up for sale, for the Earl had been the king's principal commander in the north until he chose exile rather than disgrace in the aftermath of the catastrophic defeat at Marston Moor. Newcastle's second wife, the prolific and notorious author Margaret Cavendish made an unsuccessful, and on her own account rather shamefaced attempt to obtain some allowance from his estates:

> at last necessity enforced me to return into England, to seek for relief; for I hearing my Lord's Estate, amongst the rest of many more estates, was to be sold, and that the wives of the owners should have an allowance therefrom, it gave me hopes I should receive a benefit thereby.

Cavendish characteristically presented herself as distinctive:

> indeed I did not stand as a beggar at the Parliament door, for I never was at the Parliament-House, nor stood I ever at the door, as I do know, or can remember, I am sure, not as a Petitioner, neither did I haunt the Committees, for I never was at any, as a Petitioner, but once in my life, which was called Goldsmiths-Hall, but I received neither gold nor silver from them, only an absolute refusal.

As she had married Newcastle after he had been condemned as a 'delinquent' royalist she was entitled to nothing, and so:

> without speaking to them one word good or bad, I returned to my Lodgings, and as that Committee was the first, so it was the last, I ever was at as a Petitioner; 'tis true I went sometimes to Drury-House to inquire how the land was sold, but no other ways, although some reported, I was at the Parliament-House, and at this Committee, and at that Committee.

Her own singularity was established through criticism of other women:

> the Customs of England being changed as well as the Laws, where Women become Pleaders, Attorneys, Petitioners and the like, running about with their several causes, complaining of their several grievances, exclaiming against their several enemies, bragging of their several favours they receive from the powerful, ... for the truth is, our Sex doth nothing but jostle for the pre-eminence of words.[63]

This was a disingenuous and rather tactless account for William's and Margaret's comfortable exile in Antwerp depended on generous regular funds from Margaret's adult step-children who had made their peace with parliamentarian regimes. The eldest daughter Jane had become virtual head of the family after her mother's death in 1643 with her father away at war and then in exile. When their house, Welbeck, was seized by parliament's forces in August 1644, she sought to preserve the family's prized possessions by negotiating with the enemy commanders and after the war she was more successful than her step-mother in petitions to the parliamentarian authorities. The standard 'fifth' of the estate (the allowance granted to dependants) was granted to herself and her siblings, and the grant was confirmed on her petition in April 1650 before the sale of Newcastle's property.[64]

Given Newcastle's condemnation by the parliament, it was politic for his children to present themselves as the heirs of their dead mother rather than their absent father. Thus the sequestered estates of their mother (a substantial heiress in her own right) were restored to Jane's elder brother Charles, Viscount Mansfield after he was presented as an unwilling participant in his father's army, and, with the help of agents, much of the confiscated property was purchased back from the state. Throughout the 1650s Charles and his younger brother publicly distanced themselves from their father, and used alternative networks to ingratiate themselves with the Cromwellian regime. Money went regularly to Antwerp, but the children had become effectively independent. Familial harmony and paternal authority did not return with the Restoration, and the inevitable tensions between a young step-mother and adult children had clearly been intensified by the survival strategies adopted in the 1650s.[65]

If many women managed to rescue some at least of their family's property, they were less successful in their most desperate petitions to preserve the lives of husbands condemned for political crimes. Nonetheless, as with property, so with lives, it was thought worthwhile to try to melt the hearts of enemies or opponents with female pleading. Lady Ann Fanshawe did obtain the release of her husband Sir Richard who was imprisoned after the royalists' final defeat at Worcester in 1651. He was kept in a little room in Whitehall where 'at last he grew so ill in health by the cold and hard marches he had undergone, and being pent up in a room close and small, that the scurvy brought him almost to death's door'. Every day 'when the clock struck four in the morning, with a dark lantern in my hand, all alone and on foot', she went to his prison from her lodgings in Chancery Lane:

> There I would go under his window and softly call him … Thus we talked together; and sometimes I was so wet with rain that it went in at my neck and out at my heels. He directed me how I should make my address, which I did ever to their General Cromwell.

Cromwell's advice was crucial, and he helped her to obtain evidence on Fanshawe's health from Dr Bathurst, the physician to Cromwell's family as well as her own: 'I delivered it at the council-chamber door at three of the clock that afternoon to his own hand, as he commanded me and himself moved … that he might have his liberty upon £4,000 bail, to take a course of physic, he being dangerously ill.' Cromwell supported Fanshawe in the subsequent Council debate and Fanshawe was released despite the opposition of Sir Henry Vane and other republicans.[66]

Other wives were not so fortunate. On 7 March 1649 'the Earl of Warwick, the Countess of Holland, with divers other Countesses and Ladies' came to parliament to plead for the life of Warwick's brother, the Earl of Holland, who had joined royalist insurgents in 1648. Newsbooks listed Holland's daughters, daughters-in-law and other kinswomen: the Countess of Manchester, Lady Kensington, Lady Paget and Lady Rich. On the same day, Lady Capel, whose son had been paraded before the walls of Colchester, lobbied on behalf of her husband, but the House of Commons voted by thirty-eight to twenty-eight not to hear the petitions and the men made good deaths at Whitehall, two days later.[67] Lady Capel was able to rescue a substantial pro-portion of the family's vast estates. On her petition the sequestration of her own inheritance from her father and of the lands settled on her by her husband was lifted by parliament on 9 May.[68] After the abortive royalist rising in 1655 in the West Country by John Penruddock, his wife and the wives of others condemned for their involvement petitioned the Cromwellian authorities, offering repentance on their husbands' behalf. This was clearly a coordinated campaign, with some parallels to the mass petitioning by Leveller women discussed below. Arundel Penruddock acknowledged that her husband's punishment was 'justly deserved through his rashness and folly', but she begged Cromwell to pardon her 'miserable husband' for the sake of her self and her seven small children; when this failed and her husband was exe-cuted she then petitioned Cromwell for some subsistence for herself and her children: 'She humbly prostrates herself at your highness' feet' begging him to 'shut your eye to her late husband's offence, and open your ear to the sad complains of the widow and fatherless'. Similar tactics were used by Mary Thorpe whose innkeeper husband was condemned, and by Jane Woodward, the widow of a clothier. After these humble prostrations in the 1650s, the women bided their time, and at the Restoration they petitioned Charles II in more vengeful mode, asking for the exclusion from pardon of the judges who had tried and condemned their husbands.[69]

'Brave feminine spirits': women and politics

Political commitment often strengthened women's efforts to preserve their homes and their family's estates: female petitioning, however humbly phrased and practically focused, had a political edge. We will now explore aspects of women's political activities in the 1640s and 1650s; in a necessarily selective discussion, the godly matrons and radical petitioners on parliament's side will be compared to the contrasting royalist experiences of militancy and adventure during the war, and defiant retreat thereafter. A fundamental unease about women who were overtly influential in public life did not prevent male propagandists on either side praising the loyalty and bravery of their 'own' women while denouncing their opposites as corrupt and lascivious (as parliamentarians described royalists), or domineering Puritan hypocrites (as royalists denounced parliamentarians). The techniques are well demonstrated in rival newsbook accounts of Lady Anne Waller, the wife of the parliamentarian general Sir William.

Lady Anne Waller was constructed as a stereotype of the domineering Puritan woman in a series of derisive stories in the royalist newsbook *Mercurius Aulicus*. In August and September 1644, there was a story about her nearly every week, designed of course to mock her husband (known contemptuously to royalists as 'William the Conqueror') along with herself. Lady Anne had come:

> lately to her Knight ... cast aside all her noting tools, and (with her arms upon his conquering shoulders) said aloud, O thou man of God, come kiss me ... a few such expressions will spoil her new plot for a reformed nunnery, where none must be admitted but first, such as are married; secondly such as can preach; thirdly, such whose husbands have been exceedingly well beaten.[70]

A report of disputes between Sir William and his subordinate Colonel Browne claimed Browne 'shook up' Sir William:

> as his lady used to doe at Winchester Church, where if he offered to speak about doctrines or uses, her ladyship would rebuke him, saying, peace Master William, you know your weaknesses in those things, since which time Sir William hath ever gone for the weaker vessel.[71]

Finally, the newsbook claimed Lady Waller was blamed in parliament for the delays in Sir William's march to the west, offering exclusive extracts from debates:

> 'Master Speaker, I have read in story of a fish in the sea called a Remora, which though a little one, is able and doth often hinder a ship from going,

though never so big and under sail. Master Speaker, my Lady Waller is this Remora (a mermaid), Sir William is the ship now under sail, and hoisting for a voyage of great concernment; but this Remora stays him.'

The editor spelled it out: ''tis certain the conqueror hath been vanquished by his Lady, and 'tis as certain that she first was a main cause and encourager of her husband's rebellion, which is the very reason why her ladyship of late hath been found so oft in print'.[72]

Parliamentarian newsbooks, in contrast, used Lady Anne as a godly exemplar to criticise decadent royalist women:

> She is not like your Court-Madams, *Aulicus*; uses no oil of talc, no false teeth, no wanton frisking gate, no caterwauling in Spring Garden. She bestows not all her time upon her body and leave none for the soul. She cannot measure out a whole morning with curling irons, and spend the afternoon in courting and vanity, and toying in Hyde Park, but every morning her soul is made ready before her body ... she studies not fashions but graces, and in these she is a leading example to the women of the kingdom. They hate her for her good-ness, and more especially because she loves reformation, which they can as ill abide to hear of as the Bishops. The fullness of the Gospel will not admit of carnality, masquings, close meetings, looseness and lasciviousness. And therefore they will keep it from Court, tooth and nail ... and abuse, mock and deride all Ladies that run not together with them to the same licentious courses.[73]

These contests in print over the character of Lady Anne served also as struggles over the broad cultural affiliations of each side, expressed through gendered stereotypes. For royalists, parliamentarianism drew on a self-righteous, self-indulgent hypocritical Puritanism that was subversive of all order and authority, including male authority. For parliamentarians, royalism was immoral, 'licentious', lacking in true godliness, and its female adherents were likely to be wanton whores.

Consequently, along with a steady stream of hostile reporting of the queen, to be discussed below, the parliamentarian press countered royalist praise of women like the Countess of Derby, and showed parallel contempt for the pusillanimity of royalist men, like the Earl of Derby:

> Now he tells us of the Amazonian Dame, the Countess of Derby, who he says holds out still, I am sure it is more then ever the female Lord himself could do with all his regiments, whom the gallant Lancastrians annihilated, took and killed all his men, and sent him for a recruiter to the Isle of Man ... But I would you heard what masculine prodigies he lays to the charge of this Countess; first, that she still holds Lathom House, being besieged full twelve weeks ... I am persuaded if these countesses and ladies hold on to do thus, they at Oxford will cashier all their old male commanders, and choose some females in chief.

Parliamentarian 'brave feminine spirits … the Lady Manchester, the Lady Waller, the Lady Fairfax' were counter-posed to the 'Duchesses and Countesses, and Ladies' who were soon to command '(as I can tell ye they do pretty well already) in the Court, as well as the Camp' and to Henrietta Maria who led the 'court countesses' who hoped to become 'generalissimos of all the forces for popery'.[74]

Beyond propagandist testimony, there is extensive evidence for the political engagement of women. Some widows and spinsters came to the attention of the authorities as independent political actors, so that among 286 parliamentarians accused of treason at the royalist-controlled Chester Assizes in February 1644, there were three women, two widows and one single woman, Jane Done of Ukinton, a confidante of Brereton and a well-known patron of godly ministers.[75] The potential influence of women is indicated in the widespread anxiety about divided families, and fears that women would divert men from their true political loyalties. In an auto-biographical passage in his *Second Defence* (1654) John Milton looked back to the 1640s when he had written on 'domestic' liberty, on marriage, education and free expression, as 'the very time when man and wife were often bitter foes, he dwelling at home with their children, she, the mother of the family, in the camp of the enemy, threatening her husband with death and disaster'.[76] The 'often' is a rather odd remark. It is a description of Milton's own situation, and that of parliament's first Lord General, the Earl of Essex, and a still fresh personal humiliation perhaps coloured Milton's prose. But political divisions within families were relatively rare. Shared upbringing, close networks and common inclinations worked against disagreement although the religious fragmentation of the 1640s and 1650s frequently split families.

Some well-known families, like the Verneys, were divided by civil war, while the Feildings, Earls of Denbigh, are another striking example. Basil, Viscount Feilding (second Earl of Denbigh after April 1643), was a nephew of Charles I's assassinated favourite the Duke of Buckingham. His elderly father fought in Prince Rupert's troop of horse until he was killed in an assault on Birmingham, while his mother was a close attendant and confidante of Henrietta Maria. Nonetheless, Basil Feilding became a parliamentarian commander, prompting a series of eloquently reproachful letters from his mother:

> I beg of you my firstborn to give me the comfort … which is to leave those that murthured your dear father … there was no mercy to his gray hairs but wounds and shots, a horror to me to think of, o my dear Jesus put it into my dear son's heart to leave that merciless company … now is the time that God and nature claims it from you, before you were carried away with errors but now it is hideous and monstrous. The last words your dear father spake of you was to desire God to forgive you and to touch your heart. Let your dying father and unfortunate mother make your heart relent.

Modernising spelling does not do justice to the desperately poignant nature of this appeal: 'do not think it out of fear and timorousness of a woman I persuade you to this', the Countess insisted, 'No, no, it is that I scorn. I would have you leave this bloody way in which you are crept into'. The tone of letters from Feilding's sister Elizabeth Lady Kinaelmeaky was harsher, condemning the brother who had 'so willingly thrown away at once your honour, gratitude and all that's good'.[77]

Basil Feilding, by now Earl of Denbigh, also had to contend with the more restrained reproaches of his wife, who loved him passionately and hated his absence on campaigns, but deplored his political views. *Mercurius Aulicus* highlighted this awkwardness, as usual citing Lady Anne Waller as the antithesis of true womanhood. The royalist newsbook claimed 'the noble Countess of Denbigh', wife of the 'Rebellious Earl', had given alms to royalist prisoners held at Coventry but refused any charity to 'rebel' soldiers: 'should this be known to the Lady Anne Waller, it would much distract her Saturday's meditations'.[78] The Countess does seem to have had royalist sympathies. She wrote to Denbigh about:

> a book in print about the Duke your uncle. It troubles me and I believe will do the like to you … It says both the Duke and the king poisoned King James. The Parliament … though they deny the putting it forth yet they defend it. Your good grandmother is in the book. So God bless you and send you all the happiness and, for your sake, their army: else they do not deserve my prayers nor nobody else. If my letter be broken at the Committee I care not for your friends' honours is equal with my own, and it is a damnable book … The king may have faults but not like the publishing this villainous pamphlet.

The language here is restrained but clear; parliament and its army are 'they', her husband 'you', and only affection for him limits her hostility to them. Nonetheless she remained devoted: 'I should be glad to hear of your safe arrival at Stafford, for none prays more for your safety than I do and it is a great grief to me to have you put yourself into those hazards you do and to think you are to be so long from me'. And she was a loyal and useful wife. Left short of money at Coventry, the Countess refused to borrow: 'I hope I shall have no need, but if I had never so much I would not because you command the contrary', and she did her best to cultivate potential political allies for her husband, who was not popular among Warwickshire parliamentarians.[79]

Families who shared political views might still find that civil war unsettled their relationships, as we have seen with the Cavendishes. Bitter quarrels between the royalist Earl of Northampton and his younger brothers, which disturbed their garrison at Banbury, culminated in angry scenes between the Earl and his mother, who sided with her younger sons.[80] Where families seem to have been both politically and emotionally harmonious, we cannot assume that women simply did as their husbands or fathers told them, and that their own convictions were not genuine. In some cases, the husband's instruction was crucial, at least in their own opinion. Sir Hugh Cholmley explained how he had disabused his wife Elizabeth of her parliamentarianism, once he had switched his own allegiance:

being within London and not yet understanding the causes why I quit the Parliament nor the true state of the difference between the king and the parliament [she] was very earnest and fierce for their party, but after I had unmasked to her the parliament's intents and clearly presented to her their proceedings and the state of affairs, she then was as much against them, and as earnest for the King and continued so to her death.[81]

Lady Anne Waller was clearly as dedicated as her husband to godliness, and to the parliament. To balance the contemptuous version in *Mercurius Aulicus*, we have the affectionate testimony of her husband, which confirms her autonomy, and her zeal. In autobiographical meditations, Waller described how, newly widowed, he had prayed for a second wife, and God's providence had led him to Lady Anne Finch:

> she and I agreed together to set a day apart to seek God for his blessing in it. It pleased the Lord to answer our prayers in as full a measure of comfort as ever was poured out upon a married couple: and though at first there were some little differences in our natures and judgements (as to some particulars) yet within a little while, that good God wrought us to that uniformity, that I may say we were but as one soul in two bodies.

By the later 1640s, Waller was at odds with radical parliamentarians and he was imprisoned in Denbigh castle by the army after Pride's purge in 1648. His wife 'came to me disguised in mean apparel when I had groaned in my bonds seven months, thinking it the duty of a wife to risk all things for the satisfaction of her husband'; many times she feared discovery but 'at length over mountains and unknown roads, sometimes with a guide, and sometimes with none, she arrived at my prison'. Like the Angel who appeared to St Peter 'she did not indeed bid my prison gates fly open, but by her sweet converse and behaviour, she made those things seem light which were before heavy and scarce to be borne'. These adventures exhausted Lady Anne and she died at Denbigh during the hard winter of 1651–52.[82]

Both Elizabeth Cholmley and Anne Waller were civil war activists, supporting their husbands' political and military activities in good times and bad. Women who never entered a garrison or a prison, or even delivered a petition, might nonetheless have determined political views, as surviving sources demonstrate. For Elizabeth Jekyll, a London Presbyterian woman, in a manuscript later preserved by her husband, the successes of the parliamentary cause merged with her gratitude to God for personal triumphs. In 1644 parliament's victory at Marston Moor, 'the great deliverance of this kingdom', was coupled with 'the great and wonderful mercy of God to me' in the safe delivery of twin boys, while the following year the recovery of Bristol – 'It pleased God, also to crown the endeavours of our Army' – was similarly joined with thanks for her fourth delivery from the 'pain and peril of childbirth'.[83] In the comments she added to her printed almanacs in the 1640s and 1650s, the moderate royalist Isabella Twysden combined high political narratives with the more mundane affairs of her own household and acquaintance. The king's escape to the Isle of Wight in

November 1647 was juxtaposed with 'Mary Hearn came to serve me'.[84] The commonplace books of Anne Sadleir also indicate a staunch royalist perspective, even though Anne's revered father was the common lawyer Sir Edward Coke, whose memory was more easily harnessed by parliamentarians. She denounced parliament's army as tyrannical and profane and presented Cromwell as an amalgam of Judas, Herod, Nero, Caligula and Julian the Apostate. It is misleading to see Jekyll or Sadleir as operating only in some 'private sphere' of individual reflection, for their manuscripts were circulated among sympathetic friends, kin and allies. Jekyll's text bolstered non-conformist resolve in the hard times following the Restoration, while Sadleir's was read by royalist kinswomen, including her cousin, Elizabeth, Lady Capel. Sadleir also conducted a brave and angry correspondence with the New England radical, Roger Williams, in the 1650s. Williams had been a protégé of Sadleir's father, and recommended her to read Milton on Charles I, attracting a robust response. Sadleir denounced 'the foul and false aspersions' Williams had cast on 'that king of ever blessed memory, Charles the martyr', and abused Milton in even stronger terms: 'that is he that has wrote a book of the lawfulness of divorce, and if report says true he had at that time two or three wives living'. A providential judgement had rendered him blind.[85] More 'literary' royalist examples will be discussed further below, among them Hester Pulter who vented her 'anger, dismay and contempt about specific political groups' in poems such as 'The complaint of Thames 1647 when the best of kings was imprisoned by the worst of rebels at Holmby'.[86]

'Christ hath purchased us at as dear a rate as he hath done men': parliamentarian petitioners

Many determined godly matrons played a significant role in parliamentarian politics, through influence, patronage and practical activism. We have already met Anne Waller and Brilliana Harley, and will discuss Lucy Hutchinson and others later. The most striking political interventions by parliamentarian women, however, were collective petitions on public affairs. The ways in which these initiatives were distinctive need to be carefully defined. It is too easy to locate the significance of women's petitioning solely within a history of female or even proto-feminist activism.[87] It is extremely significant that during the profound crises of the civil war years groups of women petitioned for specific religious and political ends, and, when challenged, justified their right to some influence on the affairs of the commonwealth on principled grounds. The printing of women's petitions, like those from groups of men, was also a novel development underlining the importance of 'public opinion' as readers debated the merits of rival political stances.[88] The humble petitioning of local or national authorities by groups and individuals for personal or social ends was a central element in the negotiations fundamental to relationships between elites and subordinates in early modern England, but civil war petitions, while drawing on such traditions, were clearly different. But women's subordination in early modern England is reflected not only in outright hostility to their political activism, but in the more subtle ways in which men at the same time both sanctioned and limited women's interventions in particular causes. Women petitioners faced much derision, contempt and, on occasion, violent opposition, but it was much more likely to come from men who disagreed with their particular stances, than from men in general. In February 1642 when women thronged the parliament, pressing the House of Lords to agree with the reforming measures of the Commons, an exasperated peer was reported as spluttering 'Away with these women, we were best to have a parliament of women'. The peace petitioners of August 1643 were denounced then and later as lewd whores, while Leveller women were told by the House of Commons in April 1649: 'the matter you petition about, is of an higher concernment than you understand, that the house gave an answer to your husbands, and therefore that you are desired to go home, and look after your own business, and meddle with your housewifery'.[89] Mock or satirical petitions were a popular print genre. They belittled women's political activism and the causes they were associated with, and revealed male anxieties about gender order and political division, by reducing all women's demands to aspects of illicit sexuality. They were particularly common during the controversial London peace campaigns of early 1643, and the tense summer of 1647 when the parliamentary cause was tearing itself apart over the post-war settlement.[90]

Women's intervention was encouraged and praised by men sympathetic to the specific cause involved. We need, therefore, to recognise the political allegiances women expressed in their petitioning, and to analyse the petitions as coming from parliamentarian women, supporters of peace, Quaker women or Leveller women, rather than from 'women' as some unitary category. We have already seen some collective or coordinated royalist petitioning and an early petition from women whose livelihood depended on the queen's court also expressed royalist sympathies, but most petitioning in the 1640s emerged within parliamentarianism. Some women's petitions, like many provincial ones, reinforced the position of the parliamentary leadership: *The Humble Petition of many hundreds of distressed Women, Trades-mens Wives and Widdows* claimed that decay of trade was caused by the 'want of due execution of justice upon incendiaries and delinquents', so they called for reform of the ministry, the abolition of episcopacy, the removal of papists from the House of Lords, help for Ireland and putting the kingdom into a state of war.[91] A more elaborate petition at about the same time placed women's claims for a role in the political nation within a distinctly radical parliamentarian stance. The affinities between the rhetoric deployed here, and the later language of Leveller women's petitions, are too close to be simply coincidental, or even to indicate simple borrowings. They suggest continuities of personnel within the radical London circles whence the Levellers emerged, and perhaps connections with the zealous MP Henry Marten.[92] This petition used the necessary intervention of women to emphasise the seriousness of the dangers facing the parliamentarian cause. In these 'Domestical dangers', 'gentlewomen and tradesmen's wives' 'find ourselves to have as deep a share as any other':

> whereas we, whose hearts have joined cheerfully with all those petitions which have been exhibited unto you in the behalf of the purity of religion, and the liberty of our husband's person's and estates, recounting ourselves to have an

interest in the common privileges with them, do with the same confidence assure ourselves to find the same gracious acceptance with you, for easing of those grievances, which in regard of our frail condition, do more nearly concern us, and do deeply terrify our souls.

Stressing the 'frailty' of women and presenting collective female petitioning as unprecedented underlined the severity of the crisis: 'it may be thought strange, and unbeseeming our sex to shew ourselves by way of petitions'. The petitioners claimed, 'we cannot but tremble at the very thoughts of the horrid and hideous facts, which modesty forbids us now to name', but in fact they went on to name the bloody wars in Germany, the ravages of the army raised to fight the Scots in 1640, and especially the 'savage usage and unheard of rapes' in Ireland. Arguments based on women's familial duties, and vividly emotional female imagery were effectively deployed. Only 'Almighty God, by the wisdom and care of this Parliament' could preserve the women, their husbands and their children who were 'as dear and tender unto us, as the lives and blood of our hearts'; 'to see them murthered and mangled and cut in pieces before our eyes, to see our children dashed against the stones, and the mother's milk mingled with the infant's blood, running down the streets, to see our houses on flaming fire over our heads: oh how dreadful would this be?' It was vital to end the tyranny of the 1630s which had in effect rendered them widows by imprisoning and banishing their husbands or forcing them 'to fly from episcopal persecution into desert places amongst wild beasts'.

The petition used an entirely conventional view of women's nature and their role in the household to justify determined opposition to Charles I's government, while combining this unexceptional stance with more assertive claims of the rights of women to a part in the affairs of the commonwealth. The women appealed to biblical examples such as Esther and the wise woman of Tekoah, mentioned in 2 Samuel 14. This woman was asked by Joab to persuade King David to recall his son Absalom from exile; significantly she was persuaded by a man to act for the general good. They insisted that women, albeit subordinate to men, shared with them a 'right and interest' in the 'common and public cause of the church', and appealed to notions of spiritual equality. Men and women shared in the 'common calamities' of oppression, and 'Christ hath purchased us at as dear a rate as he hath done men' so that the happiness of women as well as men is concerned in 'a flourishing estate of the church and commonwealth'. They did not petition 'out of any self-conceit or pride of heart, as seeking to equal ourselves with men, either in authority or wisdom. But according to our places to discharge that duty we owe to God and the cause of the church', and they noted they were following in the steps of men 'who have gone in this duty before us'. This petition was delivered on 4 February 1642 by Mrs Anne Stagg, a gentlewoman and brewer's wife, with many others 'of like rank and quality', and was granted a courteous and encouraging hearing. The opposition leader John Pym and other MPs assured the women that their petition had 'come in a seasonable time'. The women were gently urged however: to 'repair to your houses, and turn your Petitions … into prayers at home for us'.[93]

Women's peace petitioning in August 1643 was much more controversial. Female petitioners were subject to particular abuse and pressure, but parliamentarians were in any case anxiously divided over peace propositions originating in the House of Lords. Newsbook reports sympathetic to more militant parliamentarianism saw the women at best as naïve dupes of royalists or malignants, if not whores and malignants themselves. It was alleged that royalist agents encouraged women 'to come to the Parliament house to cry for peace, which was to the women a pleasing thing'. The women came with white ribbons in their hats, 'civilly disposed' on one account, but according to others, the 'very scum of the suburbs', beggar women, or even Irish, 'two or three hundred oyster wives and other dirty and tattered sluts, who took upon them the impudency' to lobby for peace.[94] The petition was not separately printed, which is significant in itself, but the version in a newsbook was unobjectionable – 'your poor petitioners (though the weaker sex) do too sensibly perceive the ensuing desolation of this kingdom' – and called for predictable reassurance on the preservation of the Protestant religion, the liberties of the subject, the privileges of parliament and the royal prerogative. But the behaviour of the women, according to many sources, was more alarming. Over a couple of days, they 'carried themselves very uncivilly' towards MPs 'using many horrid execrations, that they would have the blood of those' who opposed peace, threatening to tear Pym and others in pieces, calling for the return of the king to London, and denouncing 'roundheads'. It was 'such a fearful tumult and uproar as was never recorded by any histories either ancient or modern'. The women threw stones and bricks at the trained bands who struggled to disperse them, and perhaps two women were killed in the mêlée. Some women were sent to Bridewell and other prisons; 'a most deformed Medusa or Hecuba with an old rusty blade by her side' caught the attention of newsbooks as she was marched off with her hands tied behind her back. Groups of women crowding Westminster and jostling MPs were particularly terrifying, but this was not simply hostility to female assertiveness. When a male petition against peace, backed by the city of London authorities, urged the 'well-affected' to 'maintain their former resolutions', parliament condemned the disorderly multitudes that accompanied its presentation.[95]

The most dramatic of all petitioning initiatives were those of the women of the Leveller movement in 1649, and again in 1653. The Levellers emerged from radical London religious circles from 1645; through struggles for religious liberty and freedom of printing, they developed a critique of parliamentarian authoritarianism and challenged parliament's leaders to offer reward to humbler men and women for the blood and treasure spilled in the war. Levellers grounded their political theories on the claims of honest householders for independence and participation and attacked the concentration of power wherever it was located – in parliament, among great trading companies, in the church. Individual women, including the radical religious author, Katherine Chidley, and the wives of Leveller leaders John Lilburne and Richard Overton, were active supporters of the movement from the beginning.[96] Elizabeth Lilburne had her own committed views and was arrested in 1641 among fellow members of a radical Baptist congregation, but her difficult life was structured above all else by her husband's political activism. From John's imprisonment by royalists after the battle of Brentford in late 1642, to his death in 1657 during a brief respite from the prison to which opposition to Cromwell's regime had confined him, Elizabeth, always short of money, often pregnant, sometimes in prison herself, devoted all her energies to protecting her family and attempting to save her husband from the consequences of his self-regarding political activism. For this she was more often publicly criticised than thanked by John, who contrasted Elizabeth's weak tendencies to compromise with his own staunch loyalty to the 'cause'. In spring 1643 she successfully petitioned parliament to threaten reprisals if the Oxford royalists carried out their threat to execute John; heavily pregnant, she took the resulting order to Oxford and secured his release. In 1645 when John was then imprisoned by the parliament, Elizabeth joined him in Newgate and gave birth to a daughter there, and she was again arrested in February 1647 for circulating John's 'scandalous' books during his latest long imprisonment.[97]

Petitions from, or in the name of, both Elizabeth Lilburne and Mary Overton, protested against their own and their husbands' suffering. The careful construction of these petitions and the ways in which they were presented tell us a great deal about the place of women in the Leveller movement. As we have seen with royalist petitioning, the suffering of women was an effective means of highlighting the justness of any cause, while male Leveller political identities and claims were founded specifically on their status as proud householders, who had amicable and authoritative relationships with their wives (and indeed with their apprentices and servants). Consequently the interventions of women were presented both as uncontroversial and as under male control. Honest householders had active, loyal but ultimately subordinate wives. Overton and Lilburne claimed in their own pamphlets that they had written their wives' petitions, although they were often published under the women's own names. Overton 'prepared a petition and appeal … in the behalf of my wife and brother to the House of Commons, which for the better credence of our miserable condition, was presented by a competent number of women'. Lilburne similarly explained how 'I was led presently to take care, to do something for my wife as the weaker vessel … and for that end, I drew her presently up a few lines … unto which she readily assented, and set her name to it'.[98]

The Leveller petitions from groups of women in 1649 and 1653 were profoundly unsettling and divisive, but as far as we know, they were not controversial within the Leveller movement itself. The large-scale mobilisation of women aroused the alarm and derision of political opponents, especially in 1649 when Leveller resistance was one of many threats to the new and insecure republican regime. While a radical coalition of London sectaries, Levellers, soldiers and MPs had helped secure the trial and execution of the king in the winter of 1648–49, spring saw disillusioned Levellers turn on the regime with the publication of the provocative pamphlet *Englands New Chains Discovered*. Lilburne and Overton, along with other prominent Levellers, William Walwyn and Thomas Prince, were forthwith rounded up by troops and confined to the Tower of London. At this juncture, the intervention of women helped to underline the unprecedented crisis faced by parliamentarians, while a range of printed petitions in both 1649 and 1653 contributed to the construction and representation of a movement that was both complex and united, representing a variety of men and women, carefully fixed in place, and differentiated by age and gender. Thus when Lilburne was, again, imprisoned and tried for treason in 1653, he welcomed the 'honest papers' delivered in his support, from 'The honest women of London', but also from 'the young men and apprentices of London', 'the honest people of Kent' and the 'honest men of Hertfordshire'. This harmonious complexity was embodied also in Leveller ritual, as in the funeral procession for Robert Lockyer, a Leveller sympathiser executed in May 1649 for his part in army mutinies, where 'citizens and women' and 'youth and maids' followed the hearse in solemn order.[99]

The women's first petition in 1649 was notable for its suggestion of specific female organisation within the Leveller movement, closing with the appeal: 'All those women that are approvers hereof are desired to subscribe it, and to deliver in their subscriptions to the women which will be appointed in every Ward and division to receive the same – to meet at Westminster Hall 23 April between 8 and 9 to deliver the same.'[100] It echoed much of the rhetoric of the radical parliamentarian petition of 1642. The women were not able any longer to 'sit in silence' at this time of 'public calamity and distress'; if oppression makes a wise man mad 'how is it better to be expected from us that are the weaker vessel'. Women's petitioning was presented as an extreme measure: it was not the 'custom' of the sex to petition, but they were 'so over pressed, so overwhelmed in affliction' that they could not keep within their normal compass; 'poverty, misery and famine, like a mighty torrent, is breaking in upon us', and they would rather die than see their children starve. As we have seen, it is not really true that women did not customarily petition the authorities, but the argument highlighted the oppression suffered by the Leveller leaders. The women insisted, as they had done in 1642, that they had an 'equal share and interest with men in the commonwealth'; the petitions of their husbands, children, brethren and servants had been contemptuously rejected so now they were resolved to use their 'weak endeavours' for the same ends. They too appealed to biblical and historical legitimation: 'we knowing that for our encouragement and example, God hath wrought many deliverances for several nations from age to age, by the weak hand of women', citing more militant exemplars than Esther: as Deborah and Jael had helped to deliver Israel, so British women had defended England against Danish invaders, and the women of Scotland had begun the struggle against episcopal tyranny in 1637. The unnerving implications of an appeal to Jael can be illustrated by an early pamphlet of the Leveller activist Katherine Chidley, who was also a rare female participant in the male world of religious polemic. She provided the relevant text – Judges 4.21 – on the title page of her 1641 tract calling for religious liberty: 'Then Jael Heber's wife took a nail of the tent, and took a hammer in her hand, and went softly unto him, and smote the nail into his temples, and fastened it into the ground, (for he was fast asleep and weary) and so he died.'[101]

Leveller women in April 1649 insisted on their loyal parliamentarianism. They had supported the cause to the utmost of their strength, donating 'plate, jewels, rings, bodkins', yet parliament had turned on its staunchest supporters, destroying honest households by their forcible dragging of the Leveller leaders from their homes. They demanded the release of the imprisoned men, and the implementation of the Leveller manifesto, the 'Agreement of the People', which sought to enact a radically decentralised popular polity. This petition was contemptuously rejected and the women sent home to their housewifery but a few days later they responded indignantly in a second petition, structured around a series of anguished rhetorical questions: 'Have we not an equal interest with the men of this nation, in those liberties and securities contained in the Petition of Right, and other good laws of the land?' 'Would you have us keep at home in our houses, when men of such faithfulness and integrity as the four prisoners our friends in the Tower, are fetched out of their beds, and forced from their houses by soldiers to the affrighting of themselves, their wives, children and families?' Again the tyranny of the new republican regime was portrayed through the violation of honest households; again God sanctioned female intervention: 'it being an usual thing with God, by weak means to work mighty effects'; and again, the women claimed an independent right to petition: 'For we are no whit satisfied with the answer you gave unto our Husbands and friends', in terms that still resonate.[102]

Although the Levellers were released by November 1649, after a London jury acquitted Lilburne of treason, further quarrels with leading parliamentarians led to Lilburne's banishment in 1651. On the dissolution of the Rump in 1653 he returned from exile only to be promptly reimprisoned. The Levellers were no longer the force they had been in 1649, but they still mounted a wide-ranging petitioning campaign on Lilburne's behalf, involving servants and apprentices as well as women. The women's rhetoric drew on tropes of 1649: 'the thing is so gross that even women perceive the evil of it', and 'nothing is more manifest then that God is pleased oftentimes to raise up the weakest means to work the mightiest effects'.[103] A second petition referred to Esther and again to the efforts of the 'good women of England' against the Danes. But here they talked of their 'undoubted right of petitioning', rather than presenting it as exceptional.[104]

We have seen that the arguments justifying women's interventions in public affairs varied with context; sometimes their actions were exceptional responses to desperate crises, at others they were founded on straightforward claims to spiritual equality or to a share in the fortunes of the commonwealth. They were always attached to specific causes, rather than articulating a straightforward female position, and this complexity has to be acknowledged. There is no sense in which women, however radical, argued for, or even suggested, any sort of political equality with men, and it is anachronistic to expect them to have done. Leveller women did have a secure sense of their value to their households and their communities, and a thorough-going commitment to their political cause. Opponents of political initiatives by women always sought to discredit their activities on principle as unsuited to their sex, as well as attacking the particular stance they stood for. Women had to justify their petitioning and lobbying in ways that adult men at least usually had no need to adopt. In the process Leveller women, like the petitioners of 1642, provided eloquent justifications for women's voice in public affairs.

Within the Leveller movement, as we have seen, male leaders encouraged and approved of women petitioning, as individuals or in groups, at least in carefully defined contexts. Gendered relationships within the movement were more troubled than this discussion suggests. On other occasions, as we shall see in chapter three, male activists like John Lilburne constructed their own political identity as principled opponents of tyranny, through contrasts with the instability and weakness of women, who were all too ready to compromise with evil, and too liable to value their personal interests above the public good. The apparently harmonious mutuality that the Levellers projected through public petitioning by women, apprentices and servants, as well as male householders, might be shaken by the complexities of everyday social organisation as well as by ideological unease surrounding female assertiveness. Able and active women were necessary to well-run households, as they were useful in political crises; men were in some senses dependent on women, even as they sought to stress their ultimate superiority. Tensions between male householders and women were common, and perhaps between women and apprentices they were inevitable. In London households of the middling sort, the backbone of the Leveller movement, wives had authority over servants and apprentices, young men who were thus for the time being subservient to women. But apprentices hoped they would one day become authoritative householders with obedient wives in their turn, and consequently there were some disturbing currents beneath the surface of Leveller unity.[105]

Royalist women

Within the Levellers, radical political activism empowered women, at least when the movement was under threat. An influential current in recent scholarship, however, suggests that Royalism was equally conducive to women's influence, both during the war and in the following years of eclipse, retreat and exile. The culture of Henrietta Maria's pre-war court incorporated an elevated view of women's potential for good, and 1640s royalism too praised female initiative, contrasting the heroism of the queen in particular with the unseemly activities of low-born parliamentarian women:

> Your sweet celestial voice doth far more cheer
> Than any trumpet, and forbids all fear.
> Your maids of honour with their glorious fight
> Millions of preaching city dames will fright.[106]

We have already discussed royalist women's involvement in conspiracy, spying and military affairs, and stressed the crucial part they played in preserving family property. In exploring more directly their political impact, it is natural to begin with the most prominent and controversial female royalist, Queen Henrietta Maria.

For parliamentarians the influence, real or imagined, of the foreign, papist queen was a source of profound and troubling anxieties; the king's uxoriousness was not a private virtue but a key element in constructions of him as an effeminate tyrant, for tyranny, counter-intuitively perhaps, was seen as a product of inadequate manliness. As the republican Lucy Hutchinson wrote in the life of her parliamentarian husband:

the king had another instigator of his own violent purpose, more powerful than all the rest, and that was the queen … [she] was more fatal to the kingdom, which is never in any place happy where the hands that were made only for distaffs affect the management of sceptres. If any one object the fresh example of Queen Elizabeth, let them remember that the felicity of her reign was the effect of her submission to her masculine and wise counsellors; but wherever male princes are so effeminate as to suffer women of foreign birth and different religions or intermeddle with the affairs of state, it is always found to produce sad desolations.[107]

In a sermon to parliament in February 1643, marking the failure of peace negotiations and the queen's return from the Netherlands, the Puritan William Bridge addressed the absent king: 'If the Queen of your bosom stand in competition with your kingdom, you must not love her better than us, than it.' He continued with pointed praise for a Turkish Emperor who, when accused of over-fondness to his concubine and neglect of his realm, 'drew his scimitar and killed her before them all'.[108] As in this gratuitous reference to concubines, anti-papal rhetoric often mobilised images of sexual deviancy, not least in attacks on Henrietta Maria.[109] A year later, as the queen prepared to leave the royalist headquarters at Oxford for the greater safety of the west, parliamentarian newsbooks conjured up a steamy image of female intrigue and sexual excess in the queen's circle:

> it is high time for her Majesty to be looking towards Dublin, and to leave the doleful noise and business which her designs are likely to bring upon Oxford: She hath done there what mischief she could to the State already, with the help of that rare silken firework the Duchess and the D'Aubignies, with their soap and starch confederates of the laundry. And now that providence seems to be awakened to revenge, they are packing up their boxes of paint, their powders, and powder-treason, their plots, and all their traitrous trinkets for the west, where they may fornicate with Rome and roister the more freely in behalf of the Catholic cause.[110]

Another newsbook expanded indulgently on the royalist reports that 'This day … the Queen began her journey':

> she hath made a wofull Pilgrimage in this kingdom … I could tell ye the stages she hath made in this journey from France to Whitehall, from Whitehall to dancings, masquings, and little dogs, from thence to Friars and Jesuits, from Jesuits to Jermyns, and Gorings, and Digbies, from thence to Holland, and from Holland to gunpowder, ordnance and ammunition, and from thence to England, and so on to fighting, plotting, killing, murdering the Protestants of England, and Ireland.[111]

More enthusiastic views of the queen prevailed in royalist circles. Her court in the 1630s was a focus for cultural innovation as well as an arena for patronage, networking and political lobbying. The theatrical entertainments Henrietta Maria promoted had a serious purpose in propagating French Catholic and neo-platonic positions, highlighting the vital role played by pious, virtuous women in exhorting their husbands to honourable deeds. Feminine constancy and even assertiveness had essential public functions.[112] More immediately practical was the court's economic role as an employer and consumer of luxury goods. A petition to the House of Lords in February 1642 to prevent Henrietta Maria's journey to the Netherlands revealed much sympathy for the queen, even as it acknowledged the 'vulgar' suspicion of her influence. The petitioners – in their own terms, 'many thousands of courtiers', citizens', gentlemen's and tradesmen's wives' – explained they had 'lived in plentiful and good fashion' through trades 'depending wholly … upon the splendour and glory of the English court, and principally upon that of the Queen's Majesty'. Her departure meant 'nothing but distraction, penury and ruin'. They feared:

> this sudden resolution in her Majesty is occasioned by some just distaste taken at divers unusual and tumultuous assemblies, to the affright of her royal person, and at the unpunished printing of many licentious and scandalous pamphlets, some covertly, some plainly, wounding her sacred Majesty in the opinion of the vulgar, as an abettor or counsellor of such designs, which are pretended to disturb the peaceable government both of this kingdom and Ireland.

The petitioners, in contrast, believed she was 'a solicitous mediator for the assembling of this gracious Parliament' and 'an instrument of many acts of mercy and grace to multitudes of distressed people'. They praised the 'great happiness brought to this nation in her princely issue' and asked that her slanderers be punished so that she could return to 'reside continually amongst us'.[113]

The queen had already fled the city and did leave for the Netherlands in February 1642, escorting her elder daughter Mary who had married the young Prince of Orange the previous May. She spent the next year energetically raising money and arms for the royalist cause, while writing regularly to bolster her husband's resolve; after an eventful North Sea voyage she landed again in England at Bridlington in February 1643.[114] In Yorkshire, Henrietta Maria worked hard to encourage the defection of parliamentarian commanders. The John Hothams, senior and junior, parliamentary heroes for their defiance of Charles at Hull in early 1642, switched sides while Sir Hugh Cholmley was conducted in secret from his garrison at Scarborough to the queen at York:

> to whom Sir Hugh said he was come with great affection and desire to serve the king and her majesty, but before he fully declared his resolution he must make two modest requests to her: 1. that she would be pleased to give him her royal assurance not to divert the king from performing those promises he had made to the kingdom. 2ndly that she would endeavour the speedy settling the peace of the kingdom … to which, after her Majesty had given him a very satisfactory answer, he promised to quit the parliament and to serve the king.[115]

This was a complex, two-edged process in which the queen's status and charm worked some magic, even as Cholmley's account suggests anxiety about her influence; indeed, the commander of the king's northern army, the Earl of Newcastle, was urging the waverers to come over to the royalists because 'truly the women rule all', and more masculine wisdom was required.[116]

On her incident-packed and well-publicised march south to join the king, Henrietta Maria continued to send her husband robust letters. From York in March 1643, she insisted 'if you make a peace and disband your army before there is an end to this perpetual parliament, I am absolutely resolved to go into France, not being willing to fall into the hands of those people ... remember what I have written to you in three precedent letters, and be more careful of me than you have been'.[117] When these letters became public in 1645, parliament took a predictably literal and horrified view of them, but they were the rhetorical consequences of the Catholic and platonic stance which encouraged women to urge their husbands to virtuous conduct, and were part of an assertive 'femme forte' tradition valorising the heroism of strong women. Like other elements in Henrietta Maria's self-representation, this owed much to continental influences and was paralleled in the careers of Anne of Austria, regent of France, and Queen Christina of Sweden.[118] From Newark, Henrietta Maria proudly declared herself 'her she-majesty generalissima overall', in command of 3,000 foot, and thirty companies of horse. Here the women of the town petitioned the queen to go no further until the parliamentarian garrison of Nottingham (where Lucy Hutchinson's husband was in command) was taken. Her response was a reinforcement of more conventional gendered relationships:

> Ladies, affairs of this nature are not in our sphere. I am commanded by the king to make all the haste to him that I can. You will receive this advantage, at least, by my answer, though I cannot grant your petition – you may learn, by my example, to obey your husbands.[119]

Henrietta Maria and Charles were reunited at Edgehill on 13 July, and the queen's arrival, at long last, in Oxford was the occasion of a sustained outpouring of praise for her valour, emphasising her centrality to the royalist cause. Verses by Jane Cavendish, daughter of the Earl of Newcastle, circulated in manuscript among her family:

> Your looks are courage, mixed with such sweetness,
> Which makes all creatures justly to witness,
> Themselves your vassals and no longer stay
> Till you command, and then their tributes pay.[120]

A printed verse miscellany produced by the university had a wider impact. It included poems in Latin, French and English contrasting her love and loyalty with parliamentarian treachery. Printed in Oxford, it nonetheless found its way into the collection of the London bookseller George Thomason. 'Our muses are return'd (Great Queen) with you' rejoiced the poets; the celebrations she inspired were bringing good luck and new vigour to the royalists:

Go burn some rebel town, for such alone
Are bonfires suiting to the joys we own ...
And treason stoop, forc'd by commanding charms
Either to kiss your hands, or fear your arms.

The reunion coincided with significant royalist victories in the south, the west and
the north:

The northern army in one week did more
When they had seen you, then a year before.

Parliament's villainy was exposed in their assaults on the queen:

Nature nor law could check their villainy
(Unmanly rebels) sex nor Majesty

Now victory was assured:

Come then, and tell our King the wars are done,
Your safe approach confirms the day his own.
Tell him his peace, his crown, himself you bring
Such news a king should hear, such angels sing

The king and queen had been reunited 'yesterday / Where their twelve thousand
durst not stay' (at the battle of Edgehill). The volume also included the University
orator's welcoming speech, praising the combination of love-making and war-waging,
which marked the queen's endeavours:

> such an absence, so barbarously forced with danger, so bitterly perused with
> calumnies, so patiently born, in leaving that company out of pure love which
> you most lov'd, in sequestering your self from the arms of your royal husband
> to furnish his hands with strength, to send him the sinews of Mars.

Her constant loyalty had brought joy to her 'dear husband' and her 'sweet children';
and her womanly efforts for family and kingdom were conflated: 'You have often
lain in travail for princes, but now of late you have travailed for kingdoms, and in
your happy return your people are delivered'. In conclusion the printer and publisher
Leonard Lichfield added a poem of his own which, in attacking the 'confused
nonsense' peddled by 'Babel London', placed the contrasts between accomplished,
orderly, royalist loyalty, and ignorant, disruptive treachery within the very processes
of print:

That traitorous and unlettered crew
Who fight against heaven, their sovereign and you

Have not yet stained my hallowed fonts, the spring
Must needs be clear that issues from the king[121]

From July 1643 until she left Oxford for the safety of Exeter to give birth to her last child in April 1644 Henrietta Maria was the king's closest adviser; according to Edward Hyde, Charles 'saw with her eyes'. Although some resented her influence it is likely that her prominence helped to limit the impact of royalist divisions.[122]

We have already seen that Henrietta Maria was subject to sustained onslaughts in 'many licentious and scandalous pamphlets', onslaughts that reached a crescendo when the king's correspondence was seized at the decisive royalist defeat at Naseby in June 1645. This correspondence indicated the influence of the queen, for good or ill. Even after her flight to France in July 1644, advice still flowed through letters. She was full of schemes for foreign help, and still determined that Charles would brook no compromise with his enemies: 'Above all, have a care not to abandon those who have served you, as well the bishops as the poor Catholics'.[123] When parliament decided, controversially, to publish the correspondence, the editors concluded that 'the Queen appears to have been as harsh, and imperious towards the king, as she is implacable to our religion, nation and government'.[124] Comparisons were drawn with Herod, who had been seduced by his wife and daughter into sanctioning the execution of John the Baptist.[125]

Royalists attacked this intrusion into marital intimacy, and the violation of the king's privacy, and they defended the queen's right to a public influence, and her commitment to her religion:

But, lest this groundless seem, they reasons vex,
And tell the world she's of the weaker sex.
In what wild brains this madness first began!
They're wondrous angry, cause the Queen's no man.
For sirs forbear, do not the world perplex:
Reason and judgement are not things of sex.
Souls and their faculties were never heard,
To be confined to the doublet and the beard.[126]

Something of the penchant for intrigue and adventure in courts and camps which defined the reputation of Lady Aubigny as well as the queen, can also be discerned in the memoirs of Anne Murray, later Lady Halkett. Anne's reminiscences, recalled in a more humdrum, widowed middle age, recounted her earlier life with a mixture of regret, disapproval and undeniable excitement. Anne Murray was born in 1623 to a courtier family; her father, who had died when she was a baby, had been tutor to Charles and her mother was governess to the king's children. In 1648 Anne, in cooperation with a notorious royalist conspirator and double agent Colonel Joseph Bampfield, organised the escape of the king's second son, James Duke of York, from confinement in St James's palace. She procured women's clothes as a disguise, dressed him and guided him to the Thames barge that carried him to safety. She needed guile and determination:

> When I gave the measure to my tailor to enquire how much mohair would serve to make a petticoat and waistcoat to a young gentlewoman of that bigness and stature, he considered it a long time, and said he had made many gowns and suits, but he had never made any to such a person in his life ... he had never seen any woman of so low a stature have so big a waist.

Anne was already emotionally involved with Bampfield, and, indeed among the chaos of civil war, separated from her mother and brother, Anne had remarkable scope for independently conducted romantic entanglements. Her liaison with Bampfield followed an earlier courtship with Thomas Howard that ended when he abruptly jilted her. As Halkett's narrative ultimately reveals, Bampfield was already married but the confusions of the time facilitated his repeated deceptions. In 1648, believing his wife was dead, Anne promised to marry Bampfield. When it was alleged the wife was in fact alive, Bampfield sent a servant to confirm her death, who declared 'he was at her grave where she was buried'. Anne refused to believe a committed royalist could be a bad man: 'loyalty being the principle that first led me to a freedom of converse with him', 'it was impossible, in my opinion, for a good man to be an ill husband'. Only in 1653 was she finally convinced of his deception and in 1656 she married an older widower, James Halkett.

In the midst of these emotional trials, Anne remained an active, autonomous and committed royalist. In 1650, she travelled to Scotland to try to recover some of her inheritance and was caught up in the battle of Dunbar. She tended wounded soldiers, and was living with the heavily pregnant Countess of Dunfermline when the house was attacked by the English invaders' army: 'the first question they asked me was if I were the English whore that came to meet the king, and all set pistols just against me'. On her own account she was defiant:

> I told them I owned myself to be an English woman and to honour the King, but for the name they gave me, I abhorred it, but my coming to them was not to dispute for my self, but to tell them I was sorry to hear that any of the English nation, who was generally esteemed the most civil people in the world, should give so much occasion to be thought barbarously rude.

'What advantage,' she continued, 'can you propose to yourselves to fright a person of honour who is great with child, and few but children and women in the house?' In the face of this onslaught, the soldiers threw their pistols down, and promised to leave the women alone. Shortly afterwards, Anne was at dinner with the parliamentarian commander, the deeply spiritual and politically radical Colonel Robert Overton, who 'said to me that God had wonderfully evidenced his power in the great things he had done'. A long conversation about scripture and God's providence ensued during which Overton claimed the Book of Daniel sanctioned regicide, but Anne dissented: 'If you can show me in all the Holy Scripture a warrant for murdering your lawful King and banishing his posterity, I will then say all you have done is well,

and will be of your opinion. But as I am sure that cannot be done, so I must con-
demn that horrid act.' She claimed – with the benefit of hindsight – that she told
Overton they would 'change what ever government you try till you come to beg of
the king home and govern you again', and he retorted '"Well", says he, "if this
should come to pass, I will say you are a prophetess."'[127] These adventures may have
lost nothing in the telling as Anne Halkett wrote them up in her sedate later life, but
the opportunities within royalism for plotting, travelling and brave defiance as well as
unhappy love affairs are still striking.

Halkett's memoirs also involve an exploration of intricate relationships between
public and private virtue. Susan Wiseman has discussed how Anne's political loyalty
to the crown masks the dubious character of some of her private decisions, while
Bampfield's personal failings are ultimately compounded by his political betrayals.[128]
During the years of royalist defeat, which for some prominent figures meant exile
from England, a stress on retreat, privacy and withdrawal became a means of defying
the values of the dominant public, political world. Women's creativity and feminine
symbolism alike were central to this privatised vision, which, paradoxically, was a
public stance, representing 'the potency of feminized retreat' in Hero Chalmers's
telling phrase.[129] Women thus had remarkable agency within defeated royalism.
Households preserved by staunch women, fostering friendship, loyalty and innocent
revelry at Christmas and other festivals, represented an alternative to the republican
status quo. One means by which the feminine and the domestic aspects of royalism
were highlighted in the 1650s was through the publication of cookery books, as
recently analysed by Laura Knoppers. *The Queen's Closet Opened*, first published in
1655, with many subsequent editions, embellished with a portrait of the widowed
Henrietta Maria, invited readers into a private elite world to share recipes associated
with the queen's English courtiers. The book created a royalist image of lavish hos-
pitality maintained by gracious aristocrats, which contrasted sharply with the nig-
gardly repression of Puritan, republican rule and provided a version of the queen at
odds with the foreign papist of parliamentarian newsbooks.[130]

Royalist women's writing, circulated in both manuscript and print, was a form of
'memory work' as Kate Chedgzoy has eloquently demonstrated, relating personal
suffering to political defeat, but holding out hope of resistance and recovery.[131] As
with the more instrumental activities of royalist women in preserving family property,
we should not see these interventions as antagonistic to men. Indeed an ideology that
valued friendship, loyalty and female creativity was central to the identity of some
royalist men. The best example is William Cavendish, Earl of Newcastle, father of
Jane and Elizabeth and husband of Margaret, his anxieties at the queen's role in 1643
notwithstanding. In 1637 he advised the Prince of Wales 'To women you cannot be
too civil', and his openness to female inspiration and creative agency was part of an
aristocratic vision that challenged the low-born submissiveness of Puritanism. Important also was the simple factor of male political eclipse. Where royalist men were
banned from public office, and where the king himself and other prominent figures
were in foreign exile, a feminine withdrawal might well be seen as a 'genuine route
to collective empowerment'.[132]

Print publication was not necessary for women's writings to have a political charge. Manuscripts circulated to 'a limited, known and sympathetic readership', building on and strengthening the networks that offered royalists both solace and inspiration. The poems and drama of Jane Cavendish and her sister Elizabeth, Lady Brackley were collected in fine presentation volumes, written out by one of the family's servants.[133] Drama in particular was preserved as a royalist cultural form, its loss reinforcing a version of parliamentarianism as impoverished philistinism. The Cavendish sisters offered 'local, rural, yet courtly … versions of Englishness', at a time of national disaster. Jane Cavendish recorded the proud heritage of her ancestors, and praised the queen's valour and her father's victories, but in later poems she presented herself as 'coffined in a sad garrison of rest'. Exile, separation and incarceration were persistent and predictable themes as the sisters mourned their absent father and their ruined estates. Regret and hope, sorrow and determination were all evoked in these works. The volume included a 'pastoral', a form in European culture that was both 'a mode of mourning and memory' and 'a playful recollection of time past, as a way of holding on to a hope for better times'. It ended with the hope – a fantasy, but an empowering one – that merriment could restore their absent friends:

> Now could we ladies have but such a dance
> That would but fetch your friends, now out of France
> You then would well approve of this our mirth
> But since not so you do appear sad earth.[134]

The elegy similarly worked as mourning, consolation and resistance, as seen in the manuscript poetry of another royalist woman, Hester Pulter, who wrote of her personal and her political calamities, of her own dead daughter as well as of her martyred king and the commanders executed at Colchester. London without the king was represented as bereft and joyless: 'Spring Garden that such pleasures bred / Looks dull and sad since Cloris fled', while a 'complaint' of the river Thames denounced the imprisonment of the king in 1647, and evoked a lost past in order to promote a 'better future'. Hence nostalgia had a political function:

> Hast thou forgot (aye me) so have not I
> Those halcyon days, the sweet tranquillity
> That we enjoyed under his happy reign.[135]

The best known royalist poet, Katherine Phillips, was at the heart of cultivated royalist networks where friendship, especially between women, was valorised as a refuge from political disaster and as a means of reconstructing an honest social and political order. Phillips in the main insisted on her retirement from the world: as in her 1651 poem, 'A Retired friendship To Ardelia':

> Here is no quarrelling for Crowns,
> Nor fear of changes in our fate,

No trembling at the great ones frown,
Nor any slavery of State
Here's no disguise, nor treachery,
Nor any deep concealed design,
From bloody lots this place is free
And calm as those looks of thine
Here let us sit and bless our stars
Who did such happy quiet give,
As that removed from noise of wars
In one another's hearts we live

The references to treachery and slavery hint at political engagement, and when Phillips insisted, 'I think not on the State, nor am concern'd, / Which way soever that great helm is turn'd', it was in a determinedly royalist poem directed against a radical parliamentarian, '"On the double murther of the King" (in answer to a libellous paper written by V.[avasour] Powell, at my house)'.[136] Circulation of verse and other literary works, reading and performing theatrical texts in aristocratic households, and musical events were all forms of cultural defiance which had real political force – and in an England where royalists were perforce confined to 'private' life and domestic concerns, the value of female influence and creativity was marked. At various times the Cavendish sisters, their step-mother Margaret, Countess of Newcastle and Phillips all performed or provided texts at musical events organised by Henry Lawes in London. These apparently 'private' occasions cemented networks and raised morale for those who joined in, but they were of wider significance as a form of cultural politics openly challenging the Cromwellian regime, when the verse and songs found their way into print.[137]

Prominent women royalists in exile, like those in retreat in England, publicised their 'private' social and cultural life as an example to constrained friends and a reproach to enemies at home. 'Innocent' merriment or 'harmless' sport offered a clear alternative to a mean or austere Puritanism, as with the widespread reporting of the Christmas celebrations in Henrietta Maria's Paris household. The prolific publications of Margaret Cavendish have been discussed by Hero Chalmers as 'a form of political resistance in the teeth of royalist exile'. Despite their straitened circumstances the Cavendishes lived in magnificent style, maintaining a household rich in music, theatricals and other forms of aristocratic display. Margaret's writings featured adventurous and speculative women, and imagined female communities. She had served in Henrietta Maria's Paris court, and her work, in common with other royalist cultural practices in the 1640s and 1650s, was influenced by the court culture promoted by Henrietta Maria before and after the war and by the 'femme forte' tradition associated with her.[138] An elaborate printed frontispiece to one volume represented Earl and Countess, with his children and their spouses, sitting together in their Antwerp house; thus a 'royalist family dispersed by the political realities of "the Time" are brought together in the text'. As James Fitzmaurice has noted, this is the only frontispiece in any of her many books that Margaret Cavendish ever commented on, noting in verse:

Those friends I did conceit
Were gathered in a Company together
All sitting by a Fire in cold weather, ...
My Lord and I, here in two Chairs are set,
And all his Children, wives and husbands, met,
To hear me tell them Tales, as I think fit,
And hope they're full of Phancy, and of Wit,
Ladies, I ask your pardons, mercies I,
Since I talk all, and many Ladies, by.

In part, Cavendish was seeking to represent a harmonious family and perhaps to win over in reality the adult step-children and their spouses, from whom she was estranged, but she spoke also for her exiled and politically marginalised husband. Good company persisted in chilly times.[139] Central to the royalist alternatives, promoted by women, was a determined anti-Puritan religious stance, and it is to women's participation in the religious upheavals of the 1640s and 1650s that we now turn.

Religion

Parliament's attempts to remove the remnants of 'popery' from the English church and to establish a reformed national church alarmed many who yearned for the rhythms and ceremonies of the prayer book, enthused some who hoped to build a godly community, and disappointed others who wished to go much further and construct their own gathered and separate congregations of saints. We have already described how the determined wives and daughters of ejected royalist and Anglican ministers defied the authorities in the defence of their homes and livelihoods, while other women enthusiastically opposed the Puritan preachers who took their places: the 'intruded' minister of Henley in Arden in Warwickshire complained in 1653 that he was ordered from the pulpit by Sarah Biggs and 'divers other women with the assent of their husbands (whose custom it was to disturb such as were authorised to preach there)'. With 'threatening and abusive language' they commanded Fawkes to come forth.[140] Underlying this defiance was resentment at the religious changes enforced by parliamentarian reform. The set prayers and ceremonies enjoined in the Book of Common Prayer were swept away, in theory at least, and replaced by an austere 'Directory of Worship', drawn up by the Westminster Assembly of Divines. Anne Sadleir, like several other women, preserved a copy of a poem first printed in 1646 (by a hostile commentator) on a 'virtuous lady' who built a closet, 'wherein to secure the most sacred Book of Common-Prayer, from the view and violence of the enemies thereof, sectaries and schismatics of this Kingdom'. Sadleir maintained Anglican worship in her private chapel and protected deprived clergy throughout the interregnum. Similarly Dorothy Pakington, a Worcestershire royalist, protected prominent royalist clergy including Charles I's chaplain, Henry Hammond, until the Restoration.[141]

Women were perhaps particularly affected by loss of the rituals and communal sociability surrounding crucial personal and family events. By 1653 marriage had become a civil matter rather than a religious ceremony as we shall see in chapter four; infant baptism was controversial among radicals and for more orthodox Puritans, it was a solemn, minimal occasion, with no godparents or feasting. Mary Verney, pregnant and alone, was horrified by the religious changes. 'Truly one lives like a heathen in this place', she complained to Ralph in France. It was hard to find a place in the packed London churches but hardly worth the effort anyway for

> one hears a strange kind of service and in such a tone that most people do nothing but laugh at it. And everybody that receives [the sacrament of the last supper] must be examined before the elders, who that all swear asketh them such questions that would make one blush to relate.

Mary disliked this intrusive Presbyterian discipline that examined all who wished to take communion on their knowledge of the faith and personal morality, and she deplored the new forms of worship. So she hoped to have her baby baptised in the old fashion: 'I will obey thee, and get a minister in the house that will do it the old way, for 'tis not the fashion here to have godfathers or godmothers, but for the father to bring the child to church and answer for it.' Although Mary presented her plan as obedience to Sir Ralph, her exiled husband advised caution for matters of form and ceremony differed in 'almost every country': 'I pray give no offence to the state, should it be done in the old way perhaps it may bring more trouble upon you than you can imagine'.[142] When another royalist sympathiser, Isabella Twysden, recorded the baptisms of her own and her friends' children in her almanacs, she always noted whether 'gossips' (godparents) were present or not. In September 1647: 'my sister Twysden was brought a-bed of a girl ... it was christened that afternoon ... without gossips, the new way'; while another daughter was christened by the noted Presbyterian Mr Calamy, again 'without gossips'. Isabella also noted that the Kent royalist Sir Edward Dering was married 'by the book of Common Prayer' in April 1647.[143] Religious affiliations were reinforced by commitment to a social world of kinship, neighbourliness and friendship exhibited in godparenting relationships and renewed through ceremony and festivity, particularly at Christmas. The diarist John Evelyn's wife was 'churched' according to custom after the birth of her children, and the babies were baptised according to the Book of Common Prayer. The family usually managed to celebrate Christmas.[144]

While Sadleir, Verney and the Evelyns took risks to continue outlawed religious practices, the initiatives of other women were sanctioned, albeit within limits, by mainstream parliamentarian Puritans. The achievements of the well-known learned and religious Dutch woman Anna Maria van Schurman were associated with parliament through the publication of letters between her and the MP Simonds D'Ewes, in which she praised D'Ewes as a 'great patron of learning', praising parliament as that 'Honourable Assembly'.[145] The Cheshire preacher Samuel Torshell was tutor to the king's youngest children, who were in parliament's custody, and a sermon marking

Princess Elizabeth's birthday was expanded into a printed treatise, *The Woman's Glorie*, intended for her use. Torshell praised a series of learned and active women from biblical and secular history, and insisted 'the soul knows no difference of sex'. Women had, of course, to be modest and obedient, but they also had extensive religious duties, domestic and public. Torshell encouraged women to read the scriptures, to attend and discuss sermons, to 'privately and familiarly exhort others', to lead family prayers if male heads of household were absent, and, in sum, 'to get public spirits'.[146]

We have already met some of these public spirits, such as Brilliana Harley, or the much mocked Lady Anne Waller. The wife of another parliamentarian commander, Lady Cicely Brereton, whose husband Sir William acted so ruthlessly at Lichfield, was equally active, venting Puritan zeal against 'popish' images in 1641. When the minister and churchwardens of Weston-under-Lizard in Staffordshire ignored her orders to remove the 'ancient imagery' in the church, Lady Cicely herself 'with a staff most zealously brake all the windows'.[147] Puritan women, like Anglicans, used their wealth and position to promote their preferred worship and ministry. Widows with independent means had the best opportunities. Sir William Waller's third wife, another Anne, was previously the widow of Sir Simon Harcourt. She was praised in her funeral sermon in 1661 by the eminent Presbyterian Edmund Calamy, as an 'elect lady' who had made religion her 'daily labour', 'a fixed star in the firmament of God's church', and 'a diligent attender upon Gospel Ordinances'. Anne Harcourt/ Waller embodied much of Torshell's programme. She was a conscientious observer of the Lord's day, a 'constant writer of sermons' who 'wrote them in her heart as well as in her book', and made sure to instruct her maids and serving boys, 'pressing them to be doers of the word, and not hearers only, concluding all in prayer with them'. While running her estates at Stanton Harcourt after her first husband's death she managed, despite the hardships of the war years, to provide a preaching minister and a lecturer, 'the poor old incumbent being superannuated'.[148]

Lady Frances Hobart was a zealous defender of the Presbyterian interest in Norwich. As a daughter of the Earl of Bridgewater, she had connections with the royal court but – again according to a funeral elegy – 'this excellent lady was ordained to higher things than balls, and masques and visits', and was brought up 'to be a Calvinist in point of doctrine, and a Presbyterian as to Discipline' by a French Protestant governess. She was a most obedient wife but 'by her prudent monitions, and passionate entreaties her husband was won from what had been the vanities of his youth'. Both Lady Frances and Sir John Hobart had been converted by the Norwich Puritan John Carter, but Lady Frances found it easier to live up to godly expectations. Sir John found it difficult to avoid swearing and so made her 'privily to pinch his arm when she heard any oath slip from him'. Both Hobarts were generous patrons of orthodox Puritan and Presbyterian ministers, and in 1647, by then a widow, Lady Frances built a chapel in the lower rooms of her Norwich house, to protect the orthodox from radical assault: 'The times began to be troublesome, through the distempers of the army, and some fears began then to arise that ministers, who could not comply with the extravagancies of that time should not be suffered to enjoy their public liberty.' There her chaplain John Collinges delivered a lecture every week, and repeated his Sunday sermons in the evening to 'a very full auditory', attracting many young persons who otherwise would have spent the day in 'idle walks, discourses and recreations' in the town fields.[149]

Harley, Hobart and the Wallers were broadly 'Presbyterian' in sympathy, supporters of an orthodox reformed national church, that was, ideally, comprehensive and compulsory. The collapse of Episcopal government, the opportunities and speculation of the war years, and the commitment of parliament's army to liberty of conscience, ensured that the 1640s and 1650s were years of religious fragmentation, controversy and choice, officially sanctioned for most Protestants after 1649 when the commonwealth government repealed the Elizabethan laws enforcing church attendance. Women played a prominent part in these developments as rich, recent scholarship has demonstrated. Godly Puritan women like conscientious Anglicans might come to ponder the ways in which the national church marked crucial events in their lives. Lucy Hutchinson explained how she had read notes on infant baptism drawn up by radical troopers in her husband's garrison and was convinced that the arguments against it were sound: 'but being then young and modest, she thought it a kind of virtue to submit to the judgment and practice of most churches, rather than to defend a singular opinion of her own'. Shortly afterwards she became pregnant and confided her doubts to her husband. John Hutchinson 'diligently searched the scriptures' and 'all the eminent treatises on both sides' and discussed the issue with the local orthodox ministers. Remaining unconvinced, the Hutchinsons decided not to have their new baby baptised, prompting the orthodox to revile them as 'fanatics and anabaptists'.[150] Characteristically, Lucy Hutchinson emphasises her husband's spiritual and intellectual superiority but the initiative, it appears, was her own.

Despite their rejection of infant baptism, the Hutchinsons did not, at this stage in the 1640s, forsake the public assemblies, but many other women participated in the building of gathered congregations, voluntary bodies that developed as alternatives to a compulsory, imperfect national church. In Bristol Dorothy Hazzard was a leader – a Deborah or mother in Israel – among the small group who moved from criticism of Laudian 'innovations' in the 1630s to the founding in the early 1640s of a gathered congregation where some, but not all members, practised adult baptism as a sign of their faith.[151] For a period in the 1630s she was a prosperous, independent widow, Mrs Kelly:

> She was like a he-goat before the flock, for in those days Mrs Kelly was very famous for piety and reformation, well-known to all, bearing a living testimony against the superstitions and traditions of those days, and she would not observe their invented times and feasts, called holy days. At which time she kept a grocer's shop in High Street ... where she would keep open her shop on the time they called Christmas day, and sit sewing in her shop, as a witness for God in the midst of the city, in the face of the sun, and the sight of all men, even in those very days of darkness, when, as it were, all sorts of people had a reverence of that particular day above all others.

Shortly afterwards Mrs Kelly married a Puritan minister Matthew Hazzard, but retained her independence of mind. The Hazzard household provided refuge for families en route to New England and for women who wanted to avoid the ceremony of 'churching' after childbirth that was offensive to many Puritans. Dorothy rejected some of her young husband's compromises, refusing to hear him read the service from the Book of Common Prayer. Most provocatively, the minister's wife met in private discussions with her closest associates, sweeping later into the church to hear Matthew's sermon. Once the civil war broke out, the gathered church could meet openly and its members formed the core of the parliamentarian party in the city. In 1643 Dorothy led 200 women and girls who defied royalist besiegers at Frome gate, and after the city's fall she was prominent among the Bristol godly who went up to London, to give evidence against the parliamentarian governor Nathaniel Fiennes, accused of cowardice for his precipitate surrender.

The Broadmead church had been founded by Hazzard and four men, but its membership as it grew was increasingly female. The attractions of gathered congregations to women are evident in many of them. A Canterbury congregation led by the radical Independent John Durant had fourteen male and nine female founding members in 1645 but by 1658 there were almost twice as many women (seventy-nine) as men (forty-three). The officers of this congregation were male, and did not take kindly to women who challenged their authority. Nonetheless several women had clearly been emboldened by religious choice and were confident participants in controversy. One Sarah Day denied the fundamental doctrine of the Trinity, 'followed seducers' and 'was drawn away into corrupt opinions … to deny Jesus Christ's remaining still in our human nature … also that he was not distinct from the father'. Although such views might have rendered her liable to prosecution, Day remained 'pertinacious and obstinate' and uttered 'unfitting speeches' when admonished by three men. Another woman denounced for unorthodox views responded more subtly: 'Sister Fancocke' 'alleged 1 Corinthians 13. last'. This text, not included in the church's own account, was 'And now abideth faith, hope, charity, these three; but the greatest of these is charity'.[152]

Durant's church struggled to maintain unity around orthodox Calvinist theology, but all radical groups faced controversy and defection, with women often proving hard to control. The 'general' Baptist churches of East Anglia (so called because they rejected the exclusivity of Calvinism, and preached the possibility of general redemption as well as adult baptism) were in serious competition for support with Quaker activists by early 1655. Male elders struggled to keep the women in line. Sister Pharepoint 'refused to hearken' to reproof, and 'exhorted us to look within, for the light within was the only rule to be guided by'. The straightforward Quaker doctrine of salvation through seizing on the 'light' of Christ within humanity seems to have resonated particularly with Baptists, whose focus on the precise administration of the formal ceremony of baptism might prompt anxiety and despair. Another sister told the elders that 'water baptism was ceased, and the baptism of the spirit was the true baptism' while Sister Sneesby was found to be 'in a very sad and deplorable condition' after reading Quaker books. She was less defiant, explaining 'it was her husband's desire, and she could not help it'.[153]

The women in these congregations, revered mothers in Israel or pertinacious rebels, were well known within their particular communities, but it is the research of later scholars that has made them known to us. Female prophets and assertive Quaker women were inspired by religion to a more provocative, public role in the 1640s and 1650s, their contemporary impact was felt in print and in direct action. Zealous Puritans saw God's hand at work directly in the world, and in the terrible exhilaration of the revolutionary months around the regicide, it was entirely plausible that God would work through the weakest of human instruments. Had not the prophet Joel promised that God would 'pour out my spirit upon all flesh; and your sons and your daughters shall prophesy, your old men shall dream dreams, your young men shall see visions. And also upon the servants and upon the handmaids in those days will I pour out my spirit' (Joel 2.28–29)? The supposed passivity and weakness of women meant that God's choice of them as instruments was a particularly effective demonstration of God's power and purposes. These purposes were varied. Prophetesses were not always associated with radical movements. There was the eccentric Lady Eleanor Davies, long opposed to Charles I, but an individualist without associations to any coherent movement, while in Cornwall, in the later 1640s, one Ann Jeffries told of encounters with 'small people clad in green' and prophesied the restoration of Charles I to power.[154]

The female prophets who wielded the most remarkable if precarious influence operated within the broad coalition that was radical parliamentarianism. Within this milieu, many were willing to believe, or at least not to reject the possibility, that the women were inspired by God.[155] Consequently when Elizabeth Poole approached the General Council of Officers in late December 1649, claiming she had a message from God, the army leaders, in the midst of pressing debates on the fate of the king and the future of the kingdom, broke off to hear her. Poole declared herself a 'servant to the most high God' who had commanded her to deliver a 'Vision, wherein is manifested the disease and cure of the kingdom', framed, as discussed in the introduction, in conventional marital language and vividly gendered imagery of the body. Poole was a 'sad mourner' for the ills of the kingdom, struggling as if in labour until she brought forth this vision in which a man represented the all-powerful army that stood for the liberty and freedom of the country. This man was to cure the diseased kingdom which was represented as female. Poole had seen 'a woman which should signify the weak and imperfect distressed state of the land ... This woman was full of imperfection, crooked, weak, sickly and imperfect.' This validation of the army's authority was welcome to the officers but they did not accept Poole's detailed arguments, delivered a week later, that the proposed trial, and certainly the possibility of regicide, were illegitimate. Continuing her figuring of the kingdom as female, she argued that an abused wife could defend herself but could not kill her husband: 'you may hold the hands of your husband that he pierce not your bowels with a knife or sword to take your life' but you could not take his life. Both husband-killing and king-killing were, as Marcus Nevitt has noted, forms of treason.[156] At this point the officers decided she was not God's messenger and Poole was disowned by her London congregation.

Susan Wiseman has argued convincingly that Poole's intervention should be seen in the context of radical dilemmas and divisions over the revolutionary events of 1648–49. Poole had long-standing and enduring connections with gathered congregations and radical print networks of a distinctly mystical and spiritual character. She was bitterly attacked by the Baptist William Kiffin, who was prominent in denunciations of the Levellers in the same weeks. The Levellers too regarded the trial and execution of the king as illegitimate. This is not to say that she was merely a tool of male leaders – rather that her appearance before the officers was a serious effort to move the revolution in a particular direction.[157] The most unlikely demonstrations of God's power upon weak female bodies can also be linked to political crises within parliamentarianism. In 1647 Sarah Wight, a fifteen-year-old girl with close links to London gathered churches, took to her bed, refused food and uttered ecstatic messages of the power of God's grace. At first her associates doubted the validity of her inspiration; then they understood her experiences as preparation for a godly death; and finally, as it became clear that she was not dying (she lived well into the 1660s), her experiences were published by the radical Congregationalist pastor, Henry Jessey, under the revealing title, *The Exceeding Riches of Grace Advanced By the Spirit of Grace, in an Empty Nothing Creature viz. Mris Sarah Wight* (London, 1647). It was the bodily weakness of the 'Empty Nothing Creature' that gave Wight her spiritual authority and although her influence was more subject to male control than other, older visionary women, she became a respected spiritual counsellor to the godly who flocked to her for advice and reassurance. The published account included a list of those attending Wight, 'of esteem amongst many that fear the Lord in London', and a preface from another radical minister, John Saltmarsh, as well as Jessey's framing narrative. It was issued as Independents and more radical congregations with separatist tendencies led by men like Jessey or Saltmarsh faced serious threats from more authoritarian Presbyterian elements in parliament and the city of London, threats that were only defeated when the army occupied the city in August 1647. While Wight herself was perhaps not primarily concerned with immediate political conflicts – and the lasting spiritual impact of the text is demonstrated through its frequent reprinting in the 1650s and 1660s – the first issue of *Exceeding Riches* was in part a demonstration of radical solidarity and spiritual power to friends and enemies alike.[158]

Jessey was among the Congregationalist and semi-separatist pastors enthused by millenarian expectations that led, by the early 1650s, to a movement campaigning for the rule of the Saints under 'king Jesus', in other words for a fifth monarchy in place of the four monarchies overthrown in turn over the course of human history. Millenarianism, building on the prophecies of Daniel and the violent upheavals promised in the Book of Revelation, was receptive to female prophetic power. Mary Cary, about whom we know little apart from her publications, tracks millenarian arguments from the later 1640s. Her *Word in Season* responded to the same crisis addressed by Jessey's account of Wight; it appealed to the Book of Joel to justify public speaking by all gifted persons, and attacked Presbyterian attempts to suppress what they regarded as error.[159] A volume of commentaries on the Book of Revelation was published in 1648 and reissued in 1653 at the height of Fifth Monarchist agitation, while *The Little Horns doom and downfall* (1651) dealt with the central prophetic chapters of Daniel.[160] Although Cary professed herself to be 'a very weak and unworthy instrument' she gave a very accomplished account of the scriptures. The 'little horn' on the fourth or last beast in Daniel chapter 7, that overcame three other horns, was identified as Charles I; Charles's fall thus presaged the overthrow of the kingdoms of this world by Christ and his Saints:

> As the Saints have had a suffering time, so they shall have a time of deliverance and freedom from suffering; and the rod of the wicked shall not always rest upon the lot of the righteous, but God will (though he have borne long) at last avenge the quarrel of his people upon their enemies.

A new Jerusalem would arise; Cary presented an utopia of plenty without corruption, where poverty was at an end. The book was licensed by the prominent Independent Joseph Caryl, and had three epistles from leading ministers, Hugh Peter, Henry Jessey and Christopher Feake. Jessey endorsed Cary's view of Charles I, while Feake, who was the key Fifth Monarchist preacher, attacked those who scorned the visions of 'illiterate men, and silly women'. Cary's dedication was to three prominent women: Cromwell's wife, Elizabeth, and his daughter, Bridget Ireton, and Lady Margaret Rolle, the wife of Chief Justice Henry Rolle. They were placed in 'some of the highest places of honour' among the 'many pious, precious, prudent, and sage matrons, and holy women, with which this Commonwealth is adorned'. Male approbation for Cary was thus combined with an assertion of the vital role of godly women in the new republic.[161]

By 1654 when Anna Trapnel, the most notorious woman associated with the Fifth Monarchists, burst into public notice, Cromwell had taken the place of Charles I as the 'little horn', for his assumption of personal power as Lord Protector in December 1653 had dashed millenarian hopes for the rule of the Saints. Trapnel, a Stepney shipwright's daughter, fell into a trance in January 1654 among the crowds witnessing the Council of State's examination of the imprisoned Fifth Monarchist preacher, Vavasour Powell, at Whitehall. Her trances continued for some twelve days, interrupted by 'visions of God, relating to the governors, army, churches, ministry, universities, and the whole nation, uttered in prayers and spiritual songs, by an inspiration extraordinary, and full of wonder'.[162] The most vivid vision again drew on the central texts from Daniel that underlay the Fifth Monarchist narrative of the fall of earthly powers, succeeded by the rule of the Saints and the second coming of Christ. Trapnel saw a 'great company of cattle' with human faces and horns:

> For the foremost his countenance was perfectly like unto Oliver Cromwell's; and on a sudden there was a great shout of those that followed him … they bowed unto him. … with a great kind of joy that he was their supreme … He run at many precious saints that stood in the way of him.

Like most prophets, Trapnel added a gloss to ensure her listeners got the point:

> With that I broke forth, and sang praise, and the Lord said, 'Mark that scripture, Three horns shall arise, a fourth shall come out different from the former, which shall come out different from the former, which shall be more terror to the saints than the others that went before.'[163]

Despite her humble status, Trapnel had been 'trained up to my book and writing', and her views developed within the radical Puritan congregations of 1640s London, familiar already from the careers of Poole, Wight and Cary. Trapnel singled out John Simpson, pastor of her own church at All Hallows the Great, Hugh Peter and Henry Jessey for praise, and she had been acquainted with Sarah Wight.[164] On her own 1654 account the visions had begun with parliament's stunning victories of the 1640s, and the army's assault on London Presbyterians in 1647 had been a crucial stimulus. But the high hopes of the later 1640s evaporated, and Trapnel developed a classic Fifth Monarchist narrative of betrayal, with Cromwell as consummate villain.[165] In the 1640s, in Trapnel's account, Cromwell was a second Gideon, a military leader who had delivered the Israelites and then refused supreme political power, but by 1654 he was the little horn on the terrible beast in Daniel chapter 7 who made war with the Saints. Like Cary, Trapnel combined the spiritual elitism of the rule of the Saints with a more egalitarian stress on social reform. In one of her later Whitehall visions Trapnel declared:

> If he were not (speaking of the Lord Cromwell) backslidden, he would be ashamed of his great pomp, and revenue, while the poor are ready to starve, and art thou providing great palaces? Oh this was not Gideon of old, oh why dost thou come to rear up the pillars, the stones which are laid aside?[166]

By early in 1654 the male leaders of the Fifth Monarchists were mostly in prison, so Trapnel's public attacks on Cromwell were increasingly important. Pamphlet accounts of her visions were produced and she embarked on a trip to the West Country that attracted large crowds, who often asked about the 'vision of the horns'. Godly radicals who believed she was God's instrument gave her shelter, but others saw a woman adopting a dangerously inappropriate public role. Trapnel was denounced with the labels given to other women speaking or acting out of turn, as a scold, a witch or a vagrant.[167] Soldiers arrested her and escorted her back to London, where in June 1654 Trapnel was confined to Bridewell by the Council of State. Neither her spirits nor her supporters were daunted by this punishment even though the usual inmates of Bridewell were prostitutes and vagrants, and the matron accused Trapnel of being one of 'a company of ranting Sluts'. The institution faced 'many disorders by great numbers resorting daily to Anna Trapnel', and her publications continued to appear, announced as from 'Anna Trapnel … prisoner in Bridewell for the Testimony of Jesus the Lord'. Trapnel exhorted the godly not to give their love to the Protector 'more than to another, nor so much as to old King Charles's for they should love only 'King Jesus'. When that king came there 'shall be no mockers, nor deriders to scoff at the Fifth Monarchy'.[168]

Anna Trapnel illustrates some of the ambiguous implications of female prophecy. In some ways her activities reinforced notions of female passivity and subordination. Some of the visions came indirectly to the public, through a 'relater' who provided 'some short account of some things she uttered … as the relater could take them in some scattered expressions'.[169] Like Wight, whose visions were also 'related', she was not exactly the author of the words delivered. Another 'Trapnel' work, *A Legacy for Saints*, was largely autobiographical but printed under the auspices of leading members of the All Hallows congregation, the Fifth Monarchist stronghold.[170] More profoundly, of course, it was not Anna Trapnel in her own right whose words caught public attention, but Anna as the passive vehicle for God's message. She presented herself as God's handmaid inspired like so many others by the verses of Joel.[171] Trapnel was 'a weak worthless creature, a babe in Christ, which makes his power the more manifest' as her associate Sarah Wight was 'an Empty Nothing Creature'.[172] Furthermore the credibility of Trapnel as a female prophet was based on her detachment from her own body, which was the ground on which God worked. At Whitehall she was confined to bed, insensible, not eating or drinking: 'I neither saw, nor heard, nor perceived the noise and distractions of the people, but was as one that heard only the voice of God sounding forth unto me.'[173] In Cornwall she did not hear the people shouting that she was 'A witch, a witch', or feel the magistrates pinching her nose and pulling her pillow from under her. The female body is here insensible, passive and permeable, a site on which God's power rather than female agency is displayed.[174]

But there are counterbalancing or contradictory elements, where a strong individual identity is portrayed. The main text of her *Cry of a Stone* opens with the defiant assertion, 'I am Anna Trapnel', and, alongside the disclaimers that every part of her message came from God, Trapnel presented herself as defiant, committed and proud. She actively cooperates with God: 'I was desirous to be out of the body, I longed to be dissolved';[175] and she glosses or explains her visions for hearers and readers, rather than simply transmitting them passively. This dual approach is ambiguous or contradictory in theory, but it was demonstrated over and over again in practice in her months of notoriety. There is no better example than Trapnel's account of her appearance before the Cornish magistrates, where she is by turns passive: 'in all that was said by me, I was nothing, the Lord put all in my mouth, and told me what I should say', and assertive: when the Justices asked her why she had come to Cornwall when she had 'no lands, nor livings, nor acquaintance' there, she replied, 'I am a single person, and why may I not be with my friends anywhere … why may not I go where I please, if the Lord so will?'[176] Trapnel's family circumstances, her modest economic independence, and her secure position within the Fifth Monarchy movement, reinforced her assurance that she was God's instrument.

Furthermore, Trapnel actively welcomed her public role, citing another important scripture explaining that six weeks before the battle of Dunbar in 1650:

I told them how I prayed against this publick-spiritedness; and how the Lord silenced me, from those words in 1 Cor[inthians] 1.27, 28. But God hath chosen the foolish things of the world, to confound the wise; and God hath chosen the weak things of the world to confound the things that are mighty, and base things of the world, and things which are despised, hath God chosen; yea and things that are not, to bring to naught things that are.[177]

There is some contrast here with Sarah Wight whose political role is less direct and perhaps unsought, and Trapnel's impact made her the archetypical prophetess, the touchstone by which all others were measured. When the eccentric royalist Arise Evans presented an account of another prophetess Elinor Chanel, for example, he was quick to differentiate her from Trapnel: readers would find 'more truth and substance' in his pamphlet than in 'all Hanna Trapnels songs'. She featured in Hobbes's account of the civil war, and her notoriety came to worry some of her former associates. Her name is missing from the list of Sarah Wight's visitors in later editions of Henry Jessey's account of Wight's visions.[178]

Trapnel's prominence means that she is probably the woman from the humblest background who had significant public influence in the 1640s and 1650s.[179] Newsbook reports as well as the authority's alarm testify to her impact. In February 1654 the government-sponsored journalist and intelligencer Marchamont Nedham complained that she was doing a 'world of mischief' as the Fifth Monarchist movement consciously exploited her influence through print and the tour of the West Country.[180] Her actions were compared to:

the old story of Elizabeth Barton, the holy maid of Kent (as she was called) in the days of Henry 8 who was made use of by certain fanatic popish priests by feigned miracles and trances, to raise admiration in the multitude, and foment seditious humours against the Government, for which she had in the end her reward.[181]

As Barton was executed for sedition so journalists hinted the same fate might await Trapnel for her attempts to 'alienate the heart of the people from the present Government'.[182] Like Poole or Wight, but to a greater extent, Trapnel should be regarded as a crucial member of a movement as much as an example of an exceptional woman. Again this is not to denigrate her as a dupe of male leaders, but to recognise that she valued her relationships with ministers like Simpson, Powell and Feake: she visited them in prison and consciously associated herself with them in print, determined 'while I have tongue and breath I shall go forth for the Fifth Monarchy-Laws teaching and practice'.[183]

Trapnel's prominence, like that of the Fifth Monarchy movement as a whole, waned after 1654 but she had a further period of intermittent, bed-ridden trances in 1658, reported in doggerel verse in two lengthy, rather abstract works very different from the topical pamphlets of 1654. Although she is often associated with Quaker women visionaries in modern scholarship, Trapnel was a convinced spiritual elitist, from an uncompromising Calvinist framework. She was sure the Quakers were false prophets and warned readers against them:

Now then friends treasure up these notes,
Lay them up in your breast,
That you may know the difference
Between false visions and the best[184]

The Quakers were the most provocative of all the radical sects that emerged in the years after civil war; they had the most decisive impact on both rival radical groups and horrified orthodox Puritans, and they were notorious for the apparent freedom to preach and publish allowed to transgressive women. Dramatically and apparently immediately successful in the early 1650s, Quaker numbers grew as charismatic itinerant preachers won many adherents from disillusioned members of other groups, particularly Baptists, and gathered together scattered spiritual and mystical congregations, particularly in the far north-west of England. Claiming direct inspiration from God, Quaker evangelists offered salvation to all who accepted identification with the 'light within' them. They rejected all 'formal' worship and an obsession with particular 'ordinances' such as adult baptism, and their mystical, allegorical use of the scriptures contrasted sharply with the literalism of most Puritans.[185] Quakers were the most practical of spiritual enthusiasts, using print in a particularly strategic way, coordinating publications with well-organised missionary tours, and systematic assaults on rival sects and orthodox ministers. Parish ministers found themselves heckled in the streets, interrupted in their preaching and denounced as 'hireling priests', pelted with hostile pamphlets and challenged to contemptuous debate. Quakers were far from the benevolent pacifists of more recent times, and their refusal to accept distinctions of sex, class or education in spiritual matters made them very attractive to assertive women.

Quaker women denounced the ungodly to their faces, wrote pamphlets condemning corrupt authority and travelled through England and beyond seeking converts. Women were present in about a third of the incidents when Quakers attacked parish ministers. In response they were humiliated, whipped and imprisoned – in Carlisle, Exeter, Evesham and Banbury, but also in New England (where one woman was among the early Quakers executed as heretics), Jamaica and Malta. One early convert, a young servant called Dorothy Waugh, attacked the ungodly in Carlisle market-place. The audacity of a lower-class female denouncing her betters in public aroused the authorities to a humiliating response, assimilating Waugh to a more familiar but equally distasteful female role, that of the scold, who did not keep silent or know her place. Waugh was made to stand for three hours in the marketplace with a scold's bridle on her head: 'I stood their time with my hands bound behind me with the weight of iron upon my head, and the bit in my mouth to keep me from speaking.'[186] An even more humiliating and sexualising punishment was meted out to two Quaker women who travelled to Evesham in Worcestershire, a town already disturbed by conflicts between local Quakers and the town magistrates. The women were put in the stocks, with their feet wide apart in the holes because their hands were too small to be secured. When they asked for a block of wood to sit on, the mayor 'bid the constable fetch a block and thrust it between their legs, and said they should not have them between their legs which they would have'. The women of Evesham were not deterred and when a Quaker meeting was raided in 1661, thirty-three women were among those imprisoned.[187]

Margaret Fell, the Westmorland gentlewoman who later married the Quaker leader George Fox, made her house the vital headquarters of the movement, through which financial resources were mobilised and correspondence networks maintained. Fell was among the most productive of Quaker women authors; remarkably Quakers published almost half of all printed works by women in the 1650s, and some 20% of all female publications in the seventeenth century. They contributed only a small proportion of all Quaker works, however.[188] Quaker women published uncompromising attacks on 'priests' and governors, and defences of 'women's speaking' in public. Hester Biddle issued tracts, *Woe to thee, City of Oxford*, *Woe to thee, City of Cambridge*, against the arrogance of the superficially learned as well as a splendid denunciation of the city of London:

> Howl ye lawyers, weep bitterly ye rulers and judges, lament ye priests, for the day of God's account is coming on, and it hasteneth, wherein the book of conscience shall be opened, wherein your sins are written, as with the point of a diamond, and out of the book of life you shall be judged, according as your works shall be, so shall your reward be, for our God is pure and immortal, he will torment the wicked, and plague the ungodly, and cast into the pit for ever.[189]

Like Trapnel, Biddle presented her words as 'a warning from the lord God of life and power', but also as her own public duty: 'this is my testimony friends, which I must bear amongst you, for the true light against all that doth oppose it, who hath been a citizen with you'. Like many Quakers she made creative and subversive use of conventional gendered and scriptural language:

> the poor in thee are ready to famish, for whose estate and condition my heart is pained … yet thou canst pass by them in thy gaudy apparel, and outstretched neck, with the face decked with black spots, which are the marks of the whore, the beast and the false prophet, which is not the attire of Sarah, Abraham's wife.

Stereotyped distinctions between good and bad women, between the whore of Babylon and the bride of Christ, were directed by Quaker writers against oppression and spiritual error rather than applied to real women or gender hierarchies. In a defence of women's public preaching, Priscilla Cotton and Mary Cole playfully deconstructed the classic biblical requirement for women's silence in the church in an address to the 'priests and people of England' issued from Exeter jail:

> Silly men and women may see more into the mystery of Christ Jesus, than you, for the Apostles, that the scribes called illiterate, and Mary and Susanna (silly

women, as you would be ready to call them, if they were here now) these
know more of the Messiah, than all the learned priests and rabbis …

Thou tellest the people women must not speak in a church, whereas it is not
spoke of only of a female, for we are all one, both male and female in Christ
Jesus, but it's weakness that is the woman by the Scriptures forbidden, for else
thou puttest the Scriptures at a difference in themselves.[190]

Indeed Cotton and Cole claimed that it was the men who opposed women preaching
who should keep silent.

As well as dynamic risk-taking activity by small groups of women, Quakers could
mobilise very large numbers. A petition against tithes, the compulsory levies for
parish ministers opposed by most sectaries, was signed by 7,746 women, indeed
three-quarters of the pamphlet was taken up with signatures. Women were perhaps
the more determined to add their names, as most tracts against tithes were published
by Quaker men, although a contemporaneous anti-tithe petition from men had no
signatures. These women were not all Quakers: research on Somerset, for example,
has identified just under half of the names listed for that county in Quaker records,
but the numbers are still extremely significant, as is the support from other women
for this Quaker initiative.[191]

There are hints here of tension over the public prominence of women, even
within the most apparently sympathetic sect. The implications for gendered hierarchies
and family life of religious diversity, gathered congregations and female prophecy were
complex. Most sects, unsurprisingly given their scriptural inspiration, had conventional views on both the role of women in the church, and on family hierarchies. As
we have seen already many congregations simultaneously acted as cradles of female
assertiveness, and sought to control women's behaviour. Negotiating gender roles was
always difficult, even for Quakers. As Kate Peters has suggested Quaker men had
little choice than to defend women's public preaching and prophesying, for the
movement from the start attracted many forceful and gifted women, while the prominence of women ranked high among the Quaker characteristics denounced by
their enemies. Public defence took place alongside much anxiety, however. Shortly
before the leading Quaker Richard Farnworth published a pamphlet supporting
women preachers, he had issued a tract which was thoroughly conventional in its
views: 'let not the woman usurp authority over the man but be in subjection as Sarah
was, who obeyed Abraham'. Private correspondence expressed male alarm. Priscilla
Cotton's husband (perhaps understandably) urged in 1656 that 'rather men friends'
be sent to spread the word, for many 'do not care to hear any woman friends', while
Mary Howgill, it was said, 'ministereth confusion'.[192] The blaming of women for the
ruin of James Nayler is particularly instructive. Nayler, a rival to Fox for leadership in
the mid–1650s, re-enacted Christ's entry into Jerusalem at Bristol in 1656 attended by
adoring women. He was harshly punished by parliament for this blasphemy and died
shortly after release from prison in 1659. Fox and others argued that Nayler's downfall was a product of the baleful influence of women, particularly Martha Simmonds
(the sister of the radical bookseller and publisher Giles Calvert), to whom he was

apparently 'subject'. It seems that Simmonds's support for Nayler had been prompted in turn by her treatment at the hands of powerful male leaders Richard Hubberthorne, Edwards Burrough and Francis Howgill who had condemned her preaching in London as 'out of the power, out of the wisdom and out of the life of God'.[193]

Turning to the broader gender politics of the sects it is important to stress that they demanded high standards of godly men and that congregational discipline sought to shame disorderly men as well as women. Among the Cambridgeshire General Baptists, drunkenness and marital violence were regularly condemned. John Brighton who 'did mightily frequent the ale-houses, keeping company with idle persons' and John Salmon for 'sitting up whole nights in the alehouse' were excommunicated, as was Thomas Bedford, a teacher in an associated church, for idleness, drunkenness and 'beating of his wife, and that in the open street'. It is not clear that any of these men took a great deal of notice of these censures, but at least the congregation acted as a counter to male excesses.[194]

Where husbands and wives, parents and children, or masters and servants differed over religion, congregational leaders insisted that God should be obeyed before man, inevitably complicating family life. The prominent Baptist William Kiffin discussed infant baptism with one Robert Poole, 'according to your daughters' and servants' desires', while Poole himself complained that his subordinates had been 'seduced'.[195] Some 'Particular' or Calvinist Baptists were stricter separatists than Kiffin; they were particularly zealous in their desire to follow biblical teachings, and thus particularly perplexed. The issue of women's place in the church was most straightforward. In June 1656, the churches that made up a midlands association discussed 'How far women may speak in the church and how far not'. The answer was nuanced, and comprehensive: 'we answer that women in some cases may speak in the churches and in some cases again may not.'

> They may not so speak as that their speaking shall not show a not acknowledging of the inferiority of their sex and so be a usurping of authority over the man and more particularly, thus: (1) A woman may not publicly teach in the church. This appears to have been much in the apostle's eye: 1 Corinthians 14.2. (2) She may not speak in the church by way of passing sentence upon doctrines or cases in the church. (3) She may not stand up as a ruler in the church and so speak upon that account. (4) She may not speak in prayer as the mouth of the church, that is very clear in 1 Timothy 2.

In other words, women could have no formal, public role in these congregations. However, there were contexts, private, personal and delegated, when women could speak 'and not be found to offend against the rule of the apostle'. A woman could 'make a profession of her faith to the church' if she wished to be baptised and admitted to the congregation; she could act as a witness in disciplinary matters; 'if she be sent from another church as a messenger she may deliver her message'. A woman could ask for assistance from the congregation, and, finally, 'if a woman have sinned and cast out of the church and God hath given her repentance, undoubtedly she may manifest it in the church.'[196] The West Country Baptists summed up the approach more briefly in November 1653: 'a woman is not permitted at all to speak in the church, neither by way of praying, prophesying nor enquiring ... but, if any have a gift, we judge they may exercise it in private, observing the rule mentioned, 1 Corinthians 11.5.'[197]

Ideally whole families would be members of such separatist congregations, shunning the corruptions of the world together. A 'sister' was to be condemned if she ignored the church's urging that those 'in the fellowship of the Gospel' should not 'join themselves in marriage with any that are not in the same fellowship'. In practice, then, households might include divergent religious beliefs, and provoke anxious discussions. What, for example, was the duty of 'believing servants towards their master and governors'? Of course, a good servant 'must readily endeavour to obey all their lawful and just commands, and this with reverence and singleness of heart and goodwill herein acting as the servants of Christ'. But – and the but is in the text – if masters commanded 'anything against the Lord, they must remember that God is to be obeyed rather than men'. Where a master was an unbeliever, servants were to act 'accordingly as the name of God and his doctrine be not blasphemed'. A believer should not join in prayer with unbelieving members of the family, for 'as the worship of the Lord is spiritual so are his worshippers'. Exceptionally, however, 'a master of a family, when he doth instruct and teach his family, may pray for them before them'. Remarkably, given the restrictions on women's public participation within these congregations, a believing woman with 'a husband not in order' (that is not within the church) was encouraged to defy her household head. In May 1657, the West Country Baptists considered whether a sister in this situation might 'dispose of outward substance' without her husband's 'knowledge or consent'. They concluded that the wife could use household property for the church – indeed it was her 'duty', 'and that for these reasons':

> First, because the law of God hath given the wife an interest in her husband's estate, being made one flesh with him ... Secondly, this appears by the practice of holy women recorded in the scriptures ... Thirdly, believing women as well as men are created in Jesus unto good works ... it's held as a property of a good woman to be stretching forth her hand to the poor and needy ... Fourthly, God hath promised a blessing in the faithful performance of this duty, which he hath nowhere excluded the women in this case.[198]

In the end, however, the Baptists' leaders seem to have got cold feet, adding the rider, 'Yet in this matter we desire that wisdom may be exercised that so the name of the Lord, the honour of truth and her own peace as much as in her lieth may be preserved.'

The General Baptists – more radical in their belief in general redemption than the Calvinists just discussed – suffered comparable stress over family matters. As we have seen they were adamant that women should not obey husbands if the husbands defected to the Quakers or other churches. The wife of John Noble, 'departed very angry and refused to continue with the congregation' when her husband was excommunicated. When the elders asked her why, 'she told us, we knew the reason, for her mind is the same with her husband … we therefore reproved her for her sin and exhorted her to consider her folly'. The elders were clearly very annoyed by her defiance because when husband and wife both repented and asked for readmission, John was allowed back in at once, while the decision on Mrs Noble was delayed. Another woman, Jane Adams of Over, used her husband's command as the reason why she would not come to church: 'He had sworn she should not come, and she was unwilling to make him break his oath'. Jane was told in no uncertain terms that this was 'not a sufficient cause to keep her from the meetings', but retorted that 'she was minded to seek her peace. We replied that she ought to seek it lawfully; and seeing he did not hinder her by force, she was in a great fault, for which we rebuked her sharply.' This case prompted a general discussion: 'After this it was propounded whether the threatenings of a husband are a sufficient warrant for a woman to keep from the assemblies. After consideration it was concluded and resolved, that unless a person was restrained by force, it was no excuse for the absenting themselves from the assemblies of the congregation.'[199] Again, by far the best solution was for co-religionists to marry, but again, enforcing this was difficult. In Fenstanton, Anne Woodward refused to listen when the church condemned her marriage plans, while Jane Johnson who had married 'a known enemy to the truth' was clearly distressed; she 'wept exceedingly' and bemoaned her 'miserable condition' but refused to repent.[200]

Religious affiliation thus took precedence over adherence to worldly hierarchies. The Fifth Monarchist sympathiser John Rogers published a volume of the spiritual testimonies delivered in the Dublin congregation he ministered to in the early 1650s. He insisted that the only distinctions to be made were 'between the precious and the vile, the clean and unclean; and not to be a difference of sexes, ages or relations', and consequently argued that in the church all members, 'sisters as well as brothers, have a right to all church affairs'. Everyone admitted to this church had to give 'some experimental evidences of the work of grace upon his soul (for the church to judge of) whereby he (or she) is convinced that he is regenerate'. Public testimonies of faith by women as well as men were printed, including one from Elizabeth Avery who had published her own radical prophecies in the late 1640s, explaining how she had come to find 'Christ in me, ruling and reigning' within Rogers's church after years of searching and suffering through an overwhelming sense of sinfulness. Rogers's policy was controversial and he had to justify it through an appeal to Joel and other familiar scriptures, as well as to a range of other authorities. When commentators wrote of the church, Rogers argued, they meant the whole membership, and thus women as well as men should have a say in its affairs. Everyone – women and men – was made free in Jesus Christ: 'in the civil there are such differences of fathers, children, masters, servants, magistrates, subjects, men and women; but in the spiritual rule and government of Christ in his church and saints, all are one, without respect of persons'. Women's subjection in their secular life did not apply to spiritual matters: 'though there is a civil subjection to men in their oeconomical relations … there is not any servile subjection due to them, whereby poor souls are enslaved'. Rogers noted that women often excelled men in 'piety and judgement', and although the scriptures forbad women from public preaching, this should not apply to 'the common ordinary liberty due to them as members of the church, viz to speak, object, offer or vote with the rest'. Indeed Rogers hoped that soon, 'handmaids shall prophesy, and have more public liberty than now they have'. He accepted that this was controversial, and so urged women not to be too aggressive in claiming what he believed were their spiritual rights: 'I wish ye be not too forward, and yet not too backward ... maintain your right, defend your liberty ... be courageous ... and yet be cautious too ... be swift to hear, slow to speak'; they should seek an 'orderly liberty'.[201] Rogers's Fifth Monarchist affiliations made him particularly receptive to women's involvement but more conventional congregations provided a place for female participation in the life of the church, albeit in carefully circumscribed contexts. In the Broadmead church women formed a majority of the congregation by the 1660s, and some served as deacons, with charitable or welfare responsibilities for church members. When a new minister was chosen in 1671 women's consent was recorded along with men's and in a typical compromise it was declared that 'if anyone did dissent from the election, that they should speak, every brother for himself, every sister might speak to some brother to declare for her, or them, their dislike and their reasons'. Thus the scriptural prohibition on women's public speaking was respected, but women's opinions were not wholly disregarded.[202]

The contexts for women's religious experience and influence shifted after the Restoration. Anglicans who had worshipped in their closets or defied the authorities in the 1640s and 1650s were the establishment once again; Dorothy Pakington, for example, numbered eminent figures in the re-established church among her close associates. The elderly Frances Hobart, on the other hand, wrote to her brother the Earl of Bridgewater in December 1661 dreading the imposition of conformity and the Book of Common Prayer. For fourteen years 'in my little chapel' she had had 'constant prayer, preaching and reading the scriptures on the Lord's day and on weekdays, my chaplain is a Doctor of divinity'. 'Dear brother I am hastening to my long home, I would not willingly go out of the way and think myself obliged to go that way which my conscience upon the best information I can get telleth me is the best.' Hobart's connections do seem to have secured for her some liberty for her own household, and until her death 'she was a nonconformist as to some modes of worship in present use'. Other Presbyterians and godly Puritans suffered harassment until the end of the century, and the manuscripts of women like Elizabeth Jekyll, Lucy Hutchinson and Mary Love circulated within dissenting circles as memorials of better times and staunch principles.[203] Gathered churches and more radical movements were harshly treated. Dorothy Hazzard did not die until 1674, an old woman revered as the founder of the Broadmead church: 'she lived to a great age, and came to her grave a shock of corn fully ripe'. She escaped the worst of the persecution in Bristol in the later 1670s. The church records stress how women were a particular target of the Tory-Anglican assault on dissenters: they 'mocked gentlewomen, and masters of ships' wives, with such filthy expressions not meet to be named'. One elderly woman was abused as 'old carrion' and sent to Bridewell for refusing to declare her marital status.[204]

The Quakers responded to persecution by consolidating their organisation through a series of committees or 'meetings' at national and local level, and by moderating their more ecstatic or provocative behaviour. As part of this process – which was divisive within the movement itself – women were given a significant, but significantly domesticated role. Women's meetings were established in the 1670s with responsibility for marriage and welfare in the sect. This process, to which Margaret Fell Fox was central, was resented and opposed by some activist women who saw it as a restriction of their impact within the broader movement. All Quaker publications were vetted by a national 'meeting' and it was relatively anodyne autobiographical and pious works by women that predominated rather than aggressive public denunciations as in the 1650s. It is not easy to discern a clear line from women's activism in the rival religious groupings of the seventeenth century to modern claims for emancipation or liberation. Nonetheless the seventeenth-century Quakers were remarkable in their granting to women some formal authority as well as informal influence – including authority over men's behaviour within marriage. The Quakers remained a movement that facilitated public female activism, as well as female piety, and indeed from the seventeenth century to the nineteenth, religious commitment, of many different forms has been a crucial foundation for female agency and creativity.[205]

3

MANHOOD AND CIVIL WAR

A pioneering feminist historian has commented, 'Historians have either taken for granted, or noted without comment, the equation of political status with manhood in the seventeenth century.'[1] In much political history until very recently the manliness of formal politics has been 'both omnipresent and invisible'.[2] For the civil war, there is much suggestive work by literary scholars including Diane Purkiss, Jerome de Groot and Susan Wiseman on politics and manliness, discussing, in Purkiss's terms, the 'tentative connections between two arenas hitherto treated separately: masculinity and the public realm of politics'.[3] But social historians, as we have seen, have focused on men in the household, looking at sexuality, violence and the socio-economic rather than the political aspects of manhood, so that the barriers between the social, cultural and political history of early modern England, often remarked on, have restricted the analysis of masculinity and politics. This chapter seeks to avoid taking the maleness of politics for granted, by exploring the variety of ways in which civil war complicated and challenged understandings and experiences of manhood. It proceeds by means of case-studies or snapshots that highlight problems, anxieties and contested stereotypes and identities, for a more systematic or descriptive treatment such as was provided for women in the previous chapter might simply reproduce a conventional narrative of the war as a male preserve.[4]

True manliness was always – as suggested in the introduction – something achieved rather than naturally assured – established through processes of striving, of distinctions made or oppositions established, in relation to women, or to inadequate men, and so 'inherently unstable'. Manliness, as the literary critic Bruce Smith puts it, was 'a matter ... of circumstances, of performance'.[5] War demanded particularly zealous performance; it was the quintessential masculine endeavour even as it threatened the ultimate dissolution of a man's strength and being through dismemberment and death.[6] If manhood was inherently unstable, war thus made contradictions particularly apparent. Physical bravery was always an element in ideals of manliness, valued not only by aristocrats engaged in competitive defence of their honour, but praised also in the chivalric romances found in cheap pamphlets and enacted in the military exercises undertaken in grammar schools, and by citizens active in London's Honourable Artillery Company and similar provincial bodies. Such 'civic chivalry' was displayed in idealised form in an account of London apprentices at the outset of the war: these 'servants to honest and sufficient men' marched cheerfully to battle as if to a wedding, and with magnanimous courage aimed to bring 'honour and renown' to the city. Anger, flamboyant displays of courage and martial prowess were vital to men's success in war, but in the heat of battle, men might lose the moderation and rational self-control that equipped men to head households and wield authority in the commonwealth.[7] Men made friends in war, even as they confronted enemies, and new relationships might cut across existing patriarchal and marital ties. Women followed early modern armies, as we have seen, but men's need to rely on fellow soldiers encouraged comradely and fraternal, homosocial bonds.

Any war thus challenged understandings of what it meant to be a man. The Puritan minister William Bridge, preaching to volunteers in Norwich in early 1643, offered a partisan account of the qualities required, but nonetheless hinted at some general dilemmas. His text acknowledged the performative aspects of manliness stressed by modern scholars, taken as it was from the Old Testament commander Joab's exhortation to his troops: 'Be of good courage, and let us play the men'. Playing a man depended on courage: 'good courage is the strength of man, it is the spirits of a man, it is the sparkling of a man's heart'. A courageous man was 'a stout man whom adversity doth not quail … whom prosperity doth not allure'. But playing the man was not easy, and men might fail to perform. Parliamentarian soldiers had to know what true courage was; they had to 'take heed of all those things that will debase your spirits … especially idleness, worldliness, false courage'. Worldliness 'doth effeminate and set a man below himself', while false courage was associated with the enemies of parliament, when Bridge denounced 'a vaunting, bragging, boasting Cavalierism' and 'a fierce, angry, revengeful disposition'. If false courage unmanned a soldier, setting him below himself, true courage might be displayed by civilians and indeed by women. 'Men, women and children' all had to be of 'good courage in these sad times'; magistrates, ministers and parents, mothers as well as fathers, had to rally to the cause: 'It is a lamentable thing that the carnal wisdom of a worldly parent should be the quench coal of the gracious devotion of a godly child.' So Bridge quoted with approval the stories of mothers who had put to death sons who had fled from battle.[8]

Bridges's sermon, whose printing was ordered by the House of Commons, offered complex, polarised visions of courage and by extension of true manhood; it begins to suggest to us some of the particularly disruptive effects of civil war, when men, who might have been neighbours, fellow students, justices of the peace or members of parliament together, opposed each other on battlefields. These intimate dislocations help explain the profound anxieties over witchcraft, over sexuality and gender hierarchies discussed elsewhere, and they also provoked troubling contestation over what it meant to be an Englishman, or even properly a man at all.[9] In early modern

England, as we have seen, one central attribute of manliness, at least for men of some property, was the capacity to wield public authority and acquire formal office in community or realm; consequently the profound cleavage in the English polity raised questions about the nature of male authority and identity.[10] Fundamentals of political obedience were challenged as the king, whose authority was often compared to a father's role, was opposed by men who were themselves often husbands and fathers. It was painfully obvious that political obligation was not natural or innate, but a matter to be negotiated and constructed. These negotiations were not only or even usually conducted in terms of abstract principles or political theories; they involved questions of interest and passion, of imagination and emotion. What manner of men were appropriate political agents, and what relationships or narratives locating men in relationships validated their political roles?[11] Political principles and loyalties evoked contrasting ideals of manhood, as rivals denounced their opponents as inadequate, imperfect or effeminate men. Many different disputes were figured as struggles over male honour. In his bitter arguments with Thomas Edwards over religious liberty, John Goodwin presented the debates as duels, opening one pamphlet with 'I here cast the glove to him'; while Goodwin's critics condemned him as a feminised 'scold'.[12] With men, as with women, we will see that contested representations over the nature of manhood were intertwined with the experiences and self-assertion of different groups of men.

In 1644 a royalist cleric defined the ideal royalist or Cavalier as

> a child of honour, a gentleman well born and bred; that loves his king for conscience sake, of a clearer countenance and bolder look than other men, because of a more loyal heart … He is furnished with the qualities of piety, prudence, justice, liberality, goodness, honesty. He is amiable in his behaviour, courageous in his undertakings, discreet and gallant in all his executions; he is thoroughly sensible of the least wrong that is offered to his sovereign … he dares accept of death's challenge to meet it in the field, and yet can embrace it as a special friend when it comes into his chamber … he is the only preserve of English gentility and ancient valour, and hath rather chose to bury himself in the tomb of honour, than to see the nobility of his nation vassalaged, the dignity of his country captivated by any base domestic enemy, or by any foreign conquered foe.[13]

Here a perfect man is described, brave and straightforward, controlled, religious and generous, with clear social as well as gendered characteristics as a gentleman of ancient stock. The parliamentarians, in contrast, are base, dishonest and cowardly upstarts, not properly English at all. Or as the poet Alexander Brome had it in the later 1640s:

> And the scum of the land
> Are the men that command
> And our slaves are become our masters[14]

On the other hand, parliamentarian propaganda denounced the royalists as foreign and popish. The newsbook *Mercurius Britanicus*, writing after the parliament's great victory at Marston Moor, mocked:

> Malignants, 'what asleep yet? Rupert fled, Newcastle, [Colonel] King, Widdrington and the rest for Flanders, and still asleep? ... So many Irish and Papists about the king, so many lascivious French and Friars about the Queen, and are you not awaken?'[15]

The unEnglish nature of royalism was indeed a perennial theme, made plausible by the king's role as monarch of several kingdoms and nations, by the perceived influence of his French wife, and by persistent (and partially justified) suspicions of murky plotting with the Catholic Irish. The term 'Cavalier', derived from the continental term for a soldier, in itself evoked the alien and foreign.[16] After the regicide the republican John Hall offered a hostile history of the Stuarts in which 'French effeminacies' were introduced to Britain by Mary Stuart, evidence for the 'strange influence loose education hath upon youth and that weaker sex', and for the connections between subservience to women and to foreigners. John Milton praised the republican 'few, who yet retain in them the old English fortitude and love of Freedom', while another parliamentarian poet George Wither also identified brave, independent manhood with true Englishness. Also writing after the regicide, Wither explained how the tyrant Charles I had made his 'Lords and courtiers' into slaves, so that the 'king's mere creations' were pitiful specimens compared to the 'Bold barons' of former ages. Those men were:

> Lords over, not apes unto the French, and he was counted the bravest Lord who conquered most of their men, not the finest, that followed most of their fashions; scars were the ornaments of a noble face, not black patches, and hair powdered with dust and dewed with sweat and blood, not with perfumed powders and jasmine butter, was the dress wherein England's nobles courted their mistress, heroic fame.

This is also a social ideal which combined aristocratic benevolence with an independent tenantry, hierarchical to be sure, but rather different from the despair of defeated Cavaliers at a world turned upside down. Wither's noble English barons had let their estates at 'easy rates' to ensure their tenants were 'able men', independent and active, rather than 'broken-spirited'.[17] Both Wither and the royalist cleric who praised the 'bold looks' of his gallant commanders supported their arguments through a stress on the clothing, hair and deportment of the Cavaliers, drawing on potent themes from 1640s propaganda which posed hypocritical or godly Roundheads against debauched or gallant Cavaliers according to taste.

Roundheads and Cavaliers

At the most basic level, royalists and parliamentarians hoped for similar qualities in their officers and men: officers should be resolute and charismatic leaders, skilled in strategy and careful of the welfare of their men; those men should be loyal, obedient and brave. On both sides men and officers failed to live up to expectations as many proved incompetent, unreliable and cowardly, although the self-image of parliament's reformed and relatively well-paid New Model Army after 1645 as disciplined 'Saints' as much as soldiers is to some extent corroborated by modern scholarship.[18] In their mutual public denunciations, however, Cavaliers and Roundheads were utterly different in body and in behaviour. In the early 1640s in particular, a host of pamphlets defined, denounced and defended these identities. Propagandist techniques varied; there were rival, exclusive claims to qualities (bravery, constancy, loyalty) that all agreed were praiseworthy; there was simple abuse and there was a slightly more subtle tactic, condemning as faults, attributes and attitudes (particularly religious views) claimed by enemies as virtues. 'If a man have a religion in him, then (say they) he is a Roundhead ... He that is no swearer, curser, cheater, drunkard, whoremaster, quarreller, he is scandalized with the name of a Roundhead ... indeed every honest man is now called Roundhead' as a parliamentarian version had it. Or as royalists argued of 'the devil turned roundhead':

> he conformed himself to hate all good manners, all orders, rule, orthodox divinity, rule and government in the commonwealth and church, for in their opinion they were all superstition and popery; he denied likewise all good works, academican learning, charity and the public liturgy of the Church of England.[19]

It is clear that there were opportunist motives at play as well as genuine commitment in the multiplication of pamphlets responding to each other in the closed world of London commercial print culture. One early pamphlet denounced both sides, claiming it was better to be a 'ram-head' (with a cuckold's horns) than a Roundhead or a Cavalier. If a Roundhead, 'I could neither pass along the street or sit in my shop without receiving a jeer from one knave or other, some calling me a troublesome fellow, some saying I was a despiser of government, others telling me I was an enemy to Bishops and the discipline of our church'. But, 'should I wear long locks, I should be esteemed either a roaring boy, or a swaggerer; and all this laid upon me, though I were innocent of them all'.[20] Nonetheless, the stereotypes had some connection with genuine characteristics and we can discern a real process of identity formation at work as hostile smears interacted with self-constructions to set godly citizens against hard-drinking, devil-may-care Cavaliers.[21]

In the propaganda war between Cavaliers and Roundheads, rival allegiances or identities were given physical and active form. You could recognise a Cavalier, claimed one pamphlet, 'By his clothing, by his posture, by his discourse or language, by his associates and his bastard brood, by his actions'.[22] The Bible taught that 'if a man have long hair, it is a shame unto him'.[23] The Cavalier stereotype was a complex amalgam of 'violent aggression and effeminate display', portrayed thus even in representations by sympathisers as in the arrogant, lavishly dressed portrayal of the brothers John and Bernard Stuart by Van Dyck as well as in a hostile verse, 'Upon the roaring Cavalier':

Bless us! Why here's a thing as like a man,
As nature to our fancy fashion can
Beshrew me, but he has a pretty face,
And wears his rapier with indifferent grace.
Makes a neat congie, dances well, and swears;
And wears his mistress' pendant in his ears.
But strip off his rags, and the poor thing is then
The just contempt of understanding men.[24]

In hostile accounts, Cavalier behaviour belied their 'pretty faces'. Drunkenness, swearing and sexual excess defined a godless enemy as evil as the Midianites who fought the Israelites of the Old Testament: 'we will drink, and be drunk, and whore and be damned, and will not be beholding to God to save us … we had rather be in hell with our comrades, than in heaven with the Roundheads'.[25] Accounts of the 'swearing, roaring, whoring cavalier' – as with some of the family dramas discussed in the last chapter – might veer off into anxious fantasy. In late October 1642, a Cornish Cavalier, the most debauched among the 'roarers and roisterers', declared 'he would have a sea of drink, a wilderness of tobacco, and ten legions of whores' as if 'he would ingeniously confess the truth of this assertion, that one strumpet by her wiles and false allurements, has unmanned him of his best part, his reason, and left him to the mercy of her devouring appetite'. Finally he drank a health to the devil, and unwisely dared the Devil to come to him. Immediately, 'a damp faint air begun to move in the room, and an unacquainted person stood in the midst of them, who said in a terrible and hideous voice, Andrew Stonesby, I am here'.[26]

If royalists were unmanned by debauchery and whoredom, Roundheads in Cavalier propaganda were emasculated through cuckoldry, in a parallel and inter-dependent sexual smear. Again, bodies and clothes were connected to attitudes and behaviour. The short hair and big ears of Roundheads 'hindreth not the sound of the shepherd's voice', or more directly made it easier to hear blasphemy; their long noses suggested a hypocritical lust, and 'promiseth an easy appetite to some good work towards the younger sisters', while their cuckold's horns were as long as their ears and noses. Roundhead clothes, like their slovenly short hair and long nails, suggested their low birth and a mimicking of continental Calvinist style: 'the roundness of the ruff, the length of the doublet, and the shortness of the breeches being a habit correspondent to the pictures of the Apostles in the Geneva print'.[27]

These were caricatures of course, but influential ones, and some Cavaliers at least embraced an identity of insouciant, swaggering gallants who liked a drink. The character of some desperate royalist soldiers facing defeat at the end of the war – brutal, drunk and profane – corresponded to the stereotype, but many royalists criticised such behaviour, and other ideals were available in royalist culture. A eulogistic account of the life of Sir John Smith, a royalist hero who had recovered the royal standard when it was captured at Edgehill, and died of wounds suffered at the battle of Alresford, was perhaps deliberately intended as a counter to the Cavalier stereotype. Even as he offered an alternative, Edward Walsingham, the author of Smith's life, bore witness to the influence of parliamentarian smears. He suppressed crucial aspects of Smith's career, for in 'real life' Sir John was a Catholic and soldier by trade, a swordsman who had spent much of his adult life in Catholic forces in the Spanish Netherlands.[28] Walsingham however presented Smith as a reluctant soldier, always self-controlled, careless of his dress and certainly never drunk. In his youth in the Low Countries he had 'demonstrated his virtue in conquering himself to satisfy the desires of his parents and friends, declaring he knew as well how to master his passions', applying himself to his studies, despite his impatience at a scholarly existence. He had only turned to soldiering after helping to put down the unruly 'dregs and rude multitude of the city' where he lived, but quickly excelled at the martial life, in Flanders and in the wars against the Scots. His soldiers in England's civil war were always disciplined, and despite his exploits at Edgehill, 'the modest Gentleman did what lay in him to avoid the honour'. As commander of the cavalry in the king's army of the west he 'prosecutes his affaires with that prudence, courtesy, and magnanimity, that all sorts of people were enamoured with his true excellency. He won the soldiers with his courtesy, the people with his modesty, and even from his enemies he drew admiration for his gallantry.'

During the 1640s, rival political visions were frequently evoked through narratives of individual lives and deaths, and Smith's was a particularly heroic and religious death, stoical and resigned to God's will. Though mortally wounded, he descended the stairs of his inn and entered a carriage for Oxford without help, and 'all the symptoms of pain you could perceive in him, was sometimes he would bite his nether lip'. Walsingham summed up Smith as an ideal Cavalier, a man who embodied a sort of anti-stereotype, 'completely lacking in pride, ostentation or arrogance'. There was nothing affected or vain in his clothes or his 'carriage and gestures', but rather 'a certain, decent neglect'. Although Walsingham 'curiously observed him, I could never yet conclude that I saw him overcome by drink'; neither had he seen 'a soldier more reserved in courting Ladies'. In conclusion, this 'gallant gentleman was one of the prime flowers in our English garden'; 'a most valiant, loyal and Christian Knight'.[29] To his enemies, Smith was a violent papist; this idealised portrait presented in print a noble warrior as a manly exemplar.

Thinking with women

During the civil war, political conflicts evoked rival identities as much as they involved contrasting political principles. Men were invited to adhere to specific allegiances – to choose between royalists and parliamentarians, or among rival groups of royalists or parliamentarians – through imagining what sort of men they wished to be, as well as what principles they were prepared to adopt. We have suggested that formal life writing such as the published biography of Smith might serve as a political rallying call, while prominent autobiographical passages in pamphlets of the leading Levellers John Lilburne and Richard Overton presented themselves as staunch, honest men assailed by cowardly tyrants. More private biographical narratives and autobiographical reflections also helped men justify to themselves, their families or sympathetic friends the traumatic decisions they had made to join one cause rather than another. The bachelor soldier John Smith is unusual, for in most of these narratives men's public or political stances were validated through accounts of their wives, their families or their households. We have explained that boundaries between private and public were fluid, and that before the civil war a man's failings as husband or head of household might be used to attack his public or political role. We will return in chapter four to the ways in which the overthrow of personal monarchy prompted debate over the familiar association of authority in the household with power in the commonwealth; among parliamentarians, particularly those influenced by classically based republican ideas, sharper distinctions were drawn between public affairs and private lives. The parliamentarian cause, based as it was on an exclusively male institution, was inherently more 'public' than a royalism based on personal loyalty to a monarch, and focused on a court that was itself a household. Indeed, as we have also seen, to its enemies the royal court was 'secret, coded and feminised'. But parliamentarians and republicans also held that it was through rational, authoritative control of their households that men developed and demonstrated their fitness to participate as citizens in the commonwealth, so that for men the public and private were both distinct, and mutually reinforcing. And in classical traditions women featured in contradictory fashion, sometimes, as with Lucretia, their sufferings inspired men to overthrow oppression, sometimes they urged their menfolk to heroic deeds, but they might also tempt them to a selfish indulgence or extravagance that brought disaster to the commonwealth.[30]

The influence of women over parliamentarians was satirised by John Taylor, portraying a 'mis-led, ill-bred, rebellious Roundhead' urged to rebellion 'by the sway and command which mother Midnight my wife bare over me, and the false instigations of such pulpiteers, which she (upon the pain of her scolding, scalding, hot indignation) enforced me to hear and believe'.[31] The wife of the parliamentarian general Sir William Waller was portrayed as a real-life 'mother Midnight' in the royalist press but Waller himself presented the more optimistic and more straightforward view that his private roles were the foundation for his public service. In personal reflections tracing his aim 'to become better in all relations, both to the public, in church and state, whensoever I shall be in a capacity to serve them, and in private, as a father, husband, master etc', he began with his duties as a father, then:

> as an husband, dwelling with my dear yoke-fellow according to knowledge, loving her as mine own body, as mine own self, as Christ loved his church, so taking care with her for the things of this world, that as we study to please one another, we may likewise remember the homage we both owe to God, and labour above all things to please him.[32]

Similarly Edmund Waller claimed Cromwell's domestic qualities before the civil war fitted him for public office:

> Your private life did a just Pattern give
> How Fathers, Husbands, Pious Sons should live,

Born to command, your princely virtues slept,
Like humble David's, while the flock he kept.

Lucy Hutchinson, a republican opponent of Cromwell's assumption of personal power, disagreed, but argued on the same terrain, attacking Cromwell's 'private' role as a provider for his family:

Who lavished out his wife's Inheritance
Ruined the children that he should advance
And gamed away his little thriftless stock
Slept not like David for he kept his Flock.[33]

In a famous autobiographical passage in the 1650s, the republican poet John Milton explained his prose writings of the 1640s as defences of connected forms of liberty. There were:

three varieties of liberty without which civilized life is scarcely possible, namely ecclesiastical liberty, domestic or personal liberty, and civil liberty, and since I had already written about the first, while I saw that the magistrates were vigorously attending to the third, I took as my province the remaining one, the second or domestic kind.

Domestic liberty in turn encompassed marriage, the education of children and freedom of expression. Hence, Milton wrote on education, against pre-publication censorship of the press and, notoriously, in favour of divorce on grounds of incompatibility. A submerged personal narrative of a disastrous marriage animates his tracts on divorce but an unhappy marriage was not simply a personal tragedy, for it was 'unprofitable and dangerous to the commonwealth, when the household estate, out of which must flourish forth the vigour and spirit of all public enterprises, is so ill-contented'. It made a man (and it was with men's happiness that Milton was mainly concerned) 'useless to friend, unserviceable and spiritless to the commonwealth'. In 1654 he insisted on male authority in the household as the basis of true freedom:

For in vain does he prattle about liberty in assembly and market-place who at home endures the slavery most unworthy of man, slavery to an inferior. Concerning this matter then I published several books, at the very time when man and wife were often bitter foes, he dwelling at home with their children, she, the mother of the family, in the camp of the enemy, threatening her husband with death and disaster.[34]

Milton's account of household happiness and authority as an essential, but precarious foundation for honourable public service is echoed in other narratives in which men's political legitimacy is reinforced or qualified by their relationships with their families, and particularly with their wives. 'Thinking with women' was a potent means of confronting the painful dilemmas of male public life in the 1640s and 1650s.[35] Lady Ann Fanshawe provides an intriguing royalist example, in which she demonstrates her husband's integrity through an exposure of her own feminine weakness. Lady Rivers, an older woman who acted as a kind of mentor to Lady Ann, was an advocate of female involvement in politics: 'she tacitly commended the knowledge of state affairs, and [said] that some women were very happy in a good understanding thereof, as my Lady Aubigny'. Flattering Ann that she could become a capable political woman, Lady Rivers persuaded her to ask her husband, secretary to the Prince of Wales, what was in the latest letters Henrietta Maria had sent from Paris: 'she would be extremely glad to hear what the Queen commanded the King in order to his affairs'. Ann, being:

> young, innocent, and to that day had never in my mouth "What news?" begun to think there was more in inquiring into business of public affairs than I thought of, and that it being a fashionable thing would make me more beloved of my husband (if that had been possible) than I was.

She followed him around asking about the letters but he fobbed her off: 'He kissed me and talked of other things.' A predictable quarrel ensued, with tears and reproaches: 'I could not believe he loved me, if he refused to tell me all he knew', before Sir Richard explained:

> when you asked me of my business, it was wholly out of my power to satisfy thee; for my life and fortune shall be thine, and every thought of my heart, in which the trust I am in may not be revealed. But my honour is my own, which I cannot preserve if I communicate the Prince's affairs; and pray thee with this answer rest satisfied. So great was his reason and goodness, that upon consideration it made my folly appear to me so vile, that from that day until the day of his death I never thought fit to ask him any business, but that he communicated freely to me, in order to his estate or family.

Sir Richard's honourable public service was thus secured by Lady Ann's confinement to domestic matters, although her decisive action secured Sir Richard's release from prison in 1651.[36]

Fears that a man might be compromised or seduced from his public duties by undue devotion to his wife and family emerged at several points of crisis or division. Authoritative government of a harmonious household might guarantee a man's fitness for public affairs, but a happy family life and a devoted but too influential wife could be an enervating distraction. For the most part women were deemed less brave, more likely to compromise or fall away from the cause, and so more likely to sacrifice the public good to private interests than men. The Leveller leader John Lilburne wrote frequently about his wife and family in a series of pamphlets in which his own sufferings were presented as proof of the cruelty of his unprincipled opponents; in the process he became, in Mike Braddick's words, England's 'first celebrity radical'. The Levellers' adroit use of the press was central to their political movement. One of Lilburne's most characteristic modes was the concrete, manly, egotistical pamphlet with titles that were both very particular and hinted at general identities: *The Christian Man's Trial* (1641); *The Free-Man's Freedom Vindicated* (1646); *The Resolved Man's Resolution* (1647); *The Upright Man's Vindication* (1653). In many of these works, Lilburne established his own loyal, staunch manhood through contrasts with his unreliable wife. Although Elizabeth Lilburne consistently supported John's activities, as we saw in chapter two, she appears more often in his pamphlets as more concerned with a peaceful family life than with her husband's cause. In 1647, both John and Elizabeth were being examined by a parliamentary committee when, according to John's pamphlet, Elizabeth 'burst out with a loud voice and said, I told thee often enough long since, that thou would serve the Parliament and venture thy life so long for them, till they would hang thee for thy pains'. Parliament was 'a company of unjust and unrighteous judges', more concerned with 'themselves and their own ends, than the public good of the Kingdom', so why should not Lilburne himself seek a private compromise. But John asked the committee to excuse 'what in the bitterness of her heart being a woman' she had said, and insisted for himself that he could not be silent even out of love for his wife and children, 'when my conscience, from sound grounds tells me God would have me to speak'; true manliness required the sacrifice of household happiness for the sake of the cause.[37]

In 1647 Elizabeth Lilburne could at least acknowledge that the Levellers represented a righteous cause. By the early 1650s, when opposition to the new republic and to Oliver Cromwell had condemned John Lilburne to years of banishment and imprisonment, his pamphlets contained stronger condemnations of his wife's 'irrational persuasions' for him 'to be quiet and silent' and submit to Cromwell. The argument is founded on the contrast between his wife's credulity and adherence to her private interests and ease, and his own rationality and dedication to the public interest. John Lilburne saw himself as the representative of honourable, free English manhood:

> I am an Englishman born and bred, and to breathe in the air of England, is as much my right as yours; and I have contested and fought with my sword in my hand for the enjoyment of my share in the laws and liberties thereof ... by the assistance of God, I will turn all the stones in the world, that it is possible for a resolute man, and an industrious man and a man of brains to turn, to make way for my coming to England again and for my living there in a rational security.[38]

He was 'a man that even in the field have adventured my life with as much hazardness, gallantry, and bravery, as any man whatsoever in the whole Army', and now he was not only under open attack from his enemies, he was being undermined by his 'poor simple wife' who had lobbied Cromwell for a pass to return to England and 'irrationally hindered' the publication of his latest pamphlet, so that her 'late childish actions ... hath in some measure, produced an alienation of affection in me to her'. For the sake of his wife, John had made a respectful address to Cromwell: 'for that tenderness of affection that I owe to her, whom I formerly entirely loved as my own life: though your late barbarous tyrannical dealing with me, hath exposed her to so much folly and lowness of spirit in my eyes', but Cromwell's double-dealing had vindicated John's scepticism as it condemned Elizabeth's gullibility.[39] Lilburne's 'poor simple wife' was contrasted with John's self-construction as 'a manly and a faire adversary', 'a single-hearted, honest, just plain-spoken Englishman, that hath been valiant and courageous'.[40] The emphasis on Elizabeth's weakness vividly points up Cromwell's hypocrisy – putting John in mind of passages in Machiavelli's *Prince* that advised rulers to pretend to clemency, but her inadequacy also underlined Lilburne's own credentials as a manly actor for the public good.

Other men might give in to female persuasion, and political or military failure was especially liable to be expressed in terms of failures of manliness. One obvious sign of effeminacy was 'excessive devotion' to women.[41] One good example is found in the heart-searching prompted by the Western Design of 1655, the expedition to conquer Spanish possessions in the Caribbean, which was the first significant military failure of the Cromwellian army. The failure had many causes, notably over-confidence and disease, but the very susceptibility to disease prompted questioning of the commanders' strength and ultimately of their manhood. As one leader admitted, 'we act not at the helm like men imbued with common reason'. The overall-commander, Robert Venables, who had unwisely brought his new wife on the expedition, was disgraced by the failure, condemned as a weak and emotional coward, a man unable to control his own household or to drag himself from the arms of his bride.[42]

But women were not always presented as diversions from true manly commitment; in other accounts, 'thinking with women' worked to reinforce or bolster male political stances. This was particularly apposite where male political trajectories were open to question or suspicion. The royalist Sir Hugh Cholmley, for example, had initially supported the parliament. In Memoirs written for his sons and in memory of their mother – 'I was first and chiefly moved to this work by the love I bore to your indulgent mother my dear wife, ... being desirous to embalm her great virtues and perfection to future ages' – Cholmley's ability to convince his wife of the justness of his shift, validates his change of allegiance, as we saw in chapter two.[43]

After the Restoration, the parliamentarian lawyer Bulstrode Whitelocke produced voluminous writings chronicling and reflecting on his life during the revolutionary decades, drawing on his own contemporary notes as well as pamphlet and newsbook sources. In part private attempts to come to terms with defeat, but also intended for circulation among his family and broader nonconformist networks, Whitelocke's writings began by distinguishing between his 'public business' and his 'private family', but these two aspects of his life were so intermingled that the distinction often broke down. In one version – his 'Annals' – Whitelocke included domestic matters in one column, and public business in another, on the same page, until from 1656 the difficulty of distinguishing led him to abandon this form. Unlike Cholmley, Whitelocke was consistent in his support for one side, but his ever-present service in the shifting regimes of the 1650s, from commonwealth to Protectorate, laid him open to accusations of time-serving. In many of his descriptions of his successive happy marriages and his 'quiverful' of children, Whitelocke demonstrated how his governance of this happy family reinforced his integrity in public life.[44] One of the columns in the 'Annals' for April and May 1649 was preoccupied with the illness and death of his second wife, Frances, while in the other Whitelocke described public events – particularly his own service as a Keeper of the Great Seal, an office he had accepted with some hesitation because of unhappiness at the army's purge of parliament and the regicide. The entry for 16 May, the day she died, 'the saddest day of all the days of my life hitherto', included only a brief account of Frances Whitelocke's behaviour and appearance, but a much longer discussion of her role in Bulstrode's public life.[45] Whitelocke adopted the common practice of praising Frances as an exceptional woman, free from the irrationality and self-interest of the majority: 'in the most perplexed and difficult matters, which befell me, in my public employments, I received sound and wise counsel from her, beyond imagination to come from a woman's brain, unexperienced in such affairs.'[46]

In this appreciation, Whitelocke camouflaged his own rather hesitant political career through a stress on his staunch and steadfast wife whose sound advice had overcome all his doubts about where the godly cause could be found:

> She was constantly and in all the time of the war, whilst she lived, most firm to the parliament's interest, and to the army, and upon any doubts in my self in the carriage of business she would still confirm me to go on and join with them, in the cause of God, which she took to be the parliament's cause … she was much unsatisfied with the king's proceedings, but more with the final proceedings against him … She could have no private end or interest to sway her judgement, butt it must proceed merely out of conscience and the dictate of Gods spirit, … this caused me much to depend upon her counsel which was always backed with solid reason.[47]

We cannot tell whether Frances Whitelocke was in fact such a public spirited figure, but Bulstrode's account of her clearly functions as way of justifying his own role. That he listened to this committed, rational woman was testimony to the validity of the difficult course Bulstrode Whitelocke took in 1649, of opposition to the regicide but loyal service to a republic established by military power.

Inadequate men

Thinking with women – with loving wives who reinforced their stances, or fearful wives who sought to divert them from the cause – was one means through which men came to terms with civil-war dilemmas. Of course men also measured themselves against other men. Their own cause was defended, and rival allegiances condemned as opponents were denounced as imperfect or inadequate men. It is notorious that the king himself (and by extension royalism in general) was undermined by accusations of effeminate submission to his foreign wife, and his case will require extended treatment. Here we will use examples from the extremes of the parliamentarian coalition, exploring the trials of the twice-cuckolded Earl of Essex, the relatively moderate first Lord General of parliament's army, and then discussing the ways in which the masculinity of Lilburne's fellow Levellers Richard Overton and William Walwyn was asserted and impugned.

Sexual slander was a common weapon in contests between men, and it was especially effective when it was broadly true. The Earl of Essex had a particularly unfortunate marital history, and Thomas Hobbes for one argued that the humiliations that drove him from the court, also led him to reassert his manhood as a military leader in the struggle against the king.[48] In 1613 Essex's first marriage to Frances Howard had been annulled on grounds of non-consummation through the Earl's impotence, so that she could marry the royal favourite Robert Carr; his second had collapsed when it was reliably suspected that the short-lived son born to his second wife in 1636 was a result of her affair with Sir William Uvedale. His situation, like Milton's own, is one of the few that fits the poet's bitter remarks in 1654 about wives living 'in the camp of the enemy, threatening her husband with death and disaster' for the Countess of Essex 'adhered to the enemies of the king, parliament, and kingdom' (in parliament's formulation) emerging only to petition for her share of Essex's estate after the Earl's death in 1646.[49] By the time of the civil war, then, Essex had long been the butt of salacious talk and derisive verse that circulated widely in manuscript. In 1615 it was joked that 'from Robert's coach to Robin's car, Frank flings, climbs and travels far', while in 1636 a popular verse urged:

> A health to my Lady Essex
> Who once had lost her fame
> And to my Lord her husband
> That is so ill at the game.[50]

Essex was an easy target for royalist contempt, 'abused in pictures, censured in pulpits, dishonoured in the table-talk of the common people', according to the royalist newsbook *Mercurius Aulicus* in August 1643.[51] His shame was made visible on the military banners carried into battle by royalist regiments; in 1642–43 at least seven banners portrayed Essex as a cuckold. One or two were subtle, but most preferred obvious images of cuckold's horns or the unambiguous message, 'cuckolds we come', thus associating all parliamentarian soldiers with Essex's humiliation.[52] A Wiltshire cleric denounced Essex as a 'cuckold and a rebel', and the popular royalism which owed much to an overtly anti-Puritan festive culture prompted ritual mocking of Essex, in the manner of the 'ridings' that disciplined village cuckolds. In Hereford, for example, in August 1642, 'one Richard Taylor (a lewd seditious fellow)' shouted 'Down with the Roundheads, a pox take them all', and also 'did place upon his bulk a round block and fixed a pair of horns, calling it "Essex's head and horns"'. Taylor, a tobacco-seller, embellished his block with tobacco pipes. The hostile commentator also alleged Taylor had posted pictures of parliamentarian peers in his privy; he deduced that 'Drinking, gaming, tobacco-taking, watching and wenching is enough to take away care and reason'.[53] Even in death Essex was not respected, and his tomb in Westminster Abbey was vandalised within weeks of his funeral. For the royalist poet Hester Pulter, this was the inevitable result of allowing such a discredited man such lavish obsequies:

> Yet he that ne'er gained honour here on earth
> By order they made triumph after death
> And in derision of our ancient kings
> His horned image they to th'temple bring.[54]

Royalists' unmanning of Essex aimed, in the end without success, to convince all parliamentarians of their inadequacy. Conflicts within parliamentarianism could also be understood as rival forms of manhood. Essex himself was attacked posthumously in a pamphlet attributed to the republican Henry Neville: 'For a general he had ill luck / That other men his wife should——'.[55] The Leveller Richard Overton, like John Lilburne, sought to make his individual suffering into an emblem of the general tyranny of authoritarian parliamentarians who harassed Leveller campaigns:

> Wherein (as in a Glass) every freeman of England may clearly behold his own imminent insufferable bondage and slavery under the Norman-Prerogative Men of this Kingdom, represented by the present sufferings of Richard Overton.[56]

In a vividly physical account of being dragged off to prison in 1647, Overton established his own manly bravery through contrasts with the fake masculinity of his excessively violent gaoler. In the end the humiliation to which Overton is subjected, and which he endures with an almost passive stoicism, degrades his aggressors rather than himself.

> Away I was born to the boat, and when I was landed at Blackfriars, they would have forced me along up the hill on my feet, yea, they entreated me, but at that time I was not minded to be their drudge, or to make use of my feet to carry the rest of my body to the gaol, therefore I let them hang as if they had been none of my own, or like a couple of farthing candles dangling at my knees.

They 'let my body fall upon the stones ... and just as if I had been a dead dog, they dragg'd and trail'd my body upon the stones, and without all reverence to my cloth, drew me through the dirt and mire, and plucked me by the hair of the head'. Once they reached Newgate prison, a gaoler tried by force to get Overton to give up his precious copy of the famous common lawyer Sir Edward Coke's commentary on Magna Carta, resorting to violence when he refused. At this Overton's patience ran out:

> I replied, that he should not, if to the utmost of my power I could preserve it from him, and I would do my utmost, where upon I clapped it in my arms, and I laid myself upon my belly, but by force, they violently turned me upon my back, then ... (just as if he had been staving off a dog from the bear) smote me with his fist, to make me let go my hold ... thus by an assault they got the

great charter of England's Liberties and Freedoms from me which I laboured to the utmost of power in me to preserve and defend, and ever to the death shall maintain.[57]

Overton's staunch political stance, and the legitimacy of the Leveller movement, is established through contrasts with other men, as in 'normal' times different modes of manhood might be worked out or displayed through conflict among men.[58] Other men might be discredited by their attitudes towards women, and in this same pamphlet Overton provided a bitterly angry account of the mistreatment of his wife by a House of Lords' marshal, wherein the true, virtuous woman exposed the bombastic falsehood of the man. In an attempt, claimed Overton, 'for ever to obliterate the honour of her modesty, civility and chastity' the House of Lords ordered that Mary Overton, who had supported her husband's illegal pamphleteering, should be:

> cast into the most infamous gaol of Bridewell, that common centre and receptacle of bawds, whores and strumpets, more fit for their wanton retrograde ladies, than for one, who never yet could be taxed of immodesty, either in countenance, gesture, words, or action.

But Mary, like her husband and John Lilburne, refused to obey the warrant of the House of Lords, 'in plain downright terms (like a true bred English woman brought up at the feet of Gamaliel) she told the Marshall that she would not obey it'. But:

> no sooner had this turkey-cock Marshall heard of her uprightness to the Commons of England, but up he bristled his feathers and looked as big and as bug as a Lord ... out he belched his fury and told her, that if she would not go, then she should be carried in a porter's basket, or else dragged at a cart's arse. [He ...] struts towards her like a crow in a gutter, and with his valiant looks like a man of mettle assailed her and her babe, and by violence attempt to pluck the tender babe out of her arms, but she forcibly defended it, and kept it in spite of his manhood.

The marshal's manhood is invalidated by Mary's defiance, presented in her husband's contemptuous prose with its animalistic images. Even though Mary was dragged to Bridewell through 'all the dirt and the mire of the streets, with the poor infant still crying and mourning in her arms', abused as 'strumpet and vile whore'; even if the House of Lords intended that for ever after, 'she should not pass the streets upon her necessary occasions any more without contumely and derision, scoffing, hissing and pointing at her, with such or the like sayings, as see, see, there goes a strumpet that was dragged through the streets to Bridewell', it was the Overtons who held the moral high ground, she clutching her baby to her breast, he defending Magna Carta. As Overton concluded, 'this is the honour that their Lordships are pleased to confer on the Commoners' wives who stand for their Freedoms and Liberties'.[59]

The most intimate cleavage on the parliament's side came in the spring of 1649, when the Levellers denounced the new republican regime as illegal and tyrannical, but the majority of the London-gathered congregations of Independents and Baptists, among whom the Leveller movement had emerged from the mid-1640s, welcomed it as godly rule. Vicious public controversy ensued, centred on the unlikely figure of a third Leveller leader, the socially respectable but intellectually adventurous William Walwyn. The Baptist William Kiffin denounced Walwyn as a 'whorish Delilah', corrupting the unwary, and he was subject to ingenious and implausible sexual slurs.[60] While the jokes about Essex were based on unfortunate facts, the attacks on the long- and happily married Walwyn are testimony to the cultural power of sexual slander in political disputes. Walwyn indignantly responded:

> Another new thing I am aspersed withall, is that I hold polygamy ... and that I am addicted loosely to women; but this is another envenomed arrow drawn from the same politic quiver, and shot without any regard to my inclination; and shows the authors to be empty of all goodness and tilled with a most wretchless malice; for this is such a slander as dogs me at the heels home to my house; seeking to torment me even with my wife and children, and so to make my life a burthen unto me; but this also loseth its force, and availeth nothing, as the rest do also, where I am fully known, nay it produceth the contrary; even the increase of love and esteem amongst them ... one and twenty years with my wife, and fifteen or sixteen with my daughters, without the least stain of my person, putting the question of my conversation out of all question.[61]

Radical masculinities

Republicans like Milton and democratically inclined Levellers mounted fundamental challenges to English political and religious structures, challenges that had scarcely been imagined by most parliamentarians as the war broke out. As explained in the introduction, there was a widespread feeling among civilians and especially among soldiers, that the sacrifices of blood and treasure in the war demanded recompense. Radical parliamentarians presented visions of transformed polities and transformed (male) political actors. They disagreed on many issues – on the proper powers of the state, the qualifications for public office or the parliamentary franchise, the role of the army and the extent of religious liberty, but more fundamentally they differed over what it meant to be a political man, and in particular on how far a man's authority in a household was necessary for political agency. Some initial examples will suggest a range of views, and we can then put them in a more general context of civil war and social change.

In his 'Defence of the English People', published (in Latin) in early 1651, John Milton insisted that 'Fathers and kings are very different things'. Addressing his French Protestant opponent, Claudius Salmasius, he continued:

> You [Salmasius] are wholly in the dark in failing to distinguish the rights of a father from those of a king; by calling kings fathers of their country you think

this metaphor has forced me to apply right off to kings whatever I might admit of fathers. Fathers and kings are very different things: our fathers begot us, but our kings did not, and it is we, rather, who created the king. It is nature which gave the people fathers, and the people who gave themselves a king.[62]

This argument was entirely consistent with Milton's republicanism, but the pervasive influence of familial metaphors is revealed in his immediate resort in the same work to the use of the father–king metaphor:

We endure a father though he be harsh and strict, and we endure such a king too; but we do not endure even a father who is tyrannical. If a father kill his son he shall pay with his life: shall not then a king too be subject to this same most just of laws if he has destroyed the people who are his sons? This is the more true since a father cannot abjure his position as a father, while a king can easily make himself neither a father nor a king.[63]

On the other hand, the 'Digger' Gerrard Winstanley whose vivid prose inspired the cultivation of the common land in Walton and Cobham, Surrey in 1649–50 as a means of making the land 'a common treasury for all', saw fatherhood as the source of political agency. In his egalitarian and utopian tract, *The Law of Freedom in a Platform*, Winstanley argued in terms that show some similarities with the arguments of Sir Robert Filmer, the royal absolutist quoted in the introduction:

The original Root of Magistracy is *common Preservation*, and it rose up first in a private Family: for suppose there were but one Family in the World, as is conceived, Father *Adam*'s Family, wherein were many persons.
    Therein *Adam* was the first Governor or Officer in the Earth, because as he was the first Father, so he was the most wise in contriving, and the most strong for labor, and so the fittest to be the chief *Governor*.[64]

Winstanley of course was proposing rule by many fathers rather than the single authority stressed by Filmer. His deriving of government from the need for 'common preservation' echoes another very different contemporary, Thomas Hobbes, and Winstanley also shares with Hobbes the notion that it was the consent of the children that established fatherly government. Adam, in the first family, was 'the first link of the chain Magistracy'. His 'Children wanting experience of their own preservation' had to ask the father, 'do thou teach us how to plant the Earth, that we will live, and we will obey. By this choice, they make him not only a Father, but a Master and Ruler'. In Hobbesian terms again, the children gave an implied consent: 'Though the children might not speak, yet their weakness and simplicity did speak, and chose their Father to be their Overseer.' Again Winstanley did not share Hobbes's conclusion that a single sovereign political authority was needed; instead any 'father in a family is a commonwealth's officer, because the necessity of the young children choose him by a joint consent, and not otherwise'.[65]

The issue of consent was also prominent at the Putney debates in autumn 1647 when soldiers discussed the future settlement of the kingdom. Cromwell's son-in-law, Henry Ireton, who dominated the more 'conservative' arguments at Putney, used the conventional appeal to the fifth commandment to justify obedience to all authority: the 'same law [as forbad theft] says "Honour thy father and thy mother", and that law does extend to all that (in that place where we are in) are our governors'. He there-fore argued that the parliamentary franchise should continue to be vested in men of some property. The radical spokesman Thomas Rainborough rejected this argument, making a distinction between civil and natural parenthood:

> With respect to the divine law which says 'Honour thy father and thy mother',
> the great dispute is who is a right father and a right mother? I am bound to
> know who is my father and mother … I would have a distinction, a character
> whereby God commands me to honour them. And for my part I look upon
> the people of England so, that wherein they have not voices in the choosing of
> their governors – their civil fathers and mothers – they are not bound to that
> commandment.[66]

For Rainborough, then, fathers and political actors were very different things, for consent was crucial in the political realm as it was not in the family.

Radical men thus differed on how far fatherhood or household authority qualified men for political participation. The civil war was fought in a society where, as we have seen, the household was a fundamental unit of social life as well as an influential metaphor for authority in general; and where the dominant version of manhood was that of head of household.[67] Already by 1640, processes of social change made it very difficult for poorer men to achieve secure independence as head of a household, and civil war added to the difficulties in obvious, but important ways. Heavy taxation, trade disruption, loss of earnings or physical strength while serving as a soldier all threatened the independence of poorer parliamentarian men. Women's ingenuity and activism were even more necessary to the preservation of families than in peace-time, while civil war divisions had offered women unprecedented opportunities for invol-vement in religious and political life. Diane Purkiss has contrasted the passive, fem-inised manhood of the martyr king with a republican masculinity of 'heads of households and citizen soldiers', but the arguments at Putney, and the imaginative solutions of Winstanley, hint at the anxieties about resting male political agency on household status. What should happen if citizen soldiers, or other parliamentarian men, could not be effective heads of households?[68]

There is, then, an important social-history context to the contrasting views on the household as a source of male political authority. Equally relevant are more positive trends or inspirations in parliamentarian political practices during the war. Throughout the 1640s, all men and to some extent women too were invited to give their allegiance to parliament or king through rival processes of mobilisation. On the parliament's side, the conviction that they were fighting for a godly cause against the servants of antichrist, and the self-presentation of the House of Commons, as the 'representative of the people', demanded appeals to broad sections of the population. The 'people', never clearly defined, were mobilised through a range of texts and practices, petitioning and oath-taking in particular. Widely circulated cheap print cemented these activities in popular political culture. Parliament did not direct its appeals only to heads of households; in unprecedently sustained fashion, all men were invited to become political actors. Restrictions of age, marital status or wealth that operated in some spheres (voting, or formal office holding for example), and at some times, were not relevant. Consequently, as John Walter has most eloquently explained, if even in 'normal' times, 'the deep structures of the English state actively promoted popular participation', 'the revolution opened up a new political space for popular politics'.[69]

The 'Protestation' oath of May 1641, for example, passed by parliament amid fears that the king's supporters were plotting to restore his personal authority by force, required its takers to 'promise, vow and protest to maintain and defend, as far as lawfully I may with my life, power and estate, the true reformed Protestant religion … His Majesty's royal person and estate, as also the power and privilege of Parliaments, the lawful rights and liberties of the subjects' and to work to 'bring to condign punishment' all who worked against it. It was in effect a summing up of parliament's position against the plotters around the king, and it was explicitly intended to draw together all adult men in the defence of parliament, while in some communities women were encouraged or permitted to take the oath. When renewed efforts were made to enforce the Protestation in January 1642 in the wake of the king's botched attempt to arrest leaders of the opposition, the House of Commons ordered that local authorities were to call together 'the inhabitants of their several Parishes, both Householders and others, being of eighteen years of age and upwards' to affirm.[70] Similarly, the Solemn League and Covenant of autumn 1643 which marked the alliance between the English parliament and the Scottish Covenanters was tendered to all men over eighteen, 'as well lodgers and inhabitants'.[71] The Covenant, to a greater extent than the Protestation, was also taken by women in several parishes. There were twelve wives among the 126 people who took the Covenant in Gerrard Winstanley's London parish, St Olave Old Jewry, between October 1643 and February 1644, although Winstanley's own wife, Susan, was not among them.[72] Both oaths thus 'challenged one of the fundamental assumptions of early modern political culture that it was male, married, propertied householders who claimed a public political identity, and that their household dependants were subsumed within that identity'.[73]

Petitioning also mobilised broader elements of the population, directly as their marks and signatures were collected, and indirectly as cheap print took rival petitions to the wider public. From the early 1640s rival petitioning campaigns were organised in London and the provinces – for and against episcopacy, in support of parliamentary initiatives such as the 'Grand Remonstrance' that denounced Charles's personal rule in December 1641, for and against a negotiated peace.[74] There is no evidence that signatories were confined to heads of household, and indeed throughout the 1640s, petitions from London apprentices – young and dependent men – were mobilised for divergent parliamentarian purposes, in favour of peace in 1642 and 1647, in support

of determined action against 'malignants' in 1641–42, and to back the Levellers in
1649. Whatever their particular political stance, these petitions claimed the right of
younger and poorer men to present their views on public affairs to the parliament.
Peace petitioners noted parliament's 'gracious acceptation of Petitions from persons of
as mean a quality as ourselves', while more militant apprentices acknowledged they
were 'the lowest members of the city and kingdom', yet they were still 'touched with
the common sense of all your Majesties good subjects'. These latter petitioners
evoked the 'late Protestation' by which they 'stand solemnly engaged in the presence
of Almighty God by all lawful means, with the uttermost of our lives, power and
estates' to defend its principles.[75] The apprentice and young men's petitions also drew
on their military sacrifices to legitimate their political interventions, recording that
'many of our dear friends and fellow soldiers' had fallen in the parliament's cause:

> Remember you not with what cheerfulness and alacrity our fellow-Apprentices,
> the glory and flower of the youth of this Nation, and multitudes of ourselves
> yet surviving, ran in to your assistance out of a conscientious intent, to uphold
> and maintain the fundamental constitution of this Commonwealth ... that the
> people should not be bound but by their own consent given to their Deputies
> in parliament.[76]

In an ideal world, the subordination of apprentices was a temporary experience,
preparation for their mature roles as masters of households in turn. Leveller supporters
in May 1649 pointed this out in referring back to a petition of January 1641 in which
apprentices had protested against Charles I's attempts to arrest parliamentarian leaders:
'we (though bound to our Masters for a time, by our free consent, yet) fellow commoners
with them, did join together'.[77] Apprentices thus explicitly distinguished themselves
from wives whose dependence was permanent, even as they established the grounds for
political agency for men, even if they never became masters in their turn.[78]

Religious fragmentation also complicated understanding of male authority.
Household status had an ambiguous connection to participation and leadership within
the gathered religious congregations that proliferated in the 1640s and 1650s and
were an important conduit for political influence. In the last chapter we explained
that many Quakers, Baptists and other separatists would have preferred a more
straightforward relationship where spiritual commitment did not disrupt this-world
hierarchies, but ultimately membership depended on individual faith, and continued
commitment might involve defiance of masters, husbands and fathers. The recasting
of familial relationships from the worldly to the spiritual was enacted in the common
practice of describing fellow church-members as 'Brother' and 'Sister'. Of the first
fifty members of the General Baptist congregation that met at Warboys in Hunting-
donshire, only sixteen were married couples, although some other family members
joined together.[79] Ideally households were at one in the ways they served God, but
where this was not the case, the churches always, reluctantly, decided that God was
to be obeyed before man, servants might defy masters, and wives disagree with husbands. The West Country Calvinist Baptists decreed in May 1655 that a head of a

household who was the only church member in a family, could not pray with them, although he might pray for them.[80] The same group debated 'Whether church-membership in the wife and faithful children be qualifications absolutely necessary to such brethren as are appointed to officiate in the church'. This question troubled them greatly. They believed that if an elder did not keep his wife 'in subjection' and his children 'faithfully subjecting themselves to their parents' there was 'just ground of dissatisfaction concerning his fitness to take care of the church of Christ'; but despite the force of 1 Timothy 3.5 ('For if a man know not how to rule his own house, how shall he take care of the church of God?'), they hesitated to say that an elder be judged unfit if his 'wife or children of the elder be unruly' through no fault of his own.[81]

Preachers and leaders within the sects were talented and charismatic men, from various social backgrounds, often young and often unmarried, or separated from their families by a life of itinerant evangelism. The early Quakers offer the most numerous and startling examples, including James Parnell the 'Quaking boy' who died at twenty in a Colchester prison, and the leading preachers and pamphleteers of the 1650s, such as Edward Burrough (born 1633), Richard Farnworth (born about 1630) and Richard Hubberthorne (born 1628). George Fox himself only married Margaret Fell in 1669, some twenty years after he had begun his ministry.[82] Many sectarian preachers had been soldiers – military service in the parliamentary cause and a sense of a particular call from God were mutually reinforcing for many politically active men. Edmund Chillenden dedicated a pamphlet in support of lay preachers 'to the Reader, especially my fellow brethren and Saints, commanders and soldiers with me in the army under his excellency, Sir Thomas Fairfax', and signed off as 'your brother and fellow soldier and companion in tribulation, and in the kingdom and patience of Jesus Christ'. A godly man might be young and inexperienced in matters of the world, but 'no novice or youngling in the school of Christ'; he might be poor for 'God is no respecter of persons, but gives his gifts by his spirit to whom he pleaseth, whereby all men that partake of those gifts are enabled to prophesy or preach, though not ordained'. The spirit 'bloweth where it listeth, as soon upon a cobbler, tinker, chimney sweeper, ploughman, or any other tradesman, as to the greatest learned doctors in the world'. Like the London apprentices, but more directly, Chillenden distinguished male capacities from female. The fact that the scriptures specifically prohibited women preaching must imply, he claimed, that any and all gifted men could preach.[83]

Chillenden's appeal to the brotherhood of soldiers, for him a spiritual brotherhood, suggests the central importance of military service in underpinning radical claims to male political agency. Military service had obvious dangers but it was also a potent if paradoxical inspiration for claims to citizenship.[84] An army was hierarchical, but it also fostered more egalitarian comradeship. Obedience to orders was vital, but all volunteers were welcome, cooperation and loyalty were essential, and, to some extent at least, promotion came through talent not birth, and certainly not through household status, despite the mockery of the domestic arrangements of Waller or Essex. As we have seen, bravery and martial prowess were enduring elements in definitions of proper manliness, but civil war service for the parliament had a particularly powerful ideological force. Pre-civil war local militias were usually householders training in their cities and counties, but recruits for foreign wars came from younger and more marginal groups. During the civil war some men served in garrisons near their homes and families, but those in marching armies were incorporated into a homosocial world. Parliament's armies were represented, optimistically, as volunteers, freely serving a godly cause. Pamphlet accounts of the London militia's part in the battle of Newbury in October 1643 drew on earlier traditions of civic chivalry, writing of 'the glory of that courage and valour God gave unto them this day, they stood like so many stakes against the shot of the cannon ... fighting like lions in every place'. The returning London troops were 'joyfully received home of all our friends' and given a ceremonious welcome by the Mayor and Aldermen:

> Thus God that called us forth to do his work, brought us through many straits, delivered us from the rage and insolency of our adversaries, made them turn their backs with shame, giving us victory, and causing us to return home joyfully.[85]

A cheap 'Souldiers Catechisme' for parliament's troops published in 1644 contrasted the 'base and private spirits', the 'faint-hearted cowards' of the enemy with their own 'godly and religious soldiers', 'so full of courage and resolution'.[86] These were not realistic descriptions of parliament's soldiers; the London militia men were only too glad to get home, and never again marched out from the city to battle, and the Catechism's ideal that a 'well-ordered camp is a school of virtue' was never achieved. Nonetheless, parliament did aspire to moralised behaviour from its soldiers – Chillenden himself was eventually expelled from the army, and from his gathered congregation for 'getting a wench with bairn' – and the heightened expectations of personal conduct and ideological commitment encouraged some soldiers in turn to demand real transformations of their political status.[87]

A conviction that military commitment and sacrifice for the parliament entitled men to greater liberties emerged, for example, in artisanal struggles against the twin threats of mercantile dominance and the competition from waged labourers in London livery companies, struggles invigorated by feelings of fraternal comradeship and national identity.[88] In a series of pamphlets, one former soldier Nathaniel Burt displayed his pride in his 'martial abilities', developed in the fight for 'my native country's liberty and country-men's safety and privileges of parliament' and his commitment to his 'Fellow-commoners, who are the Commonwealth, or Native Country-men, or brothers English-men'. In a pamphlet promoting greater democracy within the Saddlers' company, Burt moved from brotherhood to fatherhood, both within a powerful sense of English citizenship, urging his fellows to:

> Wait you with patience in brotherly love, bearing one another's burthens; that we and ours hereafter may happily arrive at the fruition of liberty and rest from this sea and calamity of oppression and trouble; that our children may say of us, their deceased fathers hereafter, they acted courageously as free-born English-men

in their generation, wisely as Common-wealths men in their places and capacities, and lovingly and patiently as Christians, through whom we have had deliverance, and are become a happy English people born, and left to freedom and liberty.[89]

The impact of military experience was predictably strongest on the politics of the New Model Army itself. In June 1647, a sense that army grievances were treated with contempt by the parliament prompted the eloquent declaration, that they were not 'a mere mercenary army, hired to serve any arbitrary power of a state; but called forth and conjured, by the several declarations of Parliament, to the defence of our own and the people's just rights and liberties'.[90] In other words they were a patriotic citizenry, bearing arms as a vocation, for a cause, not as a marker of elite masculinity or as paid cannon fodder. The army constituted itself as a political body defending political and religious liberties as well as pursuing practical grievances, and established a Council in which representatives of rank and file soldiers, along with officers, discussed proposals for the settlement of the kingdom. At Putney in October 1647 the Council met to discuss negotiations with the king, and to debate 'An Agreement of the People', a radical proposal for a re-creation of the English polity whereby a truly representative parliamentary system would be established. We saw earlier that moderates and radicals disagreed at Putney over the force of parental authority as a metaphor for politics. In the course of the debates the radical spokesman, Thomas Rainborough, retorted to Ireton, in one of the most quoted passages from the English revolution:

> For really I think that the poorest he that is in England has a life to live as the greatest he; and therefore truly, sir, I think it's clear that every man that is to live under a government ought first by his own consent to put himself under that government.[91]

Rainborough's words, and the Putney Debates in general, have sparked much controversy in conventional political history and the history of political thought over the extent of the parliamentary franchise claimed; the relationship between civilian and military radicalism; the role of the Levellers; or attitudes to the king.[92] But behind the iconic phrase, 'the poorest he', lie sharply polarised views on the proper connections between manhood and political participation. Putney thus serves as a good place to begin more specific discussions of radical manhood. Military service in God's cause qualified and emboldened men to defend freedom and liberty as English citizens, yet they might well not be heads of household. The economic dislocations of civil war intensified the existing difficulties men had in achieving this hegemonic independent status, while many aspects of parliamentarian ideology and political practice circumvented household status as the ground for men's political activism.

While radicals argued at Putney that military zeal, loyalty to the cause and natural rights as men, or Englishmen, gave men an interest in the political process, the moderate Henry Ireton insisted that political participation should be restricted to 'fixed and settled men that had the interest of this kingdom in them', independent householders, with freehold land (as the existing county franchise required). A lease was insufficient: 'He that is here today and gone tomorrow, I do not see that he hath such a permanent interest.' Rather, the vote must be 'restrained ... to men who have a local, permanent interest in the kingdom ... such an interest that they may live upon it as freemen'. Poor or dependent men had not fought for direct political agency, but for a more ordered and lawful form of subjection, that they might have the benefit of laws made by a representative body of propertied men, rather than living in a polity where 'one man's will must be a law'. The poor, argued Ireton, 'thought it was better to be concluded by the common consent of those that were fixed men, and settled men that had the interest of this kingdom in them'. Independence was key: 'If there be anything at all that is a foundation of liberty it is this, that those who shall choose the law-makers shall be men freed from dependence upon others.'[93]

In contrast radicals like Rainborough and Edward Sexby stressed how soldiers had been raised by parliament to fight for a cause, and explicitly separated political rights from household status. The June 1647 declaration was much evoked, as when Sexby urged:

> We have engaged in this kingdom and ventured our lives, and it was all for this: to recover our birthrights and privileges as Englishmen; and by the arguments urged there are none. There are many thousands of us soldiers that have ventured our lives. We have had little propriety in the kingdom as to our estates, yet we have a birthright ... I wonder we were so much deceived. If we had not a right to the kingdom we were mere mercenary soldiers.

Rainborough more curtly demanded, 'I would fain know what the soldier has fought for all this while? He has fought to enslave himself, to give power to men of riches, men of estates, to make him a perpetual slave?'[94]

Both argued that poor men, poor soldiers in particular, might lose the capacity to be effective heads of household but they should not thereby lose their essential qualities as men or their political rights. Rainborough separated rationality from property: 'This gift of reason without other property may seem a small thing, yet I think there is nothing God has given a man that anyone else can take from him.' The argument was sometimes specifically made on behalf of those who had lost through their service of parliament: as Rainborough demanded, 'what shall become of those many men that have laid out themselves by fighting, by hazarding all they had? They are Englishmen.' An 'interest' in the kingdom did not depend on estate, on owning the freehold land worth forty shillings a year that qualified men to vote in county elections:

> many a man whose zeal and affection to God and this kingdom has carried him forth in this cause, has so spent his estate that, in the way the state and the Army are going, he shall not hold up his head, if, when his estate is lost and are not worth forty shillings a year, a man shall not have any interest.

Rainborough's extended argument applied not just to poor soldiers but to all poor men. A man's natural rights could not be forfeit if they were impoverished through service in war, or by any other means 'which God in his providence does use':

> A man, when he has an estate, has an interest in making laws; but when he has none, he has no power to in it; so that a man cannot lose that which he has for the maintenance of his family but he must also lose that which God and nature has given him.[95]

Ireton's settled, respectable householders were opposed by Rainborough and Sexby's 'poor and meaner' men who retained their birthrights even if they had lost or never had the capacity to support households. Men's political agency was here not based on any prior authority over women and children or over younger or less powerful men, but on god-given and natural qualities and rights.

It is unsurprising perhaps that Ireton and the army radicals disagreed on independent householder status as the basis for men's political rights, as they disagreed on many aspects of politics in 1647–48. However, material discussed earlier suggests that a very different conception of politically active manhood from Rainborough's is presented in civilian Leveller writings. Specific Leveller positions on the franchise were inconsistent or contradictory between 1647 and 1649; in the manifesto, the third Leveller 'Agreement of the People' (May 1649), the supreme authority of England was placed 'in a Representative of the People, consisting of four hundred persons but no more; in the choice of whom (according to natural right) all men of the age of one-and-twenty years and upwards (not being servants, or receiving alms, or having served the late king in arms or voluntary contributions)'.[96] In their programmatic statements the Levellers never explicitly endorsed a straightforward association between male householder status and political rights, but they worried greatly about men's capacity for staunch, independent political action if they were dependent on others.[97] As I have argued in earlier work, precise Leveller demands and manifestos are perhaps less important than the political identities described and offered to potential followers in the printed propaganda which was the crucial means through which Levellers constructed a movement and appealed for support.[98] And in their pamphlets Leveller leaders consistently presented themselves as substantial family men, heads of households whose wives and servants supported their views and shared their sufferings. In the works by Lilburne, Overton and Walwyn already quoted, to be a Leveller was to be a male householder. At Putney the rival accounts of political manliness were both concrete and impersonal, Ireton's fixed men opposed Rainborough's 'poorest he'. Much Leveller writing, in contrast, was vividly personal: Walwyn defended his honour as a faithful family man, Overton attacked the cruel and degrading treatment of his wife, while Lilburne contrasted his own determined commitment with his wife's preference for private compromise. The technique invited readers to associate themselves with these concrete and emblematic accounts of domestic suffering and to join the struggle against tyranny.

Title-pages proclaimed Leveller men as solid householders, as gentlemen and freemen, 'merchant' (William Walwyn) or 'A Free man of England and one of the Merchant-taylors company of London' (William Larner). While soldiers at Putney argued that inability to maintain a household was no barrier to male political agency, civilian Leveller pamphlets attacked the authorities for sabotaging their ability to support their families, demanding their restoration to responsible householder status. In describing his arrest by the Council of State in 1649, Walwyn presented the violation of a comfortable and happy family home. Soldiers came in the dead of night: 'a strong party of horse and foot … knocked violently at my garden gate between four and five in the morning' terrifying a loyal maid, who ran up 'crying and shivering', horrifying his wife, 'who for two and twenty years we have lived together, never had known me under a minutes restraint by any authority' and making his eldest daughter ill with fright, 'who hath continued sick ever since, my children and I having been very tender one of another. Nor were my neighbours less troubled for me, to whose love I am very much obliged.'[99] When the printer William Larner was imprisoned in March 1646 for distributing a seditious pamphlet, his wife petitioned for his release, and that of the two loyal servants in prison with him for refusing to give evidence against him. Ellen Larner was, like Mary Overton, a loyal and brave wife. Her petition pointed out that her husband and the servants had served in parliament's army, that she, being with child, had fallen into a 'dangerous sinkness, to her great charge and damage' on his 'violent apprehension' while William could not, from prison, 'supply the extreme wants of his family (which is 6 persons) or relieve his aged father and mother who are past labour, and were lately plundered in Gloucestershire'. Larner himself asked the House of Lords not to 'expose your Petitioner, his wife and family to ruin, which they cannot avoid, if your Petitioner may not have his liberty, and be permitted to follow his calling for the maintenance of himself, wife and family'. Larner's role as provider was crucial to his identity, and the loss of it shamed his gaolers: 'For if I provide not for my family I am worse than an infidel; but woe be to them that are the causes thereof.'[100] Levellers thus were competent householders, or at least they were when not assailed by tyrannical, back-sliding parliamentarians. Their manly identity was often secured by the support of loyal subordinates, wives or servants, within harmonious households, although in Lilburne's later tracts, his wife's pleadings operated as a potentially enervating distraction from the cause.

The Digger Gerrard Winstanley, with his radical social vision, has been described as 'conservative to the core in terms of gender'. This is not entirely fair, for Winstanley's views on marriage or rape were sympathetic to women, but the judgement perhaps also misses the radically patriarchal character of the ideal society he described in a tract published two years after the destruction of the Digger experiments.[101] The long-term economic vulnerability of aspirant heads of household was made worse and personal for Winstanley by the crisis of the later 1640s. In the mid-1640s his London business had failed, a calamity he attributed to the burdens of war, and in 1649–50, he inspired the digging on the commons of Walton and Cobham as a solution to the terrible hardship experienced by the common people in years of harvest failure and depression. Winstanley's loss of his independent London household is poignantly recalled in the *Law of Freedom*:

> And now my health and estate is decayed, and I grow in age, I must either beg or work for day wages, which I was never brought up to, for another; when as the Earth is as freely my Inheritance and birthright, as his whom I must work for.[102]

The ecstatic hopes of transformation unleashed by regicide and the digging at George's Hill; and an idiosyncratically egalitarian understanding of the Old Testament's commonwealth of the ancient tribes of Israel also contributed to Winstanley's ideal society. His imagined patriarchal commonwealth was utterly unlike his own experience, for throughout his life Winstanley's fortunes depended on connections to more privileged women. He had been apprenticed to a serious-minded woman only four years his senior, yet in his new society:

> as boys are trained up in learning and in trades, so all maids shall be trained up in reading, sewing, knitting, spinning of linen and woollen, music, and all other easy neat works, either for to furnish storehouses with linen and woollen cloth, or for the ornament of particular houses with needle work.[103]

Two economically advantageous marriages, the second to a woman twenty years his junior, bailed Winstanley out from recurrent financial disasters, and briefly employed, with other Diggers, by the eccentric prophetess Eleanor Douglas, he denounced her during a quarrel, in traditionally misogynist terms: 'you have lost the breeches your reason, by the inward boiling vexation of your spirit'.[104]

Winstanley's response to the dissolutions of revolution was thus to propose a reconstituted natural patriarchy ordered by age as well as gender. In 1652 the middle-aged Winstanley was still childless but he nonetheless stressed fatherhood as the fundamental basis for all authority, as we have seen. Within his ideal society the patriarchal household was taken for granted as the basis of social and political organisation:

> Though the earth and storehouses be common to every family, yet every family shall live apart as they do; and every mans house, wife, children, and furniture for ornament of his house, or any thing which he hath fetched in from the store-houses, or provided for the necessary use of his family, is all a propriety to that family, for the peace thereof. And if any man offer to take away a mans wife, children, or furniture of his house, without his consent, or disturb the peace of his dwelling, he shall suffer punishment as an enemy to the commonwealths government.[105]

Male authority was carefully delineated by age, for 'mankind in the days of his youth, is like a young colt, wanton and foolish, till he be broken by education and correction'. Consequently no man 'shall be a house-keeper, and have servants under him, till he hath served under a master seven years, and hath learned his trade: and the reason is, that every family may be governed by stayed and experienced masters, and not by wanton youth'. It was essential that 'a man may be of age, and of rational carriage, before he be a governor of a family, that the peace of the commonwealth may be preserved'.[106] Officers in Winstanley's commonwealth were to be over forty 'for these are most likely to be experienced men; and all these are likely to be men of courage, dealing truly, and hating covetousness', while 'all ancient men, above sixty years of age, are general overseers ... and every one shall give humble respect to these, as to fathers, and as to men of the highest experience in the laws, for the keeping of peace in the Commonwealth'.[107]

Winstanley seems to have thought that one problem with mid-seventeenth-century England was that it was insufficiently patriarchal. One of the provisions in this projected commonwealth was the transfer of women and children to other households if they lacked an effective male head. If a father was repeatedly negligent, or if he:

> be weak, sick, or naturally foolish, wanting the power of wisdom and government, or should be dead before his children should be instructed; then the overseers of this trade, wherein the father was brought up, are to put those children into such families, where they may be instructed, according the law of the commonwealth.[108]

This is patriarchy as fantasy or wish-fulfilment because of course in practice in Winstanley's England it was regarded as normal for a woman to head the household and bring up children if the husband and father were absent or dead. In the real world perhaps as many as a fifth of households were headed by women.

We are a long way from Rainborough and Sexby at Putney, who argued for rights to political participation for individual men, however poor, however young. The varied responses of radical men to the disruptions and novel mobilisations of civil war indicate the perennial dilemmas of independence and authority in male identity as well as the particularly timely problems of how claims to citizenship related to household status. They also show us that at all times, but particularly during times of fundamental conflict, rival political allegiances are not formed simply through adherence to manifestos or adoption of particular political theories such as republicanism, but through imaginative engagement with particular identities, or narratives of existence, and at the heart of understandings of identity were different ways of being a man.

An uxorious king

Contemporary debates about the manliness of the defeated Charles I may seem very distant from the understandings of manhood found among radical parliamentarians, but they reveal some shared themes. The connections between fatherhood and monarchy, or political agency more broadly, have already been suggested, while, for parliamentarians, the king demonstrated in the starkest possible fashion the political calamities that arose when a man was in thrall to his wife; as a newsbook exclaimed in a comment on a 'weak passage' in the king's correspondence with Henrietta

Maria: 'it were ridiculous in a private man, much more a King, to submit to the will of his wife upon every trifle'.[109] When Lucy Hutchinson wrote that Charles I 'married a papist … to whom he became a most uxorious husband', this was a condemnation, not a compliment, while the most intemperate denunciations of Charles as an inadequate ruler came from the pen of John Milton, whose violent disgust at the king's effeminacy was all of a piece with his pervasive anxieties about the ways in which civic liberty might be undermined by domestic subservience.[110]

Contests over the manliness of Charles I were provoked by the publication of the royal correspondence seized at Naseby, and then by the royalist literature of martyrdom after the regicide. As we saw in chapter two, parliament's editorialising of the captured letters emphasised the pernicious influence of the queen; her dominance unmanned and, by implication, unkinged her husband. Affectionate letters, as when Charles declared to the absent Henrietta Maria in February 1643 that he was 'full of affection for thee, admiration of thee, and impatient passion of gratitude to thee', were given contemptuous commentary, while letters that more obviously indicated the queen's political influence were regarded as particularly sinister. In a letter of February 1645, Charles insisted that he would make no peace that required Henrietta Maria to remain in exile:

> As for our treaty, there is every day less hopes than other, that it will produce a peace. But I will absolutely promise thee, that if we have one, it shall be such as shall invite thy return. For, I avow, that without thy company I can neither have peace, nor comfort within myself.[111]

Parliament's commentary hammered the points home:

> It is plain, here, first, that the king's counsels are wholly managed by the queen, though she be of the weaker sex, born an alien, bred up in a contrary religion, yet nothing great or small is transacted without her privity and consent.

It was clear that 'the Queens counsels are as powerful as commands. The king professes to prefer her health before the exigence and importance of his own public affairs.'[112] This unprecedented opening of the monarch's private correspondence was justified precisely because his private behaviour rendered him unfit for absolute public authority. Anyone 'may see here in his private letters what affection the king bears to his people'. Charles was 'a prince seduced out of his proper sphere' as husband and king; his behaviour was 'unbeseeming a Prince, who professes himself defender of the true faith, a tender father of his country'.[113]

If *The King's Cabinet Opened* was a propaganda coup for the parliament, the royalists succeeded after 1649 in establishing an effectively moving image of Charles I as a noble martyr. The abject and passive state of martyrdom was perhaps a feminised image, which caused disquiet to some royalists, but its association of the dead king with the sufferings of Christ had powerful resonances.[114] Central to the image of the martyred king was the *Eikon Basilike*, a volume drafted by Charles himself to justify his proceedings since 1640, and revised for publication by an Episcopalian clergyman, John Gauden. This was the 'publishing sensation of the century', going through twenty editions within a month of the regicide, thirty-five within the year, and thirty-nine before the Restoration. In *Eikon Basilike*, through words and images, and accounts of performance, Charles presented himself both as a benevolent father to his people, and as a good husband and father to his wife and children. One chapter offered advice to his heir, Prince Charles, while later editions of *Eikon* included poignant material describing Charles's last meeting with his younger children, Henry and Elizabeth. In passing, Charles attacked 'the malice of mine enemies' in exposing his private letters to public view. This was contrary to honour, civility and nobility: 'Yet since Providence will have it so, I am content so much of my heart (which I study to approve to God's omniscience) should be discovered to the world'. Eloquent and unashamed praise was offered to Henrietta Maria: 'Her sympathy with me in my afflictions will make her virtues shine with greater lustre, as stars in the darkest nights, and assure the envious world that she loves me, not my fortunes'. Unbiased readers of his letters or of *Eikon Basilike* would see nothing but good in Charles's relations with his wife or his kingdom: 'Nor can any men's malice be gratified further by my letters than to see my constancy to my wife, the laws and religion. Bees will gather honey where the spider sucks poison.' In the *Eikon*, Charles's spiritual authority was contrasted with his physical representation as weak and vulnerable, but his private or personal qualities as loyal and constant husband reinforced his public role as monarch.[115]

In January 1650 an attack on Oliver Cromwell contrasted his illegitimate military authority and the alienating, disorderly republic with the harmony surrendered when the properly patriarchal royal family was overthrown. England had been:

> The Paradise of Europe, the pattern of piety, *beati populi*, a blessed people; where our king like sun in the firmament, by his bright rains of honour gave light to our prosperity, where the Queen like the moon kept just motion in her orb and received her light from that fountain of justice her loyal-hearted spouse; where their progeny as numerous as the planets kept their royal station in this earthly heaven.[116]

Milton was unmoved by any of this and in response to *Eikon Basilike* denounced the whole 'idolised book and the whole rosary of his prayers … served and worshipped with the polluted trash of romance and arcadias'. He pointed out that one of the poems attached to later editions had been lifted from Sidney's *Arcadia*, which was in any case unfitting literature for a proper man. Milton justified the printing of Charles's letters on the grounds of 'discretion, honesty, prudence and plain truth', for it revealed his fatal weaknesses as husband and king:

> He ascribes rudeness and barbarity worse than Indian to the English Parliament, and all virtue in his wife, in strains that come almost to sonneting. How fit to govern men, undervaluing and aspersing the great counsel of his kingdom, in comparison of one woman. Examples are not far to seek, how great mischief

and dishonour hath befallen to nations under the government of effeminate and uxorious magistrates, who being themselves governed and overswayed at home under a feminine usurpation, cannot but be far short of spirit and authority without doors, to govern a whole nation.[117]

Thus responses to the regicide of Charles I were profoundly gendered, as Marcus Nevitt has explained. The dead king himself could be seen as a feminised subject, while horror and revulsion at his execution was frequently expressed through written and visual representations of sorrowful, swooning and miscarrying women. Their misery was roundly dismissed by Milton as the hypocritical whining of 'Court Ladies, not the best of women; who when they grow to that insolence as to appear active in state affairs, are the certain sign of a dissolute, degenerate and pusillanimous commonwealth', but for most people it was an effective tactic.[118] Republicans like the king's prosecutor, John Cook, retorted by denouncing support for the king as irrational and therefore feminine: 'words are women, proofs are men; it is reason that must be the chariot to carry men to give their concurrence in this judgement [against the king]'. Cook's gendered imagery was pervasive and multi-vocal. The king was executed in the name of justice and liberty, both personified as female in bloodthirsty lines on the title page of his tract: 'the Execution of the late King was one of the fattest sacrifices that ever Queen Justice had / Being a Hue and Cry after Lady Liberty which hath been ravished and stolen away by the Grand Potentates of the Earth'. Ultimately monarchy itself was a 'foul mistress', irrational in its opposition to natural hierarchies. It was absurd for men to 'enslave themselves to the arbitrary and lawless lusts of one man and his posterity, whether they be idiots, children, knaves, thieves, murderers, fornicators, gluttons, drunkards, idolators or women'. Cook in fact believed women had the advantage of men in godliness, but they remained unqualified for political office:

> though never so wise, religious, and merciful (as by reason of the tenderness of their spirits and want of temptation, I believe there are more godly women then men in the world) yet it is against the law of God and Nature to make millions of men subject to the commands of a woman.[119]

Republican men thus contrasted their own independent citizenship, exercised in the rational control of their households, as well as in the commonwealth, with the slavish dependency of royalists, loyal to an effeminate king who was himself shamefully subservient to a corrupting wife. Milton denounced Salmasius, the French Protestant who had attacked the regicide, in terms that recall Overton's vigorous assaults on his enemies. Salmasius was commonly believed to be subject to a domineering wife; for Milton this both explained and discredited his politics:

> For you are yourself a Gallic cock and said to be rather cocky, but instead of commanding your mate, she commands and hen-pecks you; and if the cock is king of many hens while you are the slave of yours, you must be no cock of the roost but a mere dung-hill Frenchman.

For this 'dung-hill Frenchman', claimed Milton, slavery had become a way of life:

> You have at home a barking bitch, who rules your wretched wolf-mastership, rails at your rank, and contradicts you shrilly, so naturally you want to force royal tyranny on others after being used to suffer so slavishly at home.[120]

England without a king

Contrasting royalist and republican styles of manhood remained central to political culture from the regicide to the restoration of the monarchy in 1660, revealed in mutual recrimination and denunciation, as well as in positive self-presentations. Three prominent royalists were executed shortly after the regicide for their parts in the second civil war of 1648. The brave ends of the Duke of Hamilton, the Earl of Holland and Lord Capel were given extensive coverage in newsbooks and pamphlets, and were perhaps intended as subtle contrasts to the passive martyrdom of Charles I. The death of Capel in particular represented a swaggering Cavalier idiom. The royalist Isabella Twysden noted in her diary: 'the 9 of March 1649 was put to death Duke Hamilton a Scotch nobleman, the Earl of Holland, a brave courtier, and my Lord Capel a gallant man'.[121] Holland and Hamilton had pious deaths; attended by godly ministers on the scaffold, they declared their loyalty to the king, and died without fuss. Capel's end was more insouciant, and more defiant, in line with his reputation as a second Hector:

> Renowned Capel, whose undaunted spirit,
> Amongst his greatest foes did honour merit
> Whose actions manifested him to be
> A second Hector, or more in degree.[122]

According to a royalist newsbook, Capel faced his sentence with classic stoicism:

> who with a magnanimous courage, more undaunted then ever was Roman, having all the time his sentence was reading and pronouncing, his arm akimbo, out-facing boldly those bloody tyrants and messengers of murther and cruelty who sat in judgement to take away his innocent life.

On the scaffold, Capel's brisk behaviour was very different from that of Holland and Hamilton who spent a good hour in prayer and speeches. Capel, again described as a 'second Hector':

> put off his hat and saluted all those on the scaffold, walking two or three turns very majestically with an austere countenance, beheld the block, clapped on his hat and cocked it, then coming to the scaffold rails directed his speech to the guard with a loud voice full of courage and magnanimity. His garb being such that struck terror and admiration in the spectators, and made those cut-throat

cannibals who stood to guard him to look like sheep-biters, his short speech …
made the very rebels to tremble that beheld him. He put off his cloak and
threw it on the rails, cocking many times his beaver and speaking after very
earnestly, which done he took his leave with all the people and kneeling down
prayed to himself.[123]

This was a very deliberate performance of male courage, in which clothes and gesture
were deployed in apparently casual but very carefully calibrated ways. And Capel
clearly did perform bravely in the face of death, for the parliamentary newsbooks tell
a similar story in which disapproval is ultimately overcome by grudging admiration.
Capel refused a chaplain, and mounted the scaffold in 'a sad coloured suit and cloak,
and white gloves, without his periwig, and came with his hat cocked, and his cloak
thrown under one arm, outfacing death with a great deal of carelessness, as one
notably resolved'. He looked out unflinchingly at the spectators, 'put off his hat as at
a salute, and then cocked it, and strutted about the scaffold in a careless posture' in
another parliamentarian version. It was all over in a quarter of an hour, offering a
less-complicated, more forthright version of martyred royalist manhood than that
presented by the king.[124]

Adopting defiant Cavalier stereotypes consoled broader groups of royalist men.
The excessive drinking that clearly characterised the actual behaviour of some of
them, as well as being central to hostile stereotyping of Cavaliers, was often criticised
by fellow-royalists. But commitment to convivial drinking and roistering merriment
succoured defeated and exiled royalists throughout the 1650s. There was a drinking
song on the 'Goldsmiths Committee' that dealt with royalist composition fines for
example:

> Since Goldsmiths Committee
> Affords us no pity,
> Our sorrows in wine we will steep 'em,
> They force us to take
> Two oaths, but we'll make
> A third, that we'll ne'er meant to keep 'em.

Royalists quaffed aristocratic wine, not plebeian beer; and drank healths to keep their
spirits up; healths to better times, to the absent king or to denounce the parliamentarians. To the extent that exuberant male excess represented an aristocratic
vision critical of austere and low-born Puritanism, it shared something with the more
woman-focused versions of privacy and retreat discussed in the last chapter, but male
and female modes of defeated royalism did not always fit easily together.[125]

Among the victors, parliamentarian manhood after 1649 was, in its own estimation,
restrained, sober, rational, godly and often military in style. Oliver Cromwell had
little interest in his own representation, and resisted much of the monarchical ceremony
of the later Protectorate, remaining 'plain and grave in his habit', even in a second
inauguration that evoked aspects of royal coronations.[126] Cromwell's sober courtiers

were contrasted with the 'mohair linseywoolsy nits and lice gentlemen' who attended the Stuarts. Printed images presented Cromwell as a decisively masculine, active, godly ruler as in the print, 'Cromwell between the Pillars', that seems to have offered a deliberate contrast to the frontispiece of *Eikon Basilike* portraying the passive, feminised, martyred Charles I.[127] On the other hand royalist satire, according to Laura Knoppers, created a 'semiotic' other to the martyred royal body, in the grotesquely masculine body of Cromwell the mock-king, with his enormous sexualised nose. Here an excessive masculinity rather than effeminacy was used to imply illegitimate rule.[128] A lusty, out of control Cromwell featured in long-running royalist accusations of cuckoldry directed this time against Major General John Lambert, a dominant influence in the Army and the Protectorate, until he split from Cromwell in 1657. From the later 1640s to the end of the century inventive royalist satire featured Cromwell as the seducer of Lambert's wife Frances. In a 1649 play-pamphlet, among much 'farce and high jinks', the radical minister Hugh Peter at Cromwell's request persuades Mrs Lambert to become his mistress. She is Cromwell's 'Star of the north', his Poppea or Cleopatra, and he offers her 'my self, my sword, all under my command, the spoils of nations, all that the earth shall boast'; when he rushes off to London, Cromwell urges her to dissimulate and let her husband 'repose his horned head betwixt your delicate paps'.[129] The widespread smears of Lambert as a humiliated, effeminate man, subjected to a deceitful woman, gained some plausibility, not from their literal truth (as with Essex) but from his reputation for artistic and horticultural interests, which seemed incongruous in a soldier, and from the prominent role of Frances Lambert in his business and political activities. Lucy Hutchinson, a political opponent, denounced the pride of both Lamberts and wrote derisively of how when Lambert fell from power he retired to 'his house at Wimbledon, where he fell to dress his flowers in his garden and work at the needle with his wife and maids'.[130] At the Restoration mocking pamphlets had Lambert blaming his wife for his downfall, 'ignorant cuckold that I am' and lamenting, 'Farewell Wimbledon, farewell my tulips and my pictures there'.[131] Thus the Lambert–Cromwell triangle was still making people laugh at the Restoration, and it remained relevant for decades thereafter, as we shall see. It had serious political force in the 1650s, however, demonstrating for royalists the illegitimacy of the new regimes through the inadequate manliness of figures like Lambert, and the hypocritical, hyper-masculine and unrestrained tyrannical power of Cromwell himself.

4

BODIES, FAMILIES, SEX

Using gender, imagining politics

In discussing women and the civil war, or conflicts over manhood, we have demonstrated at many points the ways in which representations of manliness and womanhood, positive or hostile, had political force alongside actual initiatives or experiences. Influential women from Henrietta Maria to Anna Trapnel were praised or condemned through the use of female stereotypes of loyal wife or conniving shrew, inspired daughter of God or scold and witch; powerful men were undermined through accusations of cuckoldry or effeminacy.[1] One's own cause was supported by brave, rational men, and loyal, chaste women; the enemy's men were inadequate, and their women were unruly whores. As the royalist poet Abraham Cowley wrote:

> For to outdo the story of Pope Joan
> Your women preach too, and are like to be
> The Whores of Babylon, as much as she.[2]

The royalist press attacked parliament's 'Virgin troops', the forces raised through the support of women, by associating political disloyalty with sexual infidelity: 'these busy girls' would probably remain as 'stale virgins', 'for men I presume will suspect those women to falsify with their husbands, who are not true to their prince'.[3] Parliament's response was equally predictable: the Cavaliers had 'not left in any county or city they came in so much honesty or virginity as to raise a dragoneer'.[4]

Gendered and sexualised language was prominent in denunciations of enemies or attacks on particular political stances. In this chapter we explore further the impact of the profound political cleavages of the 1640s on gendered understandings of politics, and, vice versa, how fundamental conceptions of gender were deployed to explain political division. In early modern England gender hierarchies were assumed to be natural; most men and women, so far as we know, agreed that women were subordinate; assumptions about how men and women should behave were widely shared. So discrediting rival causes or individuals by associating them with female or deviant male characteristics was a popular tactic, adopted in disputes among parliamentarians as well as between royalists and parliamentarians. In Norwich, for example, both sides in a 1646 petitioning dispute between Independent and Presbyterian religious groups denigrated their opponents with gendered imagery. The Independents accused the Norwich Presbyterians of aping a London Presbyterian Remonstrance: the 'London Remonstrance … proves generative, and hath begotten a Norwich Remonstrance … but abortion hath been its doom'. The Presbyterians responded to this smear of a feminised, monstrous birth with an assertion of their rational masculinity: 'Sir you are mistaken, London Remonstrance was a masculine remonstrance, judicious discreet men that had a hand in it. They are your female petitions of the Independents that are the engenderers, such as are filled with maids' and girls' hands.'[5]

More fundamentally the traumas unleashed by violent civil war could be expressed in lurid, anxious fantasies of untrammelled, aberrant sexuality, deformed bodies, monstrous births and gender inversion. This chapter looks at the political origins and purposes of sexualised language, sexual fantasy and pornography, and at how civil war divisions were reflected in and in turn affected understandings of the gendered body. In previous chapters we have noted the influence of sexual slurs on the reputation and influence of particular individuals, but we should not assume that the use of gendered, sexual and bodily metaphors for understanding these broader political divisions, denouncing opponents or imagining new possibilities, tells us much about the status or experiences of 'real' women and men. Sometimes perhaps it does, but more commonly it reveals the basic importance of gendered understandings of the world, particularly of a world in crisis.

The importance of parallels between the family and the polity has been stressed already; as a basic metaphor through which political authority was comprehended and legitimised, and as a contested reference point for radical parliamentarians. The extraordinary events of the 1640s when a king, widely presented as the father of the country, was defeated in war, tried and executed in the name of the people, produced a crisis that directly raised the question of how far patriarchal authority in the family was connected to patriarchy in the state.[6] People might agree on the proper arrangements for family life but they did not agree on what this meant for politics. There was thus 'an uncomfortable and disputed border between the family and the state'.[7] We will explore some of the ambitious initiatives on family matters attempted by the novel, non-monarchical regimes of the 1650s as well as the contests over the political implications of familial metaphors, and ultimately over whether what happened (or should happen) in families had any relevance to politics.

Women, politics, sex

In 1641, as radical religious groups emerged in London, a pamphlet describing six alleged women preachers had, as its cover, a wood-cut of five women dancing. As was common with such cheap illustrations, this had been recycled from an earlier work, *The Sisters of the Scabards Holiday*, a clearly fictitious and scurrilous dialogue between prostitutes, celebrating the legal reforms of the Long Parliament which had apparently made their lives easier. The reprinting of the picture thus associated religious radicalism with sexual licence, and women preachers with whores; the frightening consequences of religious speculation were represented by the inappropriate public activity of women, whether preaching or selling their bodies. Fears of political and religious disintegration were presented through bawdy entertainment.[8] Perhaps laughing at women also helped readers of cheap print to laugh at the approach of civil war. Just as royalists and parliamentarians took up arms in August 1642, one pamphlet presented an image of a woman waving goodbye to her horned, cuckolded husband as he went off to fight. The text declared that all the women of London 'wives, widows, maids or foolish virgins', 'rich or poor, great or small, honest or half honest, even from the black bag to the oyster wench' would use their tongues in 'continual scolding' to force their husbands to the wars, so then women 'can live as merrily as may be'. Widows vow to marry Cavaliers and maids to breed more soldiers. There is criticism of the king for leaving London, but also some rather obvious sexual puns about his withdrawing from the parliament; it is hard to know if any particular political point is being made.[9]

In the early months of war, a series of dirty jokes about the impact of war presented women as sexually obsessed. In January 1643 a mock petition from midwives complained that they were out of work because women were not getting pregnant, while *The Virgins Complaint* bemoaned that there were no men left to marry except 'frosty-bearded usurers'. The lively young men they used to enjoy on shrove Tuesdays or 'in summer season under and upon hay-cocks' were all at the wars; it was a hard world where men were so scarce that 'women must be confined to their husbands'. At least two pamphlets echoed and replied to the virgins within a week. Wives and matrons insisted they had as much to complain about. They were the ones who peopled the commonwealth, yet 'not one man in a hundred since the departure of the Courtiers and Cavaliers, that in this City hath so much honesty as to ask a married woman the question, or offer his body to her service'. They were denied 'the due benevolence of our husbands, or the charitable assistance of our friends' (both polite descriptions of sexual intercourse), and the commonwealth would not be peopled. The wives rejected the 'malicious and ungracious reports' that 'we should wear the breeches, that our tongues are perpetual alarums to disturb the peace and quietness of their rest, that we are cankers in their estates. ... terribly given to the making of monsters, or converting our husbands into such, by furnishing their foreheads with large and beautiful horns', but insisted they had to petition for an end to the lamentable civil war. Widows were not to be left out, and lamented that both rich and old, and young, lusty widows also lacked suitors. These mock petitions and complaints were issued during weeks of real agitation and lobbying for a negotiated peace as it became all too apparent that the war would not rapidly end. Commercial pressures played a part in their production, but presumably these pamphlets worked also to discredit the genuine peace petitions and to mock through sexualising the women who supported them. But one suspects that genuine anxieties about war and about assertive women were also unleashed.[10]

Years of particular uncertainty followed parliament's victory in the civil war in England. Charles I had been decisively beaten by 1646, but the shape of any peace settlement was unclear; the king's influence depended on how he was valued or supported by the various political factions in England (and Scotland). In this political vacuum, as Sue Wiseman has suggested in a brilliant analysis, the role of women (symbolically and actually) in giving value to men came to the fore. When men are divided the status of women becomes 'radically unstable' in Wiseman's words, while the nature of manhood itself is open to question.[11] A satirical and sexualised stress on women out of place was a means of coming to terms with uncertainty and division on the parliament's side. In the summer of 1647, a desperate political crisis unfolded in London as Presbyterians agitated for a peace with the king which they hoped would put an end to the influence of the New Model Army and halt the growth of religious radicalism. Forces were raised to oppose the New Model, while that enraged army massed near the city, advancing and retreating to cow its enemies, and ultimately triumphing through a peaceful occupation in August. The genuine petitioning and counter-petitioning by London factions included a prominent role by apprentices, as indicated in the last chapter; many of these petitions were printed along with many mock petitions featuring sexually voracious women. *The Maids Petition*, for example, attacked the 'armified parliament' and denounced sectaries such as 'Patience the Taylor' who 'will go nigh to make us mad with his heretical thimble', and presented themselves as 'your vassalized virgins' demanding their 'lawful days of recreation' (a holiday on a Tuesday). In essence, the petition consisted of a succession of sexual innuendoes:

> to prevent all hostile incursion, the Apprentices shall freely enter us by way of listing, and if they do advance (which we hope will never be beyond the line of communication) we shall be vilely troubled to secure our sorts from the multitude of tub-preachers who will never be out of exercise.

Another 'remonstrance' from women claimed the liberty to go elsewhere if their husbands could not satisfy them. Politically broadminded, the 'women' both asked the Leveller John Lilburne to stand stiff for the subjects' liberties, and pleaded with the king to return to London with his lascivious courtiers.[12] The jokes scarcely mask the fears of disorder and chaos, as men who had been allies against the royalists were now on the verge of violent conflict among themselves, and women were visibly and collectively active in public affairs. In strikingly violent sexual imagery, the whole confrontation was expressed in terms of rape, in a Royalist-Presbyterian lament for the over-awing of the city by the army:

> What violence could ever have ravished her, had she kept herself close together, and (according to the custom) cried out to the neighbouring counties? I say, these men-fornicators have violated all her younger sisters, withal the country milkmaids and dairy wenches in the kingdom, yet they never have entered here. But now she has lost her veil, and what is become of her credit? 'Tis pawned in the Tower.[13]

One genre characteristic of these years of instability was the 'Mistress Parliament' or 'Parliament of Women' pamphlet that imagined women as law-givers in bawdy and sometimes frankly pornographic fashion. Ultimately derived from classical satire, some of the best known and most elaborate of these texts were written by the republican Henry Neville, but they were widely imitated and used to present a variety of political stances. An early version was ostensibly set in republican Rome, but it was illustrated with a group of undoubtedly Stuart women debating round a table. The title page declared that the women had enacted many 'merry laws' to 'live in more ease, pomp, pride and wantonness' and wished for superiority and to 'domineer over their husbands'. A list of laws at the end included, 'that women may twang it as well as their husbands', and that a 'man which promises a pretty maid a good turn, and doth not perform it in three months shall lose his what do you call them'.[14] Politics here was subordinated to simple sexualised derision, whereas a later pamphlet purported to portray a gathering of royalist women at Oxford. Lady Aubigny, predictably, took the chair, and other familiar figures such as the Countesses of Essex and Derby had prominent roles. This pamphlet was structured like a newsbook and took the form of a series of summonses to leading royalists to answer for their crimes and failings. Prince Rupert pleaded not guilty to the 'noble Amazons' of 'plundering at Edgehill, his wilfulness at Marston Moor, and his cowardice at Bristol', while the courtier Lord Jermyn denied that he had merely 'made all compliments towards them, not sparing them one drop of help'. All were found guilty, sentenced to gruesome punishments (Rupert was to be stuck to a porcupine until killed by its quills), but reprieved to general rejoicing on the very last page. Issued in May 1647, this was presumably a caution against a generous peace with the king.[15]

The 1647 pamphlets associated with Henry Neville seem to target the House of Lords and Presbyterianism in particular. Named Presbyterian noblewomen dominate these parliaments of ladies; real Presbyterian male politicians are satirically praised, while the Assembly of Divines is mercilessly undermined. In a parody of parliamentary procedure, the ladies send a message to the Assembly to ask them what 'due benevolence' meant, only to find the Presbyterian clergy debating that very question. The phrase was used to describe marital sexual intercourse, and the Assembly's spokesman, Obadiah Sedgwick, reassures the ladies that they have agreed that any man who had been absent from his wife, had to 'solace' her twice a day on his return, and that all married men should be 'engaged to content his mate and fellow feeler as often as the strength of his body will permit'. The ladies order the decree to be published and made '*jure divino*'; men who failed at the task would be denied the sacrament. The author thus uses a 'women on top' theme to make fun of two religious controversies that had bitterly divided parliamentarians: whether Presbyterian church government was of divine institution, and what doctrinal or moral failings disqualified parishioners from receiving the sacrament of the Lord's supper. This pamphlet ends with the ultimate symbol of sexual (and by extension political) dissolution with a hermaphrodite causing alarm and chaos in the streets of London. In a second pamphlet the ladies torment the Assembly with apparently innocent questions about the Bible, on Lot and his daughters, or Susanna and the elders. Women here feature as absurd judges of male political and religious dilemmas, but there are other messages hinted at in these tracts: a desire to demonstrate the absurdity of women's political activism by reducing it to sexual competition for men, and perhaps more profound fears of women's controlling sexuality.[16]

Later 'parliament of women' pamphlets adopted the language of radical parliamentarianism, a language of tyranny, rights and liberty, but discredited it through application, absurdly, to women's supposed claims to superiority over men. A January 1650 pamphlet by Neville mocked the rhetoric of the commonwealth, before moving on to the familiar sexual innuendoes about named Presbyterian aristocratic women:

> There was a time in England, when men wore the breeches and debarred women of their liberty, which brought many grievances and oppressions upon the weaker vessels; for they were constrained to converse only with their houses and closets, and now and then with the gentleman usher, or the foot-man (when they could catch him).

Now, considering:

> The tyranny of men, the ladies rampant of the times, in their last parliament, knowing themselves to be a part of the free people of this Nation, unanimously resolved to assert their own freedoms, and casting off the intolerable yoke of their lords and husbands, have voted themselves the supreme authority both at home and abroad, and settled themselves in the posture of a free state.[17]

Politically this perhaps suggested Neville's disillusion with the commonwealth regime, as well as a delight in sexualised comedy, and hints of unease at female activism. A late version, published by George Horton who specialised in sensationalist, often pornographic print, similarly deployed the language of liberty, servitude and tyranny, but presented stock figures such as an ancient maid, and a grave matron rather than real women, who all claimed superiority over men. Here the jokes dominate any plausible political message, but the text does reveal the easy slippage between political language and anxieties about gender order.[18]

Bodies and the body politic

As we saw in the introduction, one of the most influential ways in which authority was legitimated or naturalised was through comparisons with the human body. The 'body politic' was a stock phrase, a favourite of preachers and other moralists, but the routine nature of the reference indicated the importance of the concept of the polity as a healthy body, with the head in its proper place, the humours in balance and all members working together.[19] One tactic in *Eikon Basilike* was the presentation of Charles I as a 'good physician who heals the fevered sickness of the body politic' in the hope that one day the head, the king, would be restored.[20] The execution of the king was the culmination and most obvious evidence of the disorders in the body politic; consequently the disruptions of the civil war years were frequently evoked in accounts of monstrous births and monstrous bodies, often sexualised and often female.[21] As with the 'Mistress Parliament' pamphlets, texts and images could be recycled in different contexts, to deliver subtly distinct messages within a broad framework of unnatural inversion. Most of these accounts come from cheap print, but monstrous females featured also in more refined poetic descriptions. A female peace petitioner in 1643 had been denounced as a 'deformed Medusa' in the news-books, and for the royalist poet Abraham Cowley also, the threatening figure of Medusa represented the horror of sedition and division:

> There schism, old hag, but seeming young appears
> As snakes by casting skin renew their years …
> Sedition there her crimson banner spreads,
> Shakes all her hands and roars with all her heads.
> Her knotty hairs were with dire serpents twist,
> And all her serpents at each other hissed.[22]

On the other hand, the destruction of monsters in acts of heroic violence might be a way of understanding revolutionary new regimes; as Medusa was dispatched by Perseus, so a new polity could be erected.[23]

Violent political conflict and chaotic religious divisions were figured as monstrous, often pregnant women. Beyond the specific context or message, there was often a submerged fear of fecund women themselves.[24] An early 1640s pamphlet by John Taylor dealt with religious disorder:

> For my motherly wife had at the least 500 daughters, maids, wives, widows, married and unmarried, all breeders (or teeming women) … all devout in diversities, and all differing in their devotions, and from all these (my sincere wife Saphira) had sucked so many documents and doctrines that she could discourse and dispute of all points of religion.

This religious freedom had produced further sexual abominations:

> Some sons have made so bold with their own mothers, that they have proved with child by them, so that with incests, adulteries, rapes, deflowerings, for-nications and other venereal postures and actions which daily pass and escape uncontrolled and unpunished, and, as it may be conjectured, tolerated.[25]

For the Presbyterian Thomas Edwards, religious toleration was a monster, 'conceived in the womb of the sectaries long ago, they having grown big with it ever since, are now in travail to bring it forth'.[26]

Some of the Mistress Parliament texts also focused on the grotesquely pregnant female body, bringing forth a monstrous child after a terrible labour. The recycling of such dreadful fantasies suggests their value in expressing political disgust at the excess and subversion of the civil war years, as well as their roots in profound anxieties about motherhood itself.[27] In a royalist pamphlet of 1648, 'Mistress parliament' had become a whore who 'turned up her tail to every lousy, ill-dependent rascal in the army, Sir Thomas [Fairfax] himself and King Cromwell too'. Her seven years' 'teeming' was succeeded by 'bitter pangs and hard labour', in which she vomited up the innocent blood of Strafford and others that had lain congealed in her stomach for seven years, along with the gold for which she had sold her king and her god. A cruel midwife 'Mistress London' refused assistance, and her 'gossips', or birth-attendants, Mrs Schism and Mrs Leveller among them, could not help her be delivered. Only when Mistress Parliament confessed her grievous misdeeds to 'Mrs Truth', did she give birth amid 'terrible thunderings', the howls of cats and dogs, and the screechings of owls and ravens, to a 'monster of deformed shape, without a head, great goggle eyes, bloody hands growing out of both sides of its devouring paunch, under the belly hung a large bag, and the feet are like the feet of a bear'.[28]

A version of this grim parody of childbirth was issued again in early 1660, among many lurid pamphlet attacks on the Rump parliament. The narrative was similar but the characters were revised to fit a new political context; hence the gossips were the wives of leading republicans including Henry Neville himself:

'Tis strange a Rump that's roasted, boiled and broiled
Should after death bring forth a child,
Got by some pettifogging knight of the post
Who in her womb did leave this horrid ghost
To vex the honest people of this nation
By her base brat, pretending Reformation.[29]

Gender was central to the images of inversion that sought to evoke a polity in crisis, and promote the restoration of harmony in body and polity:

Reason, once king in man, deposed and dead
The purple isle was ruled without a head,
Monstrous Mrs Rump brought to bed.

The gendered imagery in these attacks was unstable; at some points the English body politic was a woman violated by male Rumpers, but the Rump too might be a monstrous woman.[30] The recourse to gender here and in other pamphlets was not univocal; the force of gendered language lay precisely in its capacity to take various forms and suggest a variety of messages.

Disturbing fantasies of childbirth overlapped with other pamphlet accounts of monstrous births, purporting to describe 'true' events. Monstrous births had long been seen as providential judgements, on the mother herself, and more broadly on sinful communities. In the 1640s and 1650s they were connected to specific religious or political transgressions, albeit turned into general warnings through print. So, a pregnant woman who (in 1642) hoped that her child would be born without a head, rather than have it baptised with the sign of the cross, another (a Lancashire papist) who wished in 1646 'rather to bear a child without a head than a Roundhead', and a third, a 'Ranter' who claimed in 1652 that she was 'with child by the holy ghost' – all gave birth to monstrous, headless babies. In this last example the illustration of a large deformed child overshadowing an alarmed birthing room was recycled (down to the rosary beads hanging from the wall) from the earlier Lancashire pamphlet. Even as these women (and by extension all who share their opinions) are condemned through their own weakness and folly, testimony is paid to the power of the maternal imagination.[31] There are echoes of these sensationalist accounts of pregnancy and birth in more sober atrocity stories where parliamentarian propagandists stress Cavalier violation and mutilation of pregnant women. At Leicester, for example, 'a good religious honest woman named Jane West' reproved Cavaliers who were blaspheming, 'whereupon one of this wicked rabble shot her with a brace of bullets through the back and belly, upon which she immediately died, she being great with child, and within three weeks time of her delivery'.[32] Here, of course, women feature as victims whose fate highlights the transgressive violence of the enemy.

Crude (in all senses) images of naked bodies were provided in alarmist accounts of religious radicalism. The erect penis in the woodcut on the title page to a 1641 pamphlet, *A Nest of Serpents*, was perhaps the first example of such an illustration in English print history. This was an account of an unlikely and probably fictitious sect, the 'Adamites', who went naked as in the garden of Eden as a symbol of prelapsarian innocence, but were defined here by their depraved, unbridled lust and shamelessness. There are several examples of this woodcut and it was again recycled much later to smear the loose collection of radicals, known to their opponents the Ranters. These argued that the truly godly were free from sin, and were popularly believed to indulge in lurid sexual orgies. There was a long-standing association of religious heterodoxy with sexual excess so again these cheap, sensationalist pamphlets had some serious intent, but readers of course may have just used them for sexual titillation.[33]

Our final example of how the political upheavals of the 1640s and 1650s prompted a concern with the gendered body is a more serious one. Mary Fissell has explained how religious and political cleavages from the Reformation to the civil war encouraged 'thinking with the body', especially the female reproductive body, and how political upheaval itself influenced medical thinking. There were more books published on midwifery in the 1650s than in the previous hundred years, and their preoccupations were influenced by the upheavals around them, and women's part therein. Midwives' handbooks focused increasingly on the sexual act of conception, in which men of course were prominent, rather than on the processes of pregnancy and birth. Women's experience of their own bodies and of childbirth was devalued in comparison to educated, male expertise. The cleric Henry Jessey presented himself as the authoritative interpreter of the bodily weakness of the prophetess Sarah Wight, and, most interestingly, the successful medical writer and heterodox religious figure, Nicholas Culpeper, 'a radical in politics but a conservative at home', as Fissell defines him, published *A Directory for Midwives* in 1651, in which he insisted that female midwives had to defer to the scientific knowledge of men. Women's bodies became more certainly knowable, but also more disturbing; the womb was increasingly regarded as a source of women's health problems rather than a marvellous generative organ (and here there are perhaps some echoes of the monstrous births and disgusting pregnancies already discussed). Fissell sums up thus:

> Part of the resolution of the turbulence of the 1640s was the reassertion of men's authority over women, a reassertion accomplished by means of new ideas about the relationship of men's and women's bodies.[34]

We might be sceptical about whether this reassertion of male authority was always successful, while medical expertise took its place among many other strategies, but there were clear connections between metaphorical, satirical and pornographic treatments of the 'body politic' as an abstraction or concept, and the more directly practical works which structured people's understanding and experiences of real bodies.

Women, family and political change

'Exemplary' women from the Bible or classical mythology and history figured in attempts to comprehend traumatic political change. We have already met Medusa, and the vengeful figure of Jael, whose brutal assassination of the Canaanite Captain Sisera helped to deliver the ancient Israelites, was an inspiration for the radical religious activist, Katherine Chidley.[35] A further complex and much debated exemplar was Lucretia, whose rape by Tarquin had prompted the overthrow of monarchy and the birth of the Roman republic. Parliamentarian newsbooks in the early 1650s referred to the exiled Charles Stuart as 'young Tarquin'.[36] A new regime was founded through an act of rape and a tragedy of violence and sacrifice. But again, the lives of real as well as metaphorical women were affected by the novel and precarious republican regime of the 1650s. As Christina Larner has suggested, it is 'characteristic of new regimes in their search for legitimacy that they demanded a high level of social control and of conformity in behaviour as well as belief'.[37] Habits of connecting disorder in the family with disorder in the state intensified anxieties about unruly women and dislocated gender relationships, and strengthened the concern with familial stability.[38] This is part of the context for the spikes in witchcraft prosecutions, as we have seen; it also encouraged a focus on marriage and sexual behaviour which drew additionally on long-standing and long-thwarted Puritan reforming ambitions.

These concerns predated the Republic of 1649. John Walter has argued that idolatry was seen in Old Testament terms as spiritual fornication, so that Puritan crowds in the early 1640s often policed sexual morality (through abusing 'whores') as well as reforming sacred space (by destroying altar rails and images in churches).[39] The morality of men as well as women might be a target. High standards of personal behaviour were demanded within the sects, as we have seen in chapter two, and within the army, as we saw in chapter three. Religious radicals like the Digger Gerrard Winstanley insisted (against Ranters) on the importance of chastity before and fidelity within marriage, while the mystical preacher John Pordage regarded marriage as a union of male and female elements with God. In this fallen world Pordage lived near

Reading in a chaste and largely female community.[40] Soldiers who gave 'themselves to whoring and uncleanness ... swear and blaspheme the name of God ... follow that swinish sin of drunkenness ... plunder and steal whatsoever they come near' were unworthy of parliament's service.[41] The disciplined morality of the New Model Army was secured by the punishment of both deviant men and their tempting 'whores'. Parliamentarian newsbooks praised the cashiering of soldiers for swearing, drunkenness and adultery, and the whipping of whores from the enemy quarters.[42]

When parliament summoned the Westminster Assembly to consider the reform of the national church, the drafting of a new 'Directory' of worship inevitably involved discussions on the nature of marriage. Was it a religious or a civil matter? In what circumstances might it be dissolved? Was the crucial reference point the marriage of Christ with his church, or some comparison with subordination and obedience in the state? After long and 'tough debate', it was concluded that marriage was a religious ceremony but also a matter for state concern. As the Directory explained: 'Marriage be no sacrament, nor peculiar to the Church of God, but common to mankind, and of public interest in every commonwealth.' Clandestine or inappropriate marriage threatened the stability of the commonwealth, so public control was essential. Parental consent was demanded, even for those of age if it was their first marriage. Marriage was an indissoluble and strenuous endeavour, that needed the support of prayer: as God 'hath brought them together by his Providence, he would sanctify them by his Spirit, giving them a new frame of heart fit for their new estate; enriching them with all Graces, whereby they may perform the duties, enjoy the comforts, undergo the cares, and resist the temptations which accompany that condition'.[43]

These debates are one context for Milton's four controversial tracts on divorce published between 1643 and 1645. Milton proposed – from a largely male perspective – that marriage could be dissolved on the grounds of general temperamental incompatibility, not simply on account of infidelity or violence. As we have seen, Milton argued that a fulfilling marriage was essential if male citizens were to serve the public interest; the testimony of respectable Protestant authorities as well as biblical and historical examples were mustered in support. But to his indignation – complaining, 'I did but prompt the age to quit their clogs / By the known rules of ancient liberty' – his views were incorporated by Presbyterians into a general association of religious heterodoxy with sexual libertinism and immorality, and used to discredit moves towards religious liberty.[44] Thomas Edwards's *Gangraena*, a Presbyterian denunciation of heresy and sectarianism, spread the story of 'Mrs Attaway', a woman preacher who had consulted 'Master Milton's Doctrine of Divorce ... for she had an unsanctified husband ... and accordingly she hath practised it in running away with another woman's husband'.[45] It is likely, however, that the verdict of a royalist broadside was more widely shared than Milton's divorce proposals:

> From the doctrine of deposing a King
> From the Directory, or any such thing:
> From a fine new marriage without a ring,
> Libera nos Domine[46]

If church marriage without the ceremonial of the Common Prayer Book was resented, the civil marriage legislation passed in 1653 by the 'Nominated' or 'Barebones' parliament, the most radical assembly of the period, seems to have been extremely unpopular. The Marriage Act was in some ways a natural conclusion to the West-minster Assembly's stress on marriage as a matter of public interest, its meticulously detailed provisions embodying the state's desire for control. Notice of intention to marry could be published in the market place, rather than a church if the couple preferred; each parish was to keep a register of marriages in 'a book of good vellum or parchment' but the ceremony itself (using the formula of the Directory) was to be conducted by Justices of the Peace. The act was printed in full in the state-sponsored newsbook *Mercurius Politicus* as of 'so public concernment'.[47] Modern assessments suggest the act was met with confusion and widespread evasion. The minister Ralph Josselin continued to officiate at weddings and the monopoly of civil marriage was modified during the conservative revisions of the Protectorate constitution in 1657. The Protector's own daughters took different paths: Frances married Lord Rich, a grandson of the Earl of Warwick, in a civil ceremony, whereas Mary married a former royalist Thomas Fauconberg in church according to the rites of the Book of Common Prayer.[48] It is possible to exaggerate the adherence to 'tradition', however. When the prohibition on marriage in Lent and Advent was removed, many couples hastened to wed in March and December.[49]

Properly controlled marriage required also the punishment of deviant sexual relations, hitherto the responsibility of the church courts. With the abolition of episcopacy there was a gap that the civil power had to fill, but the republic's concern with morality was also a sign of its (gendered) reformist ambitions. A long-standing Puritan campaign for legislation against adultery came to fruition with the Rump's act of 16 May 1650 'for suppressing the detestable sins of incest, adultery and fornication'. Here the state rather than the church was defining sexual deviance. Adultery, a felony punishable by death, was defined as sexual intercourse with a married woman (a married man's sexual misdemeanours were considered the lesser crime of fornica-tion). There were exceptions if the man did not know the woman was married or if her husband had been absent for more than three years or was reputed to be dead. There were harsh punishments for those convicted of keeping a brothel, or being a 'common bawd': offenders could be whipped, marked on the forehead with the letter 'B' and imprisoned; second offences were felonies punishable by death.[50] The ferocity of the punishments, and the difficulty of obtaining witnesses, meant that there were very few executions under the Adultery Act. In Somerset there is no evidence that the death penalty was ever imposed, although there were frequent sentences of three months imprisonment for fornication. In Warwickshire, similarly, there are records of one indictment for adultery only, along with six cases of 'carnal knowledge', and sexual regulation was based on the traditional bastardy legislation.[51] The Act exhorted Justices of the Peace to energetic prosecution of sexual offences and Stephen Roberts has found that some Devon JPs were particularly 'vigorous hounders of fornicators and bastard bearers'. Women bore the brunt of this vigour; male suspects numbered only 10% of 255 Devonians examined on charges of fornication between 1650 and 1660. During 1655 when Major Generals were appointed to encourage reforming initiatives by local government, more than 30% of prosecutions in Devon concerned sexual offences. Even here, however, adultery was very rarely prosecuted. There were no more than nine cases of adultery and no executions in Devon, while juries were less zealous than magistrates; only about half of all cases went to trial and conviction rates were very low.[52]

As Mary Fissell has suggested the numbers prosecuted are in many ways less significant than the ways in which the act contributed to the self-representation of the republic as a beacon of austere discipline and sexual reform. In any case even if many shied away from executing men and women for adultery, the act might be deployed in more routine ways to control sexual behaviour. Bernard Capp concludes that in Middlesex some twenty-four women and twelve men were tried for adultery in the 1650s, although as in other areas there is almost no evidence of executions. But the trials under the Adultery Act were overshadowed by the 'flood of recognisances' prompted by it. Hundreds of people suspected of adultery or fornication were bound over to appear at Quarter sessions and then to keep the peace, a process particular to the 1650s. Neighbours, clergymen and, most often, aggrieved spouses reported these offences. Usually the wronged husbands and wives accused their spouses' lovers but there were some cases where the erring partner was denounced. The 1650 Act had barred husbands and wives from giving evidence against each other; this would have disqualified them as witnesses in trials but did not prevent them initiating this procedure.[53] In Middlesex then we see the 1650 Act being actively employed to resolve or inflame community divisions and painful family conflicts, and employed by women as well as men, as when Susan Ward complained that her husband had brought his mistress to her home and had 'carnal copulation with her whilst his wife was in the bed'. It was not simply a means by which powerful men imposed a discriminatory law on vulnerable or unconventional women.

But some commentators clearly discerned the double standards in the enforcement of the Act, and in the skewed definition of adultery confined to married women. It is intriguing that the republican Lucy Hutchinson, whose rather conventional opinions on gender have been quoted earlier, inscribed a long ballad against the Adultery Act into her commonplace book. 'A ballad upon the lamentable death of Anne Greene and Gilbert Samson, executed at Tyburn the 2nd day of January for having been taken in the act of adultery', to the tune of 'When I was a buxom lass' is worth quoting at some length:

> What a pitiful age is this
> What cruelty reigns in this town
> To hang a poor silly wench
> For using a thing of her own
> … Is not my body my own
> Why may I not use it then
> This is not a law made by god
> But by the vile acts of men

Had you followed the sacred rule
I need not have made this moan
For where is that parliament man
That was worthy to throw the first stone?
Oh where was Harry Martin
And where was my little lord Grey
Oh where was the good earl of Pembroke
And noble Sir Harry Mildmay
Sure they did not pass this act
Nor thus did their country betray
For such trivial faults as these
To cast our poor lives away
Come gentle lover of mine
That die with me for this fact
Let us never lament to part with such slaves
As rule by this shameful act

The plaintive fate of the poor wench is contrasted with the light-hearted approach to sexual misdemeanours of notorious republican politicians like Henry Mildmay. Hutchinson presumably endorsed the ballad's opposition to these double standards.[54]

From a very different perspective the Act was mocked in cheap print, as in a dialogue issued shortly after the Act's passing, between 'a suburb bawd', a courtesan and a pimp who all bemoaned 'the late act against fornication and other venial sins, 'tis that hath undone us all'. The courtesan had already given up her fine gowns and was in danger of losing her petticoats in the courts but the bawd advised doubling the doors and hanging thick curtains to thwart witnesses. The increased risks were at least raising the charges prostitutes could demand, but in the end the courtesan decamped to Venice for better pickings.[55] Other attacks on the Act included a libel against one of the zealous Middlesex JPs, denounced as a 'bawdy-court justice' whose pursuit of female sexual offenders was attributed to revenge for his infection with venereal disease by city prostitutes. Hostility to sexual repression was openly expressed in 1660, sometimes as part of an overt royalist challenge to Puritan culture: in John Tathum's *The Rump*, performed just before the Restoration, it was claimed that thousands of the 'distressed sex' (prostitutes) had petitioned for the repeal of the act.[56] Although campaigns for sexual and moral reform occurred intermittently after 1660, there was nothing to match the impact in the 1650s of republican and Puritan zeal, backed by a state both ambitious and insecure.

The state and the household: the public and private

At several times in this book, we have touched on the complex relationship in early modern England between the 'public' and the 'private', defined as spheres of influence or as ways of understanding rival interests and concerns. In discussing women's activism during the war, male disputes about the nature of virtuous political conduct or attitudes to Charles I as man and monarch, the boundaries between public and private were, as we discussed in the introduction, blurred, shifting and contested. Nonetheless, the boundaries were continually pushed and reassessed; in chapter three we suggested that parliamentarianism conceived of itself as both more public, and more male, and it is possible to argue, without undue simplification, that royalists and parliamentarians drew different conclusions about the proper balance between public and private realms. We will pursue these abstract debates further, but first we will explore the related, but rather more concrete question of how participants in civil war divisions conceptualised the links between power in households and power in the state.

Throughout this book we have seen men and women deploying analogies between the family and the state in political argument; the household was both a source of political metaphor and an inspiration for political action. Women's household responsibilities validated their public interventions in 1640, whether defending their homes from enemy soldiers, lobbying to preserve family fortunes or, in the case of the Leveller women petitioners, arguing that attacks on honest householders demonstrated the tyrannical oppression of the new republican regime. Male Levellers also insisted that the fate of individual households was a public matter, condemning assaults on commoners' houses when men came 'forcibly to enter their bed-chambers with drawn swords and pistols ready cocked, even while such persons are in their beds';[57] along with other radical parliamentarians they pondered the political rights of male heads of household. The early modern household eludes any attempt to posit a clear distinction in theory or in practice between a public and a private world; women could not be confined to their homes as snails, despite the pronouncements of some men. At all social levels, particularly during years of political conflict and bitter fighting, female initiative was central to practical survival and to political networking and religious commitment.

And yet, there is a sense in which the household might also be regarded as a precarious refuge from a world of division, betrayal and defeat. Most obviously this stance was adopted by defeated royalists; we have explored some aspects of their stress on private retreat in chapter two and will return to the issue below. Among the Levellers too, the indictment of tyrannical intrusion into households implied some sense of a private space that should not be violated, while in the writings of John Lilburne (and John Milton) there was a darker view that seductive familial and female ties might corrupt men into preferring private advantage to their public duty. Arguments about the relationships between households and the broader polity, and views on the place of women within households, and on the proper connections between public and private concerns, were marked by contradiction and incoherence. This was a product of enduring social tension and more immediate political crisis, of the inevitable tensions between men and the women who were both subordinate and crucial to household prosperity, and of the bitter and terrifying cleavages over the proper ordering of the commonwealth, that convulsed England in the 1640s and 1650s.

Gendered understandings of politics were thus contested in arguments about the force of household analogies, but also in more abstract reflections on the public and the private. Although a man's household status was usually seen as a qualification for a public role, parliamentarians, and republicans in particular, tended to deny that political authority as such was ultimately legitimised through a comparison with the authority of a father or a husband, or through naturalising evocations of a 'body politic', but derived it rather from the consent of the 'people'. The influential parliamentarian theorist, Henry Parker, explained:

> The wife is inferior in nature, and was created for the assistance of man, and servants are hired for their Lords mere attendance; but it is otherwise in the State betwixt man and man; for that civil difference which is for civil ends, and those ends, are that wrong and violence may be repressed by one for the good of all, not that servility and drudgery may be imposed upon all, for the pomp of one. So the head naturally doth not more depend upon the body, than that does upon the head, both head and members must live and die together; but it is otherwise with the head political, for that receives more subsistence from the body than it gives, and being subservient to that, it has no being when that is dissolved, and that may be preserved after its dissolution.[58]

In Parker's formulation, then, the body politic endured if the head was changed, in contrast to the essential unity of the human body. The danger that attacks on political fatherhood might prompt criticism of male authority in families was deflected by a distinction between family and state. The submission of women was derived from a natural inequality that had nothing to do with the political world strictly defined.[59] One consequence, as already implied, might be a particularly intense stress in republican thought on the masculinity of politics. As we have seen, in Henry Neville's 'parliament of women' pamphlets, women in 'public' represented absurd political positions. Women's irrationality made them ill-fitted for citizenship, so that women in power were the antithesis of virtuous republican rule.[60] Although David Norbrook has pointed to the ways in which a republican milieu encouraged the intellectual and political activities of Lucy Hutchinson, many scholars have stressed the ways in which republicans combined civic liberty with domestic patriarchy.[61]

Although parliamentarians did in the end refuse to accept that familial authority legitimated absolute monarchy (or monarchy at all), they were not immune from deploying familial comparisons in other ways, as we have already seen in chapter three. Recent work has stressed the complex implications of familial comparisons: 'at the root of the family-state analogy was not a single ideology, but a debate', writes Su Fang Ng. Another way of explaining this is that parliamentarians used the comparisons as metaphors, rather than as analogies that clinched an argument.[62] The republican John Hall denounced hereditary succession as foolish for it might lead to women, children or lunatics inheriting, and attacked the patriarchal justification for monarchy: 'As for the antiquity from Adam it is true before his fall his dominion was large and wide … economically not despotically over his wife and children. But what is this to civil government?' For Hall, paternal metaphors nonetheless remained powerful weapons against monarchical oppression: if kings would be fathers of the people:

'it were then their duty to do like fathers, which is, to provide for, defend and cherish whereas on the contrary, it is themselves that eat the bread out of the mouths of their children and through the groans of the poor'.[63]

Edward Sexby, the radical Leveller turned bitter conspirator, used similar arguments against the tyrant Cromwell. He too rejected the parallels between family and state: 'To fathers within their private families, nature hath given a supreme power', but when several families came together to form a commonwealth 'being independent one of another, without any natural superiority or obligation, nothing can introduce amongst them a disparity of rule and subjection, but some power that is over them; which power none can pretend to have but God and themselves'. God did not establish particular forms of government so the choice of the people was key. This separation of fatherly and political authority seems straightforward, yet Sexby looked forward to the death of Cromwell as a liberation from an oppressive father:

> All this we hope from your Highness' happy expiration, who are the true father of your country, for while we live, we can call nothing ours, and it is from your death that we hope for our inheritance.[64]

Some parliamentarian discussions of liberty and political obligation also involved comparisons with the marital relationship. Where Parker distinguished, others developed more-or-less logical connections. The political writer Anthony Ascham wrote in favour of obedience to de facto government, specifically urging the taking of the 1650 'Engagement oath' to the new republic; and he also insisted in an unpublished tract that marriage should be an indissoluble contract enforced by the state.[65] Milton's linking of domestic and civil liberty in his much derided views on divorce was equally consistent:

> He who marries intends as little to conspire his own ruin, as he that swears allegiance and as whole people is in proportion to an ill Government, so is one man to an ill marriage.[66]

So parliamentarians did not ignore the familial, but the contrasts with royalist preoccupation with marriage and 'private' intimacies are nonetheless significant. Hereditary monarchy is by its nature a politics of the family; early modern courts were households in which private access and personal networks were as important as official relationships. In the 1630s, as we have seen, the royal marriage symbolised and was seen to encourage a broader harmony within the kingdom.[67] In *Eikon Basilike* the martyred king was presented as husband, father and ruler in a broad and coherent account of royal legitimacy that, in Kevin Sharpe's words, achieved 'a reconnection of the personal and public' (albeit one scornfully denounced by the republican Milton).[68] When they printed the king's correspondence in *The King's Cabinet Opened*, parliament condemned the 'deeper and darker secrecy' of the king's policies, and the gap between his public stance and his private letters. Charles's domestic or private subservience to the queen fatally compromised his public authority. By contrast, royalist responses defended the notion of private marital intimacy as well as the king's political stances. Parliament was wrong to pierce the 'sacred laws of marriage' and to trespass on the necessary distance between the people and their rulers:

> For active treason must be doing still,
> Lest she unlearn her art of doing ill.
> Who now have waded through all public awe
> Will break through secrets and profane their laws ...
> Our thoughts no commons, but enclosures are
> What bold intruders then are who assail
> To cut their prince's hedge and break his pale
> That so unmanly gaze, and dare be seen
> Even then, when he converses with his queen.

Parliament here is identified with enclosure rioters attacking the private property of landlords, while the gendered associations are fascinating: treason is figured as feminine, while voyeuristic intrusion into the royal marriage is unmanly.[69] When a royalist journalist published the (fictitious) letters of the republican Henry Marten to his mistress, he presented it as retaliation for Marten's role in opening up the king's letters to public view:

> These letters of yours to yours, had not seen the world, if you yourself had not given just occasion for the incivility. There was a time (I would it had never been) when you voted and principally caused the sacred letters of your sovereign and his queen ... to be made public.[70]

Where parliamentarians enthused about public service and the public interest, royalists valued the personal and the private. We should remember the feminised notions of retirement and privacy, offered as (public) political critiques of the parliamentarian regimes of the 1650s, and discussed in chapter two. A favourite literary genre for defeated royalists was romance, elaborate fictions of disguised and wronged rulers regaining lost kingdoms, and true lovers triumphing over suspicion and separation. Their political hopes were expressed through personal emotional dramas, for romance 'dramatizes the instability of the passions', while hinting at how rulers should behave, how they should win the love of their subjects.[71] Through romance, royalists accepted the parallel that many parliamentarians had rejected, between the marital bond and political obligation, arguing that obedience in both cases was founded on love. This was not always a straightforward matter, for discussions risked feminising (male) political subjects or empowering women within marriage. The exuberant writings of Margaret Cavendish, Countess of Newcastle, often compared wives to subjects but her female characters were not easily controlled and their obedience was certainly not guaranteed. In *A Blazing World*, the heroine was a martial Empress whose chief advisor was a Duchess; both women were lightly fictionalised aspects of

Cavendish's own self-representation, and their adventures suggested that authority might be shared between men and women.[72]

When all complications have been allowed for, then, it remains the case that parliamentarians tended to distinguish between the family and the state in a way that royalists did not, and that this distinction overlapped with a similar contrast between the public and private, that was also more characteristic of parliamentarianism than royalism. 'Public', as we have seen, was a vague but potent concept encompassing a simple contrast between the collective and the individual, but also more normative understandings of public service, public interest and the public good. For parliamentarians it was through public service that men (in particular) found fulfilment, whereas for royalists the personal and political could not and should not be separated. Parliamentarians, particularly those with developed republican sympathies, believed 'the ideal state was one where public interests prevailed over private concerns; monarchy tended inexorably towards the private interests of the prince and his favourites, subsuming the whole nation under a single household'. The 1649 Act abolishing the office of king declared that to have power in 'any single person' was 'unnecessary, burdensome, and dangerous to the liberty, safety and public interest of the people'.[73] When Marchamont Nedham opposed proposals to make Cromwell king he argued it was 'usual in free-States to be more tender of the public in all their decrees, than of particular interests: whereas the case is otherwise in a monarchy'.[74]

We know that in many cultures the distinction between the public and private is a gendered one. This is not to endorse the simple linear narrative of an increasing separation between the 'public' and the 'private' spheres in the modern world, with women remorselessly confined to a private or domestic sphere. Most recent scholarship has made such an account untenable, and throughout this book we have shown that 'public' and 'private' are contested concepts, deployed in complex fashion in political argument; while the household was both the site of private intimacy and the grounds for public agency for both men and women.[75] Nonetheless the mid-seventeenth century, like other periods of particular political division, was characterised by an intensified concern with the boundaries between public good and private life.[76] Parliamentarians contrasted their own commitment to the public interest with a selfish, private royalism, while conflicts within parliamentarianism also involved rival claims to virtuous public service. These contrasts were inevitably gendered, for several reasons. The inferior pole in any binary is commonly defined as female, while early modern women were specifically associated with privacy in the sense of secrecy or conspiracy (Lady Aubigny was the classic civil war example of this). Notwithstanding the undoubted influence of many women in religious and political affairs, the classically derived rhetorical contrast between a male polity and a household of men and women worked with the grain of parliamentarian political practice in the male arenas of army, council and committee. This chapter has sought to show how the profound crisis of the English revolution was explained and experienced in gendered language; political trauma unleashed profound anxieties about the stability of gender identities and hierarchies. Parliamentarian struggles to police the boundaries between the public and the private were also attempts to reassert the proper roles of women and men.

5

CONCLUSION

A narrative can be constructed in which the English revolution inaugurates a modern political world. A king was executed in the name of his people, and parliament declared the people the source of all just power. Political authority was no longer founded on parallels with patriarchal power; it was not to be taken for granted or accepted as god-given, but rather founded on abstract principles. The process culminated in John Locke's stress on individual natural rights and government based on contract.[1] The place of gender in such narratives is complex and disputed. The most creative theorist, Thomas Hobbes, who claimed to be founding a science of politics argued that both marriage and the state were artificial creations in which obedience was not sanctioned by God, but owed by convention, based on self-interest. In Hobbes's state of nature, the power of mothers was dominant; fatherhood, like sovereignty, was a (necessary) social and political construction.[2] In contrast, Locke, writing against Filmer, reasserted a radical separation between familial and political power:

> If this be the original grant of government and the foundation of monarchical power, there will be as many monarchs as there are husbands. If therefore these words give any power to Adam, it can be only a Conjugal Power, not Political, the Power that every Husband hath to order the things of private concernment in his family, as proprietor of the goods and land there, and to have his will take place before that of his wife in all things of their common concernment, but not a political power of life and death over her, much less over any body else.[3]

Scholars have drawn radically different conclusions about women's political agency or public role in these narratives of modernity, and about the specific contribution of the English revolution. Hilda Smith argues that when enlarged claims are made by men for political rights (as in the 1640s), there is a greater insistence on absolute distinctions between men and women.[4] It is true that many of the processes (oath-taking, petitioning, exercising religious choice) discussed in chapter three as the basis for extending male political agency could and sometimes did apply to female mobilisation, as well as to the activism of 'mean' men; military service as a foundation for citizenship is an obvious and perhaps crucial exception. So, it is striking how often the same men who argued for radical change were careful to assert absolute, natural distinctions between male and female capacities, often on the grounds of women's inferior rationality, or the fallibility of their commitment to the public good. We saw this with Winstanley, Lilburne, Milton and Chillenden, as well as the anonymous apprentice petitioners. At a local level, research in Staffordshire suggests that it was in the 1650s that the customary liability of women householders to serve as constables was declared illegal.[5] More broadly, the republican stress on a male public world of rational citizens, ideally with staunch and loyal wives, worked in the same direction. All this is to support Carole Pateman's influential argument that a Lockean stress on contract theory replaced a patriarchal view of politics with a masculine 'fraternal' vision in which all women were naturally subordinated to men.[6]

Overarching narratives of women's history have a tendency to lament a lost golden age, explaining how opportunities are stifled and conditions deteriorate, but there is a rival, progressivist account of 'empowerment', rather than victimisation.[7] The English revolution can be located within this narrative as well. The overthrow of Charles I, and the defeat of arbitrary monarchy in the later seventeenth century, can be connected to the challenging reflections on marriage, and female subordination, associated with the 'feminism' of the early Enlightenment. As Mary Astell asked (with tongue in cheek, because as a Tory she deplored the broader political developments):

> If absolute sovereignty be not necessary in a state, how comes it to be so in a family? Or if in a family not in a state? ... how much soever arbitrary power may be disliked on a throne, not Milton himself would cry up liberty to poor female slaves, or pleas for the lawfulness of resisting a private tyranny.[8]

The sharply contrasting narratives, like the ironies of Astell's 'Tory feminism', indicate the impossibility of any neat ending to this book. Conclusions are tentative and provisional.

In the first place it is clear that there were many continuities under the restored monarchy. Gendered political languages had continued force in contests over royal authority or a national church. As we have seen, the fall of the Rump parliament in February 1660 was met with a frenzy of rejoicing and revenge on the streets of London, and in print. With 'Rabelasian masculinity', Cavaliers exulted over vanquished, cuckolded Puritans, as they defeated the monstrous Mistress Rump and recovered a virtuous body politic.[9] In the midst of bitter party strife over proposals to exclude James, Duke of York from the succession, a play written by another Tory woman, Aphra Behn's *The Roundhead or the Good Old Cause*, was staged in late 1681 or early 1682 to warn of the dangers of renewed civil war. The sexual slanders of the 1650s remained relevant; Behn's play was modelled on Tatham's *The Rump* and so again featured a cuckolded Lambert, and a tyrannical, adulterous Cromwell. Lambert had already featured as the knight of the Golden Tulip, eight of hearts in a pack of cards issued in the Tory cause in 1679.[10]

Monarchical politics through to 1689 were partly family dramas. It was Charles II's failure to produce a legitimate male heir that provoked the controversial attempts to exclude his Catholic brother from the throne, and anxious debate over whether his popular, Protestant son, the Duke of Monmouth, might really be legitimate, or even whether his illegitimacy was necessarily a barrier to inheritance. In the revolution of 1688, James II's daughter Mary chose obedience as a wife (to William of Orange) above her duty to her father.[11] So personal and 'private' matters continued to animate political debate, and perhaps they always do. People argued about the 'border between the family and the state' for the rest of the century. Indeed patriarchal justifications of royal authority remained prominent precisely because authoritarian monarchy was still contested in political practice. Henry Neville's *The Isle of Pines* (1668) was part travel-narrative, part 'pornographic fantasy of polygamy' as it recounted the collapse of a patriarchal polity into depravity and conflict. It was intended to demonstrate the absurdity of patriarchal rule and the imperative to separate the state from the family.[12] This fictionalised assault on Filmer was reinforced by heavyweight, theoretical attacks from John Locke, Algernon Sidney and other Whig theorists. As in the 1640s and 1650s, men who in the abstract denied that familial authority was relevant to the state, found it difficult in practice to stop writing about families.[13]

The personal and the public interacted most obviously in discussions of the monarch himself. Charles II's sexual adventures and the broader libertinism of the court were variously regarded as signs of potency and power, or as an effeminate submission to female domination. Fears of royal absolutism in the 1670s were often expressed through attacks on the king's sexual excess, linked to long-standing, sexualised fears of popery. When these criticisms were themselves sexually explicit, opponents could avoid being accused of Puritanism. The influence of the king's mistresses, particularly the French Catholic Duchess of Portsmouth, was condemned by Whigs and others hostile to royal ambition, but more sympathetic politicians drew on mid-century royalist traditions and legacies of exile to praise friendship, loyalty and affectionate relations, in preference to abstract 'public' duty. In this framework, Charles's commitment to his mistresses was an accepted part of political life.[14] Associated with the restored court was a novel male libertinism, a 'theatrically masculine' form of behaviour that challenged conventional notions of civility and gentlemanly conduct, through group drunkenness, violence and sexual excess. Edward Hyde, Earl of Clarendon explained this partly as a product of the family dislocation among royalists in the years of exile and defeat, and partly as a result of 'Hobbist' scepticism and irreligion. It was also a reaction against Puritan discipline, and perhaps a challenge to the stronger state that was a product of the revolution. The reformist, 'civilising' aspirations of the state risked subordinating and feminising unruly men.[15] Despite its characteristic misogyny, this aristocratic 'Cavalier' libertinism might be attractive to some women; Aphra Behn, for example, admired a world of 'honor and oaths, generosity and pleasure'.[16]

But we should not exaggerate the later seventeenth-century continuities in gendered understanding of politics. There is an artificiality, a self-consciousness about discussions of patriarchal power, about sexual politics, and about the relationship between public and private life, that suggests we have entered a different world. As Michael McKeon in particular has argued, familial analogies depended for their force on being taken for granted; once they are explicitly elaborated and defended they lose their power. All familial metaphors had been fractured by the civil war upheavals; they were repeatedly recuperated after 1660 but had been decisively transformed; the 'tacit authority' of earlier monarchs now had to be aggressively demonstrated, and was in turn contested.[17] There was a parallel self-consciousness about the boundaries between public and private worlds, and a persistent anxiety about transgressing such boundaries. Arguments about the status of the Duke of Monmouth as potential heir to Charles II inevitably involved consideration of whether his 'private' family background disqualified him. The 'public' were intrigued by a poem of Katherine Phillips found in Monmouth's private pocket book after his 1685 rebellion. Characteristically, the poem praised private retreat over engagement with a corrupt public world, but was at the same time a critical engagement with that world. If his recording of Phillips's poem was a subtle critique of 1680s politics, Monmouth's armed challenge to James II was a public intervention of the most emphatic kind. In the accounts of his capture, trial and execution, the interactions between public and private concerns surfaced again and again.[18]

By the later seventeenth century a minority view was emerging that it was possible to distinguish 'public conduct' and 'private character', and to argue that disreputable or deviant sexual conduct, for example, did not disqualify a man from political office. One unintended consequence of the religious liberty of the revolutionary years was an emphasis on the validity of the private conscience. For some, again a minority, this emphasis justified more tolerant views of unconventional sexualities.[19] For the most part, however, private sexual behaviour remained significant. Monmouth was condemned as 'perfectly effeminated' by his passionate devotion to his mistress.[20] Indeed a century later, the sexual conduct of the radical politician, John Wilkes, coloured responses to his political campaigns.[21]

Amanda Capern has suggested that a female or perhaps feminised morality gave women a stake in the public sphere in the later seventeenth century, countering male libertinism and unconventional sexual behaviour. In non-conformist bodies and local communities, and as pious and practical authors, women's influence was exerted.[22] Exploring the longer-term impact of the revolutionary upheavals on the experiences of women, we can refuse to decide between 'a history of empowerment and a history of victimization', and also take account of Margaret Ezell's insistence on women's normal capacity to construct meaningful and influential lives within overall structures of subordination. Susan Wiseman's perceptive comment that 'perhaps in isolating women from the men who were around them' we have underestimated their political impact is also helpful.[23] Women as a category did not challenge male domination as such during the 1640s and 1650s. There is no straightforward line from revolutionary petitioners and prophets to modern feminism, or even enlightenment feminism, although inspiring exemplars can quite properly be found. The civil war did not directly provoke women into challenging male power, but it did enlarge their opportunities for influence, sometimes through an extension of their normal roles, sometimes in new arenas, especially religious organisations. This is not of course to suggest that women, from the Fifth Monarchist Anna Trapnel to the royalist Margaret Cavendish, were merely the tools of men. The particular inflections of women's activism, the specific ways in which they were able to speak out and affect developments, were clearly influenced by gendered expectations, restrictions and opportunities. And it remains remarkable how many different women, royalist and Leveller petitioners, prophets and poets, moved to argue for women's agency in more abstract and general terms, in the face of obstruction and ridicule.

The effects were paradoxical. Women's civil war activism had been valued and permitted in some specific contexts, even as more general anxieties about women's public roles hardened into exclusionary positions. We remember that John Cook, the regicidal prosecutor, valued women's godly piety even as he condemned their irrationality.[24] Women's informal and religious influence remained significant after 1660. Within the Quakers, women had real authority, albeit within carefully defined areas, and the movement retained its support for female preaching despite becoming more passive and respectable in the face of persecution. As Margaret Fell insisted: 'whether they be Jew or Greek, bond or free, there is neither male nor female here but they are all one in Christ Jesus'.[25] Among more moderate non-conformists, such as the Broadmead congregation, as in some Anglican circles, women were also prominent. In later seventeenth-century cultural and intellectual initiatives, women addressed gendered identities and challenged masculine domination. The religious pluralism and political debates prompted by the mid-century revolution provided crucial frameworks for these developments.[26]

Mary Fissell suggested that the 'gender troubles' of the 1640s and 1650s influenced medical thinking about men and women, and perhaps contributed to the sharper sense of sexual contrast, the conviction that men and women were utterly different, that has been seen as characteristic of the later-seventeenth century. There are some parallels with the argument of Dror Wahrman about the impact of a later civil war on gender identities. Wahrman posits a rapid and decisive change in the later-eighteenth century whereby gender identities became fixed in accordance with the earlier defining of sexual division. In this 'closure' of the 'potential for imaginable gender play', national crisis – the American war of independence, experienced as a traumatic civil war – had a major part. The war divided those who should be united, and distinguished those who should be similar; it was compared to disorder and division within a family, and so called into question all categories of identity, including gender. Political anxieties therefore contributed to a hardening or fixing of sex-gender identities, as female or feminist assertiveness became more dangerous.[27] I too have argued that gendered identities and gendered hierarchies are central to a national crisis like the English civil war; gender affects how people experience and understand politics, and how men and women influence and are influenced by developments. But the actual causal relationships between political change and profound ruptures in definitions of gender seem complex and elusive; they perhaps work on different chronologies, and it is difficult to connect the seventeenth-century civil war to a sudden and comprehensive transformation in understandings of gender.

What, finally, does a focus on gender contribute to the historiography of the English civil war or revolution? Two brief suggestions can be made. In the first place it complicates attempts to place the events of the 1640s within simple progressive or 'Whig' narratives of British or English history. There is no straightforward connection between opportunities for women's agency in religion and politics, and the most radical initiatives by men. Aristocratic women, female prophets, petitioners and sectaries had a significant impact on the conflicts of the revolution but alongside this (and perhaps in response) there was a distinctly republican masculinisation of politics. The attitudes of individual radical men like John Lilburne and Gerrard Winstanley can be compared to the valorisation of female activism and feminised modes of resistance among some royalists. Second, sensitivity to gender vindicates attempts to ground political history in social and cultural contexts. Political choices are not made simply through rational adherence to particular manifestos or lists of policies; they involve less-easily defined personal and affective questions of passion, emotion and identity. Gender is of course fundamental to identity; so civil war divisions provoked discursive struggles over gender order and harmonious family life, and involved contrasting visions of proper manhood and true womanhood. It was at the same time a most profound, and a most intimate upheaval.[28] We cannot be certain how relationships between men and women were transformed in the long run by the English revolution, but it is clear that we can only fully understand that revolution by paying attention to gender.

NOTES

1 Introduction

1 For further discussion of the points in these opening paragraphs see below pp. 22–23, 120–21, 76; S. R. Gardiner, *Constitutional Documents of the Puritan Revolution* (Oxford: The Clarendon Press, 1962), 377–81; Ann Hughes, *Women, Men and Politics in the English Civil War* (Keele: University of Keele Centre for Local History, 1999), 7; Alison Plowden, *Women all on Fire. The Women of the English Civil War* (Stroud: Sutton, 1998, 2000 pbk), 153.

2 Marcus Nevitt, *Women and the Pamphlet Culture of Revolutionary England* (Aldershot: Ashgate, 2006), 64–65.

3 *To the Supream Authority of this Nation, the Commons assembled in Parliament* (London, April 1649).

4 Joan Scott, 'Gender: a useful category of historical analysis' and 'Women's History' both in *Gender and the Politics of History* (New York: Columbia University Press, 1988), 28–52, 15–27; 'Women's History', 25, is quoted. See also Judith Butler, *Gender Trouble: Feminism and the Subversion of Identity* (London: Routledge, 1990).

5 For the debates see G. Bock, 'Women's history and gender history: aspects of an international debate', *Gender and History* 1 (1989), 7–30; D. Thom, 'A lopsided view: feminist history or the history of women' in K. Campbell, ed., *Critical Feminism: Argument in the Disciplines* (Buckingham: Open University Press, 1992), 25–51. For the comment, Wendy Wall, *The Imprint of Gender: Authorship and Publication in the English Renaissance* (Ithaca, NY: Cornell University Press, 1993), 7.

6 Martin Ingram, 'Men and women in late medieval and early modern times', *English Historical Review* 120 (2005), 732–58, 736. For a range of historical and literary work see Lorna Hutson, ed., *Feminism and Renaissance Studies* (Oxford: Oxford University Press, 1999); for a preliminary brief attempt at such a broad study see Ann Hughes, *Women, Men and Politics in the English Civil War* (Keele: University of Keele, Centre for Local History, 1999).

7 Scott, 'Gender', 46. For a range of stimulating work on the French revolution, see Olwen Hufton, *Women and the Limits of Citizenship* (Toronto: Toronto University Press, 1992); Lynn Hunt, *The Family Romance of the French Revolution* (London: Routledge, 1992); Sara Maza, *Private Lives and Public Affairs: the causes célèbres in pre-revolutionary France* (Berkeley: University of California Press, 1993); Joan Scott, *Only Paradoxes to Offer: French feminists and the rights of man* (Cambridge, MA: Harvard University Press, 1996).

8 See, for example, Keith Wrightson, 'The enclosure of English social history', *Rural History* 1 (2009), 73–82; John Walter, '*The English People and the English Revolution* Revisited', *History Workshop* 61 (2006), 171–82.

9 Ivan Roots, ed., *Speeches of Oliver Cromwell* (London: Everyman Classics, 1989), 34.

10 For some of the debates see Richard Cust and Ann Hughes, eds, *The English Civil War* (London: Arnold, 1997); Ann Hughes, *The Causes of the English Civil War* (Basingstoke: Palgrave, 2nd edition, 1998).

11 For further justification of the designation 'revolution': Ann Hughes, 'The English Revolution' in David Parker, ed., *Revolutions and Revolutionary Traditions in the West* (London: Routledge, 2000), 34–52.

12 There is a balanced discussion in Barbara Donagan, *War in England 1642–1649* (Oxford: Oxford University Press, 2008), 215–16.

13 See C. Carlton, *Going to the Wars: The Experience of the British Civil Wars* (London: Routledge, 1994), and Carlton, 'Civilians' in John Kenyon and Jane Ohlmeyer, eds, *The Civil Wars* (Oxford: Oxford University Press, 1998), 272–305, especially 272–76.

14 The broad impact of the civil war is discussed in Michael Braddick, *God's Fury, England's Fire* (London: Penguin, 2008), chapter 14; Martyn Bennett, *The Civil Wars in Britain and Ireland* (Oxford: Blackwell, 1997), chapter 7; Ann Hughes, *Politics, Society and Civil War in Warwickshire* (Cambridge: Cambridge University Press, 1987), chapter 7.

15 *The Leveller Tracts*, edited William Haller and Godfrey Davies (Gloucester, MA: Peter Smith, 1964), 55; Andrew Sharp, ed., *The English Levellers* (Cambridge: Cambridge University Press, 1998), 120, 122.

16 Gerrard Winstanley, *The Law of Freedom in a Platform or True Magistracy Restored* (London, 1652); quoted from *The Complete Works of Gerrard Winstanley*, edited Thomas N. Corns, Ann Hughes and David Loewenstein (2 vols, Oxford: Oxford University Press, 2009), II, 279, referring to 1 Samuel 30.

17 *To the Supream Authority of this Nation*; Anna Trapnel, *Report and Plea, or a Narrative of her Journey into Cornwall* (London, 1654), 50.

18 S.R. Gardiner, *Constitutional Documents of the Puritan Revolution* (Oxford: Clarendon Press, 1906), 155–56; Edward Vallance, 'Protestation, Vow, Covenant and Engagement', *Historical Research* 190 (November 2002), 408–24; John Walter, '"Abolishing Superstition with Sedition?" The politics of popular iconoclasm in England 1640–42', *Past and Present* 183 (May 2004), 79–123, shows how parliamentary declarations interacted with patterns of popular politics to produce dramatic local actions.

19 Joad Raymond, *Pamphlets and Pamphleteering in Early Modern Britain* (Cambridge: Cambridge University Press, 2003), 89–94; Paul Seaver, *Wallington's World. A London Artisan in Seventeenth Century London* (Stanford, CT: Stanford University Press, 1985), p. 156

20 Tessa Watt, *Cheap Print and Popular Piety 1550–1640* (Cambridge: Cambridge University Press, 1991); Raymond, *Pamphlets*, 160–66; John Barnard and D.F. McKenzie, *The Cambridge History of the Book in Britain, iv, 1557–1695* (Cambridge: Cambridge University Press, 2002).

21 Mary Fissell, *Vernacular Bodies. The politics of reproduction in early modern England* (Oxford: Oxford University Press, 2004), stresses the importance of cheap print to the playing out of gendered tensions in the English revolution.

22 Scott, 'Gender', 42; Diane Purkiss, *Literature, Gender and Politics During the English Civil War* (Cambridge: Cambridge University Press, 2005), 4–5. See also Mihoko Suzuki, *Subordinate Subjects. Gender, the Political Nation and Literary Form in England 1588–1688* (Aldershot: Ashgate, 2003), chapter 2 'Gender and the Political Imaginary'.

23 Michael J. Braddick and John Walter, 'Introduction' in their *Negotiating Power in Early Modern Society. Order, Hierarchy and Subordination in Britain and Ireland* (Cambridge: Cambridge University Press, 2001).

24 Louis B. Wright, *Middle-class Culture in Elizabethan England* (Chapel Hill: University of North Carolina Press, 1935); K. M. Davies. '"The sacred condition of equality": how original were Puritan doctrines of marriage?', *Social History* 2 (1927), 563–80; Jacqueline

Eales, 'Gender construction in early modern England and the conduct books of William Whateley', *Studies in Church History* 34 (1998), 163–74.

25 See Alexandra Shepard, *Meanings of Manhood in Early Modern England* (Oxford: Oxford University Press, 2003), for an eloquent presentation of these arguments. I am indebted to Margaret Sommerville, *Sex and Subjection. Attitudes to Women in Early Modern Society* (London: Edward Arnold, 1995), for the ensuing account.

26 Jean Klene, ed., *The Southwell-Sibthorpe Commonplace Book, Folger Ms Vb.198* (Tempe, AZ: Medieval and Renaissance Texts and Studies, 1997), 21.

27 Genesis 3.16; 1 Timothy 2.11–14. Modern biblical scholars do not agree these were Paul's writings but they were accepted as such in the seventeenth century.

28 William Gouge, *Of Domesticall Duties* (London, 1622), title page, and preface.

29 Erica Longfellow, *Women and Religious Writing in Early Modern England* (Cambridge: Cambridge University Press, 2004), 37–39; Rachel Speght, *A Mouzell for Melastomus* (London, 1617), here quoted from Desma Polydorou, 'Gender and Spiritual Equality in Marriage', *Milton Quarterly* 35 (2001), 22–34, at 24; see also Barbara Lewalski, *The Polemics and Poems of Rachel Speght* (New York: Oxford University Press, 1996); for Southwell see Jill Seal Millman and Gillian Wright, eds, *Early Modern Women's Manuscript Poetry* (Manchester: Manchester University Press, 2005), 62, and Klene, ed., *Southwell-Sibthorpe Commonplace Book*, 20, 80.

30 Quoted in Thomas Laqueur, *Making Sex: Body and Gender from the Greeks to Freud* (Cambridge, MA: Harvard University Press, 1990), 4.

31 Anthony Fletcher, *Gender, Sex and Subordination in England 1500–1800* (New Haven, CT: Yale University Press, 1995), 36–43; Shepard, *Meanings of Manhood*, 47–51.

32 Fletcher, *Gender, Sex and Subordination*, 44, drawing on Laqueur, *Making Sex*. Laquer's arguments have been modified by Fletcher, and by Sommerville, *Sex and Subjection*; Laura Gowing, *Common Bodies: women, touch and power in seventeenth-century England* (New Haven, CT: Yale University Press, 2003); Mary Fissell, *Vernacular Bodies*, 7–8; Shepard, *Meanings of Manhood*, 47–51.

33 Fletcher, *Gender, Sex and Subordination*, 44, 83; Shepard, *Meanings of Manhood*, 56–67.

34 Shepard, *Meanings of Manhood*, 130–40, 151.

35 Fletcher, *Gender, Sex and Subordination*, chapters 15 and 18; Hilda Smith, 'Introduction' to Smith, ed., *Women Writers and the Early Modern British Political Tradition* (Cambridge: Cambridge University Press, 1998), 10–11; Walter Ong, 'Latin Language Study as a Renaissance Puberty Rite', *Studies in Philology* 56 (1959), 103–24.

36 'Introduction' in Jennifer Richards and Alison Thorne, eds, *Rhetoric, Women and Politics in Early Modern England* (London: Routledge, 2007), 3–7, 14–15.

37 Marjorie McIntosh, *Working Women in English Society 1300–1620* (Cambridge: Cambridge University Press, 2005); Pamela Sharpe, ed., *Women's Work: the English Experience 1650–1914* (London: Arnold, 1998).

38 Tim Stretton, *Women Waging Law in Elizabethan England* (Cambridge: Cambridge University Press, 1998), 242, has a useful definition.

39 Amy Erickson, *Women and Property in Early Modern England* (London: Routledge, 1993); Laura Gowing, *Domestic Dangers. Women, Words and Sex in Early Modern London* (Oxford: Oxford University Press, 1996); Stretton, *Women Waging Law*, 39–40, 218.

40 Stretton, *Women Waging Law*, 216 (quoting 'T.E.', *The Lawes Resolutions of Womens Rights* (1632)); see also W.R. Prest, 'Law and women's rights in early modern England', *The Seventeenth Century* VI (1991), 169–87.

41 Gowing, *Domestic Dangers*, modified by Bernard Capp, 'The Double Standard revisited: plebeian women and male sexual reputation in early modern England', *Past and Present* 162 (1999), 70–100.

42 Linda Pollock, 'Teach her to live under obedience: the making of women in the upper ranks of Early modern England', *Continuity and Change* 4 (1989), 231–58; Diane Purkiss, '"Material Girls": the seventeenth-century woman debate', in Clare Brant and D. Purkiss, eds, *Women, Texts and Histories, 1575–1760* (London: Routledge, 1992),

69–101; Danielle Clarke, *The Politics of Early Modern Women's Writing* (Harlow: Longman, 2001), 50–67; Joseph Swetnam, *The Arraignment of Lewd, Idle, Froward and Unconstant Women* (London, 1615), 16; *Ester hath hang'd Haman* (London, 1617), title page; the newsletter writer John Chamberlain is quoted in Wright, *Middle-class Culture*, 493.

43 Gouge quoted in Longfellow, *Women and Religious Writing*, 37; Thomas Smith quoted in Shepard, *Meanings of Manhood*, 74.

44 Sarah B. Pomeroy, *Xenophon: Oeconomicus. A Social and Historical Commentary* (Oxford: Oxford University Press, 1994).

45 William Gouge, *A Funerall Sermon* (London, 1646), 27.

46 Sommerville, *Sex and Subjection*, 61, 67–68.

47 *"Tis not otherwise*: or: *the praise of a married life*. To the tune of *"I'll never love thee more"'* (London, 1617).

48 Shepard, *Meanings of Manhood*, 10, 76–83.

49 Shepard, *Meanings of Manhood*, 97–99, 187, 210–11, 247–52; see also Alexandra Shepard, 'Manhood, credit and patriarchy in early modern England', *Past and Present* 167 (2000), 75–106.

50 Martyn Bennett, *A Nottingham Village in Peace and War* (*Thoroton Society*, 39, 1995).

51 Gowing, *Domestic Dangers*, modified by Garthine Walker, 'Expanding the boundaries of female honour in early modern England', *Transactions of the Royal Historical Society*, 6th series, 6 (1996), 235–45; Shepard, *Meanings of Manhood*, 183.

52 Steve Hindle, 'The shaming of Margaret Knowsley: gossip, gender and the experience of authority in early modern England', *Continuity and Change* 9 (1994), 391–419.

53 Malcolm Gaskill, 'Witchcraft and power in early modern England: the case of Margaret Moore' in Jenny Kermode and Garthine Walker, eds, *Women, Crime and the Courts* (London: UCL Press, 1994), 125–45.

54 John Walter, 'Grain riots and popular attitudes to the law: Maldon and the crisis of 1629' in John Brewer and John Styles, eds, *An Ungovernable People: The English and their law in the seventeenth and eighteenth centuries* (London: Hutchinson, 1980), 47–84; reprinted in Walter, *Crowds and Popular Politics in Early Modern England* (Manchester: Manchester University Press, 2006).

55 Martin Ingram, 'Ridings, Rough Music and Mocking Rhymes in Early Modern England', in Barry Reay, ed., *Popular Culture in Seventeenth-century England* (London: Croom Helm, 1985), 129–65.

56 David Underdown, *Revel, Riot and Rebellion: popular politics and culture in England 1603–1660* (Oxford: Oxford University Press, 1987), 106–11; Natalie Zemon Davis, 'Woman on Top', in her *Society and Culture in Early Modern France* (Cambridge: Polity Press, 1987), 124–51.

57 Both quoted in Richard Cust, 'Honour and politics in early Stuart England: the case of Beaumont v. Hastings', *Past and Present* 149 (1995), 57–94, at 82.

58 Elizabeth A. Foyster, *Manhood in Early Modern England* (Harlow: Longman, 1999), 115–18; Cust, 'Honour and politics'; Ann Hughes, 'Religion and society in Stratford upon Avon, 1619–1638', *Midland History* 19 (1994), 58–84, at 68.

59 Frances E. Dolan, *Whores of Babylon. Catholicism, Gender and Seventeenth-Century Print Culture* (Notre Dame, IN: University of Notre Dame Press, 1999, 2005 pbk).

60 Cynthia B. Herrup, *A House in Gross Disorder: Sex, Law and the Second Earl of Castlehaven* (Oxford: Oxford University Press, 1999), 70.

61 Johann P. Sommerville, ed., *James VI and I. Political Writings* (Cambridge: Cambridge University Press, 1994), 181–82; cf 78.

62 Johann P. Sommerville, ed., *Filmer. Patriarcha and Other Writings* (Cambridge: Cambridge University Press, 1991), introduction.

63 Ibid., 12.

64 Ibid., 138. See also G.J. Schochet, *Patriarchalism in Political Thought* (Oxford: Blackwell, 1975).

65 Sommerville, ed., *King James VI and I*, 136 (March 1604).

66 Anne McLaren, 'Monogamy, polygamy, and the true state: James I's rhetoric of Empire', *History of Political Thought* 25 (2004), 446–80.

67 Richard Cust, *Charles I. A Political Life* (Harlow: Longman, 2005), 148–60; Karen Britland, *Drama at the Courts of Queen Henrietta Maria* (Cambridge: Cambridge University Press, 2006); Kevin Sharpe, 'Van Dyck, the royal image and the Caroline court' in Karen Hearn, ed., *Van Dyck and Britain* (London: Tate Publishing, 2009), 14–23; Sharpe, *Image Wars. Promoting Kings and Commonwealths in England 1603–1660* (London: Yale University Press, 2010), 176–77, 207.

68 Barbara Kiefer Lewalski, *Writing Women in Jacobean England* (Cambridge, MA: Harvard University Press, 1993), 103.

69 For female cultural and political activities at court see Clare McManus, ed., *Women and Culture at the Courts of the Stuart Queens* (Basingstoke: Palgrave, 2003); *The Diaries of Lady Anne Clifford*, edited D.J.H. Clifford (Stroud: Alan Sutton, 1990), 45; Lewalski, *Writing Women*, 125–35.

70 Alastair Bellany, *The Politics of Court Scandal in Early Modern England: News Culture and the Overbury Affair 1603–1660* (Cambridge: Cambridge University Press, 2002), offers a vivid, comprehensive account of the scandal.

71 This account is taken from Bellany, *Politics of Court Scandal*, 50–79.

72 Ibid., 148–49, 164–65, 179.

73 Bellany, *Politics of Court Scandal*, 257; Alastair Bellany and Andrew McRae, eds, *Early Stuart Libels: an edition of poetry from manuscript sources*, *Early Modern Literary Studies*, Text Series I (2005) http://purl.oclc.org/emls/texts/libels/

74 Cust, *Charles I*, 150.

75 Ibid., 179, citing the work of John Scally.

76 Herrup, *A House in Gross Disorder* deals with this case.

77 Bellany and McRae, eds, *Early Stuart Libels*, no. R5.

78 Roger A. Mason, ed., *John Knox. On Rebellion* (Cambridge: Cambridge University Press, 1994), 23.

79 *Sir Thomas Smith, De Republica Anglorum*, edited Mary Dewar (Cambridge: Cambridge University Press, 1982), 54.

80 Cf. Ann Hughes, '"A lunatick revolter from loyalty": the Death of Rowland Wilson and the English Revolution', *History Workshop Journal* 61 (2006), 192–204; Karen Harvey and Alexandra Shepard, 'What have historians done with masculinity? Reflections on five centuries of British history, circa 1500–1950', and Alexandra Shepard, 'From anxious patriarchs to refined gentlemen? Manhood in Britain, circa 1500–1700', both in *Journal of British Studies* 44 (2005), 274–80, 281–95.

81 Peter Lake and Steve Pincus, 'Rethinking the public sphere in early modern England', *Journal of British Studies* 45 (2006), 270–92, at 275.

82 Paula R. Backscheider, 'Introduction' in Backscheider and Timothy Dykstal, eds, *The Intersections of the Public and the Private Spheres in Early Modern England* (Special Issue of *Prose Studies*, 18/3 (December 1995)), 1–21, 1.

83 Richard Tuck, *Philosophy and Government 1572–1651* (Cambridge: Cambridge University Press, 1993), 260–61, where it is argued that patriarchal theories were directed against the Aristotelian distinction between the household and the polity; Mary Beth Norton, *Founding Mothers and Fathers. Gendered Power and the Forming of American Society* (New York: Knopf, 1966), 8–11, 19–24. I am grateful to Mike Braddick for the Norton reference.

84 Anne McLaren, *Political Culture in the Reign of Elizabeth I* (Cambridge: Cambridge University Press, 1999).

85 Sommerville, ed., *King James VI and I*, 42 (from *Basilikon Doron*, first published in 1598).

86 Sommerville, ed., *Filmer*, 96; Filmer, 'In Praise of the Vertuous Wife', from Margaret Ezell, *The Patriarch's Wife. Literary Evidence and the History of the Family* (Chapel Hill: North Carolina University Press, 1987), 183.

87 Ezell, *The Patriarch's Wife*.

88 Leonore Davidoff, 'Regarding Some "Old Husbands'" Tales: Public and Private in Feminist History' in Davidoff, *Worlds Between. Historical Perspectives on Gender and Class* (Oxford: Polity and Blackwell, 1995), 227–76, at 241–42.

89 Erica Longfellow, 'Public, Private, and the Household in Early Seventeenth-Century England', *Journal of British Studies* 45 (2006), 313–34.
90 Winstanley, *Law of Freedom*, in *Complete Works*, edited Corns et al., 312, 324–28. See further chapter three.

2 Women and war

1 *Strange Newes from Warwicke* (London, 1642), printed publication date 23 November 1642; Ann Hughes, *Politics, Society and Civil War in Warwickshire* (Cambridge: Cambridge University Press, 1987), 204, for Wright.
2 National Archives, SP28/253B, unfoliated, evidence to the sub-committee of accounts.
3 F.P. Verney, ed., *Memoirs of the Verney Family* (4 vols, London, 1892), II, 287.
4 *Strange Newes*, 5–6.
5 Ibid., 7.
6 Amanda Capern, *The Historical Study of Women. England 1500–1700* (Basingstoke: Palgrave Macmillan, 2008), 237.
7 *Mercurius Aulicus* 3–10 September 1643, 499–500; *Mercurius Britanicus* 12–19 September 1643, 27.
8 Anne Bradstreet, 'A Dialogue between Old England and New', quoted in Kate Chedgzoy, *Women's Writing in the British Atlantic World* (Cambridge: Cambridge University Press, 2007), 129.
9 Keith Wrightson, *Earthly Necessities. Economic Lives in Early Modern Britain* (New Haven, CT: Yale University Press, 2000), 229–30. The figures are 5.23m in 1651 and 5.06m in 1701. Cf Christopher Durston, *The Family in the English Revolution* (Oxford: Blackwell, 1989), 115. Some estimates suggest that births rose in the earlier 1640s but the records are very patchy.
10 For marriage legislation see chapter four.
11 Martyn Bennett, *The Civil Wars Experienced. Britain and Ireland 1638–1661* (London: Routledge, 2000), 97.
12 'A pastorall' quoted in Chedgzoy, *Women's Writing*, 142.
13 *Historical Manuscripts Commission* IV, Appendix, 267.
14 Robert Tittler, 'Money-lending in the West Midlands: the activities of Joyce Jefferies, 1638–49', *Historical Research* 67 (1994), 249–63, especially 255; C. Carlton, *Going to the Wars: The Experience of the British Civil Wars* (London: Routledge, 1994), 296.
15 The most recent account is Steve Hindle, 'Dearth and the English revolution: the harvest crisis of 1647–50', *Economic History Review* New Series 61 (2008), 64–98, at 68–69.
16 Hughes, *Politics, Society and Civil War*, 277.
17 *Quarter Sessions Order Book Michaelmas 1637–Epiphany 1650*, edited S.C. Ratcliff and H.C. Johnson (Warwick County Records, II, 1936), 142, 199–200, 251.
18 Bennett, *Civil Wars Experienced*, 30, 119; Michael J. Braddick, *The Nerves of State: Taxation and the Financing of the English State 1558–1714* (Manchester: Manchester University Press, 1996), 99, 222–24.
19 *A Blazing Starre Seene in the West* (London, 1642).
20 N. Wallington, *Historical Notices*, edited R. Webb (2 vols, London, 1869), II, 171, quoted in Carlton, *Going to the Wars*, 256.
21 For examples see *Perfect Occurrences* 2nd week, ending 16 January 1646; *Perfect Occurrences*, 22nd week ending 29 May 1646: E339 (5).
22 On rape and sexual assault see Carlton, *Going to the Wars*, 292–94; Ian Gentles, *The New Model Army* (Oxford: Blackwell, 1992), 133; Barbara Donagan, *War in England 1642–1649* (Oxford: Oxford University Press, 2008), 163–64, 185; Margaret Griffin, *Regulating Religion and Morality in the King's Armies, 1639–1646* (Leiden: Brill, 2004), 104, 124, 166. See also Donagan, 'Codes and Conduct in the English Civil War', *Past and Present* 118 (1988), 65–95.

23 Mark Stoyle, *Soldiers and Strangers. An Ethnic History of the English Civil War* (New Haven, CT: Yale University Press, 2005), 297n.

24 Marcus Nevitt, *Women and the Pamphlet Culture of Revolutionary England 1640–1660* (Aldershot: Ashgate, 2006), 102–12; Donagan, *War in England*, 105.

25 *A True Discovery of a Woman's Wickednesse* (London, 1642), printed date 19 November, 4–5.

26 *England's Monument of Mercies in her Miraculous Preservations from Manifold Plots, Conspiracies, Contrivances and attempts of forraigne and home-bred treacherous Enemies against the Parliament* (London, 1646); *Oxford Dictionary of National Biography*; Edward Hyde, Earl of Clarendon, *History of the Rebellion*, edited W.D. Macray (6 vols, Oxford: Clarendon Press, 1888), V, 19–20. For Fanshawe see chapter three below.

27 Jack Binns, ed., *The Memoirs and Memorials of Sir Hugh Cholmley of Whitby 1600–1657*, Yorkshire Archaeological Society, 153 (published in 2000, for 1997 and 1998), 105, 117; Alison Plowden, *Women all on Fire. The Women of the English Civil War* (Stroud: Sutton, 2000, pbk), 122–23.

28 Ian Atherton, 'An Account of Herefordshire in the First Civil War', *Midland History* 21 (1996), 136–55, at 144–45.

29 Verney, ed., *Memoirs of the Verney Family*, 199–204; Durston, *Family*, II 145.

30 Roger Hayden, ed., *The Records of a Church of Christ in Bristol, 1640–1687* (Bristol Record Society, 27, 1974), 293.

31 Chris Cleveland, 'The London Trained Bands and the English Civil War', MRes thesis (Keele University, 2006), 88.

32 *Mercurius Aulicus*, 13–19 August 1643, 444–45. I am grateful to Anne Laurence for this reference.

33 Randle Holme's diary 10 October 1645, quoted at: www.channel4.com/history/microsites/H/history/war/cost5.html.

34 *Historical Manuscripts Commission*, IV, Appendix, 263.

35 Ivor Carr and Ian Atherton, eds, *The Civil War in Staffordshire in the Spring of 1646: Sir William Brereton's Letter Book* (Collections for a History of Staffordshire, 4th series, 21, 2007), 356.

36 The National Archives, SP28/36/255–59; SP28/253B; Hughes, *Politics, Society and Civil War*, 215–16.

37 Plowden, *Women all on Fire*, 39–59; Jacqueline Eales, *Puritans and Roundheads: the Harleys of Brampton Bryan and the outbreak of the English Civil War* (Cambridge: Cambridge University Press, 1990), 173.

38 Donagan, *War in England*, 237; *Tracts Relating to Military Proceedings in Lancashire during the Great Civil War* (Chetham Society, II, 1844), 160–67, 184; Katharine A. Walker, 'The military activities of Charlotte de la Tremouille, Countess of Derby during the civil war and interregnum', *Northern History* 34 (2001), 47–64; Plowden, *Women all on Fire*, 96–110.

39 *Mercurius Aulicus*, 27 August–2 September 1643, 471–72. Phipps was an active member of parliament's administration: Hughes, *Politics, Society and Civil War*, 197.

40 *Mercurius Aulicus*, 6–13 August 1643, 435.

41 Donagan, *War in England*, 297–303.

42 Carr and Atherton, eds, *Civil War in Staffordshire*, 280–92, 319.

43 Donagan, *War in England*, 339–46; 'The Diary of Isabella, wife of Sir Roger Twysden', *Archaeologia Cantiana* 51 (1939), 125.

44 Griffin, *Regulating Religion*, 166–67.

45 Mark Stoyle, 'The Road to Farndon Field: Explaining the Massacre of the Royalist Women at Naseby', *English Historical Review* 133 (2008), 895–923. The reference to England is precise; there were more terrible massacres of women and men in Ireland and Scotland.

46 *Englands Monument of Mercies*, paragraph 42.

47 *Extraordinary News from Colonel John Barker* (London, 1644); Donagan, *War in England*, 202, 209; Stoyle, *Soldiers and Strangers*, 51.

48 For witchcraft and the war see Stoyle, 'Road to Farndon Field'; Malcolm Gaskill, 'Witchcraft and Evidence in Early Modern England', *Past and Present* 198 (February 2008), 33–70; Diane Purkiss, 'Desire and its Deformities: Fantasies of Witchcraft in the English Civil War', *Journal of Medieval and Early Modern Studies* 27 (1997), 103–32; Purkiss, *The English Civil War. A People's History* (London: Harper Press, 2006), 375–88 (quotation at 380); Malcolm Gaskill, *Witchfinders: a seventeenth-century English tragedy* (London: John Murray, 2005).

49 Geoff Hudson, 'Negotiating for Blood Money: war widows and the courts in seventeenth century England', in Jenny Kermode and Garthine Walker, eds, *Women, Crime and the Courts* (London: UCL Press, 1994), 146–69; David Appleby, 'Unnecessary persons? Maimed soldiers and war widows in Essex, 1642–62', *Essex Archaeology and History* 32 (2001), 209–21, at 213–15.

50 East Kent Archives Centre, Dover, Sa/C1, Sandwich Letter Book fols 128v, 129v, 132v; Centre for Kentish Studies, Maidstone, U3/12/8/1, Vestry Minutes, Sandwich St Peters.

51 Anne Laurence, '"This sad and deplorable condition": an attempt towards recovering an account of the sufferings of northern clergy families in the 1640s and 1650s', *Life and Thought in the Northern Church c. 1100–c. 1700*, edited Diana Wood (*Studies in Church History. Subsidia*, 12, 1999), 465–88.

52 *To the Supreme Authority of the Commonwealth, the Parliament of England* (London, 1650).

53 Margaret Ezell, *The Patriarch's Wife. Literary Evidence and the History of the Family* (Chapel Hill: North Carolina University Press, 1987), 130; Ann Hughes, 'William Dugdale and the Civil War' in Christopher Dyer and Catherine Richardson, eds, *William Dugdale, Historian, 1605–1686* (Woodbridge: The Boydell Press, 2009), 51–65, at 59.

54 D.H. Pennington and I.A. Roots, eds, *The Committee at Stafford 1643–1645* (Staffordshire Record Society and Manchester University Press, 1957), 100–101, 157.

55 Ibid., 38, 48–49, 60, 141, 264.

56 Ibid., 142, 247, 254, 280–81.

57 Verney, ed., *Memoirs of the Verney Family*, II, 239–40.

58 Ibid., 246, 255, 248.

59 Ibid., 249, 256–57, 263, 278.

60 Ibid., 292–93, 295–96, 304–6.

61 Ibid., 307–10, 413–14.

62 *Calendar of the Committee for Compounding* IV, 3043–44: proceedings in 1652–53. I am grateful to Anne Laurence for this reference.

63 Margaret Cavendish, 'A True Relation of my Birth, Breeding and Life' in her *Natures Pictures* (London, 1656), 368–91, at 379–80.

64 Katie Whitaker, *Mad Madge. Margaret Cavendish, Duchess of Newcastle, Royalist, Writer and Romantic* (London: Chatto and Windus, 2003), 86, 131–32; Margaret Cavendish, *The Life of William Cavendish, Duke of Newcastle*, edited C.H. Firth (London: Routledge, 1906), 116; *Calendar of the Committee for Compounding*, 1732–37.

65 For this account see Ann Hughes and Julie Sanders, 'Disruptions and evocations of family amongst royalist exiles' in Philip Major, ed., *Literatures of Exile in the English Revolution and its Aftermath, 1640–1690* (Aldershot: Ashgate, 2010), 45–63.

66 *The Memoirs of Anne, Lady Halkett, and Ann, Lady Fanshawe*, edited John Loftis (Oxford: Clarendon Press, 1979), 133–35.

67 *Journals of the House of Commons*, VI, 158; *A Perfect Diurnall*, 5–12 March 1649, 2359. See chapter three below for the deaths of Capel and Holland.

68 *Commons Journals*, VI, 202.

69 Andrea Button, 'Royalist Women's Petitioners in South-west England, 1655–62', *The Seventeenth Century* 15 (2000), 53–66.

70 *Mercurius Aulicus*, week ending 3 August 1644, 1110.

71 *Mercurius Aulicus*, week ending 24 August 1644, 1127–28; also quoted in Jerome de Groot, *Royalist Identities* (Basingstoke: Palgrave Macmillan, 2004), 118.

72 *Mercurius Aulicus*, week ending 14 September 1644, 1155. The debate is reported under 8 September, which was a Sunday, but Waller's march to the west was discussed on Saturday 7th: *Journals of the House of Commons*, III, 620. I am grateful to Anne Laurence for this reference.

73 *The Spie*, 26 April–1 May 1644, 110; also quoted in John Adair, *Roundhead General: The Life of Sir William Waller* (London: Macdonald, 1969), 236.

74 *Mercurius Britanicus*, 29 April–6 May 1644, 266.

75 Carr and Atherton, eds, *Civil War in Staffordshire*, 309, 109.

76 John Milton quoted from *Complete Prose Works of John Milton*, edited D.M. Wolfe et al. (8 vols, New Haven, CT: Yale University Press, 1953–82), IV, Part I, 625.

77 Warwick County Record Office, CR2017/C1/24; *Historical Manuscript Commission*, IV. 259; CR2017/C2/131. Purkiss, *English Civil War*, 166–72, 184–85.

78 *Mercurius Aulicus*, week ending 10 August 1644, 115.

79 Warwick County Record Office, CR 2017/C2/ 154; *Historical Manuscripts Commission*, IV, Appendix, 261.

80 British Library Add MS 29,570 f. 81.

81 Binns, ed., *Memoirs and Memorials*, 105.

82 *The Poetry of Anna Matilda ... to which are added Recollections ... written by General Sir William Waller* (London, 1788), 127–28, 105; Adair, *Roundhead General*, 252–53, 256.

83 Beinecke Library, Yale University, Osborn Ms b 221, 8–9, 13; David Underdown, *A Freeborn People. Politics and the Nation in the Seventeenth Century* (Oxford: Oxford University Press, 1996), 110; Elizabeth Clarke, 'Elizabeth Jekyll's Spiritual Diary: Private Manuscript or Political Document', *English Manuscript Studies* 9 (2000) [Peter Beal and Margaret Ezell, eds, *Writings by Early Modern Women*], 218–37. I am grateful to Sue Wiseman for discussion of Jekyll.

84 'Diary of Isabella, wife of Sir Roger Twysden', 122. See Adam Smyth, 'Almanacs, Annotators, and Life-Writing in Early Modern England', *English Literary Renaissance* 38 (2008), 200–44, at 230 and 237.

85 Arnold Hunt, 'The Books, Manuscripts and Literary Patronage of Mrs Anne Sadleir (1585–1670)' in Victoria E. Burke and Jonathan Gibson, eds, *Early Modern Women's Manuscript Writing* (Aldershot: Ashgate, 2004), 205–36.

86 Margaret J.M. Ezell, 'The laughing tortoise: speculations on manuscript sources and women's book history', *English Literary Renaissance* 38 (2008), 331–55.

87 I draw here on Ann Hughes, 'Gender and Politics in Leveller Literature' in Susan D. Amussen and Mark A. Kishlansky, eds, *Political Culture and Cultural Politics in Early Modern England* (Manchester: Manchester University Press, 1995), 162–88. Important accounts of female petitioning include Patricia Higgins, 'The reactions of women, with special reference to women petitioners' in Brian Manning, ed., *Politics, Religion and the English Civil War* (London: Edward Arnold, 1973), 179–224; Ann Marie McIntee, '"The [Un]civill-sisterhood of Oranges and Lemons": female petitioners and demonstrators, 1642–53', *Prose Studies* 14 (1991), 92–111; Sharon Achinstein, 'Women on Top in the Pamphlet Literature of the English Revolution', *Women's Studies* 24 (1994), 131–63, reprinted in Lorna Hutson, ed., *Feminism and Renaissance Studies* (Oxford: Oxford University Press, 1999), 339–75; Susan Wiseman, '"Adam, the Father of all Flesh", Porno-Political Rhetoric and Political Theory in and after the English Civil War', *Prose Studies* 14 (1991), 134–57, also in James Holstun, ed., *Pamphlet Wars* (London: Frank Cass, 1992); Mihoko Suzuki, *Subordinate Subjects. Gender, the Political Nation and Literary Form in England 1588–1688* (Aldershot: Ashgate 2003).

88 David Zaret, *Origins of Democratic Culture: printing, petitions and the public sphere in early-modern England* (Princeton, NJ: Princeton University Press, 2000).

89 Higgins, 'Reactions of Women', 185; *England's Monument of Mercies*; *Perfect Occurrences of Every Daie Journall in Parliament*, 20–27 April 1649.

90 Higgins, 'Reactions of Women', 189; *The Maid's Petition* (London, 1647); Suzuki, *Subordinate Subjects*, 151–57; see further chapter four below.

91 British Library 669 f. 4 (57), the bookseller George Thomason has changed the printed 1642 date to 1641, suggesting it was published before 25 March 1642.
92 Higgins, 'Reactions of Women', 187 (drawing on the work of Valerie Pearl); Suzuki, *Subordinate Subjects*, 2, 146.
93 *A True Copie of the Petition of the Gentlewomen and Tradesmens Wives in and about the City of London* (London, 1641).
94 *The Kingdomes Weekly Intelligencer*, 8–15 August 1643; *Certaine Informations*, 7–14 August 1643, quoted in Higgins, 'Reactions of Women', 190–91. Higgins, 189–98, gives a full account of the controversy over these petitions. See also the later comments in *England's Monument of Mercies*, mentioned above.
95 *Mercurius Civicus*, 2–11 August 1643.
96 For the Levellers see Brian Manning, *The English People and the English Revolution* (London: Book Marks, 1991, 1st edition 1976), chapters 9 and 10. This section also draws on my 'Gender and Politics in Leveller Literature'.
97 See *Oxford Dictionary of National Biography* for Elizabeth Lilburne; for details of John's criticism see chapter three below.
98 *To the Chosen and betrusted Knights, Citizens and Burgesses ... The Humble Petition of Elizabeth Lilburne, wife to Lieut-Col John Lilburne* (September, 1646); *To the right Honourable, the Knights, Citizens, and Burgesses ... the Humble Appeale and Petition of Mary Overton, prisoner in Bridewell* (March, 1647). Both petitions were also printed in their husbands' pamphlets: see for example Lilburne, *Regall Tyranny Discovered* (London, 1647), 72–77; Overton, *The Commoners' Complaint* (London, 1647), appendix; Overton, *An Appeale from the Degenerate Representative Body of the Commons of England* (London, 1647); Lilburne, *The Resolved Mans Resolution* (London, 1647), 2–3.
99 *The Kingdomes Faithfull and Impartiall Scout*, 27 April–4 May 1649; John Lilburne, *The Upright Mans Vindication* (London, 1653), 29.
100 *To the Supreame Authority of this Nation, the Commons assembled in Parliament: The humble Petition of divers wel-affected Women inhabiting the Cities of London, Westminster, the Borough of Southwark, Hamblets, and Places adjacent. Affectors and Approvers of the late large Petition of the Eleventh of September 1648* (London, 1649), 8.
101 Katherine Chidley, *The Justification of the Independant Churches of Christ* (London, 1641).
102 *To the Supreme Authority of England* (London, 1649).
103 *To the Parliament of the Commonwealth of England* (London, 1653), Thomason date 25 June.
104 *Unto Every Individual Member of Parliament* (London, 1653), Thomason date 20 July.
105 See Suzuki, *Subordinate Subjects* on women and apprentices, and further, chapter three below.
106 Jerome de Groot, *Royalist Identities* (Basingstoke: Palgrave, 2004), 127, 133 (spelling modernised); and quoted also in Hero Chalmers, *Royalist Women Writers* (Oxford: Clarendon Press, 2004), 50 from *Epibathria Serenissimae Reginarum Mariae ex Batavia Felictier Reduci* (Oxford, 1643) sig C3v.
107 Lucy Hutchinson, *Memoirs of the Life of Colonel Hutchinson*, edited N.H. Keeble (London: Everyman, 1995), 70.
108 William Bridge, *Joab's Counsel and King David's Seasonable Hearing It* (London, 1643) quoted in H.R. Trevor Roper, 'The Fast Sermons of the Long Parliament' in Trevor-Roper, ed., *Essays in British History Presented to Sir Keith Feiling* (London: Macmillan, 1964), 104.
109 See Frances E. Dolan, *Whores of Babylon. Catholicism, Gender and Seventeenth-Century Print Culture* (Notre Dame, IN: University of Notre Dame Press, 1999, 2005 pbk), 98–128.
110 *The Spie*, 26 April–1 May 1644. Lady Aubigny held a profitable monopoly on the production of soap and starch.
111 *Mercurius Britanicus*, 29 April–6 May 1644, 265–66.
112 See particularly Karen Britland, *Drama at the Courts of Queen Henrietta Maria* (Cambridge: Cambridge University Press, 2006).

113 *To the Right Honourable the House of Peers Now Assembled in Parliament. The Humble Petition of Many Thousands of Courtiers, Citizens, Gentlemens and Tradesmens Wives* (London, 1641), delivered according to the pamphlet on 10 February 1641 [ie 1642]. There is no record of its delivery in the Journals of the House of Lords although the queen's journey was discussed several times in that month.

114 William J. Bulman, 'The practice of politics: the English civil war and the "resolution" of Henrietta Maria and Charles I', *Past and Present* 206 (2010), 43–79.

115 Plowden, *Women all on Fire*; Binns, ed., *Memoirs and Memorials*, 143.

116 Newcastle quoted in Andrew J. Hopper, 'The Extent of Support for Parliament in Yorkshire During the Early Stages of the First Civil War', DPhil thesis (York, 1999), 173.

117 *The Kings Cabinet Opened* (London, 1645), 28–29.

118 Britland, *Drama at the Courts of Queen Henrietta Maria*, 195–96; Chalmers, *Royalist Women Writers*, 40–42; Bulman, 'The practice of politics'.

119 Agnes Strickland, *Lives of the Queens of England, from the Norman Conquest*, vol. 8 (London, 1848), 81–82.

120 Jane Cavendish, 'On her Sacred Majesty', quoted from Jill Seal Millman and Gillian Wright, eds, *Early Modern Women's Manuscript Poetry* (Manchester: Manchester University Press, 2005), 90.

121 *Epibathria Serenissimae Reginarum Mariae ex Batavia Felictier Reduci* (Oxford, 1643) sig A2v–A3v, A2r (second sequence), Aa2r, B4v, D2v–D4v.

122 Quoted in Richard Cust, *Charles I. A Political Life* (Harlow: Longman, 2005), 370; for royalist unease at the queen's influence see de Groot, *Royalist Identities*, 127–30.

123 *King's Cabinet*, 30.

124 Ibid., 44.

125 Britland, *Drama at the Courts of Queen Henrietta Maria*, 195–200. For more on the impact of the *King's Cabinet Opened*, see pp. 119, 141–42 below.

126 *A Satyr Occasioned by the Author's Survey of a Scandalous Pamphlet Intituled the Kings Cabinet Opened* (Oxford, 1645), 4–6; by Martin Lluellyn, see de Groot, *Royalist Identities*, 71–73, 124.

127 For Halkett see Loftis, ed., *Memoirs of Anne, Lady Halkett, and Ann, Lady Fanshawe*, 24–25, 23, 27, 29, 59–61; Neil Keeble, 'Obedient Subjects? The loyal self in some later seventeenth-century Royalist women's memoirs', in Gerald MacLean, ed., *Culture and Society in the Stuart Restoration: literature, drama, history* (Cambridge: Cambridge University Press, 1995), 201–18.

128 Susan Wiseman, *Conspiracy and Virtue. Women, Writing and Politics in Seventeenth Century England* (Oxford: Oxford University Press, 2006), 319–33.

129 Chalmers, *Royalist Women Writers*, 104.

130 Laura Lunger Knoppers, 'Opening the Queen's Closet: Henrietta Maria, Elizabeth Cromwell, and the Politics of Cookery', *Renaissance Quarterly* 60 (2007), 464–99.

131 Chedgzoy, *Women's Writing*, chapter 4.

132 Chalmers, *Royalist Women Writers*, 5–8, 26–37, 132 (quoted).

133 Chedgzoy, *Women's Writing*, 140 on the Cavendish sisters' work.

134 Chedgzoy, *Women's Writing*, 135–44. The poems were mostly by Jane, while the dramatic works were jointly written. The Bodleian library and the Beinecke library, Yale, both hold copies of the presentation volume.

135 Chedgzoy, *Women's Writing*, 144–49, 166.

136 For Phillips see Chalmers, *Royalist Women Writers*, 59–68, 108–9; Carole Barash, *English Women's Poetry 1649–1714* (Oxford: Oxford University Press, 1996), 55–59; Phillips's poems quoted from Millman and Wright, eds, *Early Modern Women's Manuscript Poetry*, 142, 132.

137 Chalmers, *Royalist Women Writers*, 18–20, 78–82.

138 Chalmers, *Royalist Women Writers*, 21–37, 46, 131–32, 145–46; Britland, *Drama at the Courts of Queen Henrietta Maria*, 205–6; James Knowles, '"We've Lost, Should We Lose

Too Our Harmless Mirth?" Cavendish's Antwerp Entertainments', in Ben Van Beneden and Nora de Poorter, eds, *Royalist Refugees: William and Margaret Cavendish in the Rubens House 1648–1660* (Antwerp, 2006), 70–77.

139 Chalmers, *Royalist Women Writers*, 22, 131–32, and plate 133; Margaret Cavendish, Countess of Newcastle, *Nature's Pictures Drawn by Fancies Pencil to the Life* (London, 1656), sig A2r, A3v; James Fitzmaurice, 'Front Matter and the Physical Make-up of *Natures Pictures*', *Women's Writing* 4:3 (1997), 353–56; Emma L.E. Rees, *Margaret Cavendish. Gender, genre, exile* (Manchester: Manchester University Press, 2003), 26–33.

140 NA SP24/47 quoted in Hughes, *Politics, Society and Civil War*, 324.

141 Hunt, 'Books, manuscripts and literary patronage', 211–12; Sara H. Mendelson, 'Pakington, Dorothy, Lady Pakington (*bap.* 1623, *d.* 1679)', *Oxford Dictionary of National Biography*, Oxford University Press, 2004 (www.oxforddnb.com/view/article/21142, accessed 12 January 2010).

142 Verney, ed., *Memoirs of the Verney Family*, II, 258–60.

143 'Diary of Isabella, wife of Sir Roger Twysden', 121, 132, 123.

144 E.S. de Beer, ed., *The Diary of John Evelyn*, vol. 1 (Oxford: Clarendon Press, 1955), 61, 76, 185, 203; Durston, *Family*, 119–20.

145 *The Learned Maid ... by that incomparable Virgin Anna Maria a Schurman of Utrecht* (London, 1659), 49–50, letter to D'Ewes, November 1645.

146 Samuel Torshell, *The Woman's Glorie* (London, 1645), 11, 159–60, 225, 228.

147 Carr and Atherton, eds, *Civil War in Staffordshire*, 13. Weston was the seat of Lady Cicely's first husband.

148 Edmund Calamy, *The Happiness of those who sleep in Jesus* (London, 1662), 28–29. I owe this reference to Anne Laurence.

149 [John Collinges] *The Excellent Woman* (London, 1669), also published as *Par Nobile. Two Treatises* (London, 1669), 4, 7, 13, 20–22, 25–27, 31.

150 *Memoirs of the Life of Colonel Hutchinson*, 210–11; cf Durston, *Family*, 117.

151 This section is based on Hayden, ed., *The Records of a Church of Christ*, especially 84, 88–90, 293.

152 Canterbury Cathedral Library U37, 'A History of the Church which was first gathered and settled in the city of Canterbury', ff 1r,13r, 14v.

153 E.B. Underhill, ed., *Records of the Churches of Christ Gathered at Fenstanton, Warboys and Hexham* (Hanserd Knollys Society, 9, 1854), 117, 119–20.

154 Esther Cope, *Handmaid of the Holy Spirit: Dame Eleanor Davies, Never Soe Madd a Ladie* (Ann Arbor: University of Michigan Press, 1992); Peter Marshall, 'Ann Jeffries and the fairies: folk belief and the war on scepticism in later Stuart England', in Angela McShane and Garthine Walker, eds, *The Extraordinary and the Everyday in Early Modern England* (Basingstoke: Palgrave Macmillan, 2010), 127–41, at 130.

155 See Phyllis Mack, *Visionary Women: Ecstatic Prophecy in Seventeenth-Century England* (Berkeley: California University Press, 1994).

156 For Poole's visions see her pamphlets, *An Alarum of War given to the Army* (London, 1649), published in May and incorporating the earlier and shorter *A Vision wherein is manifested the disease and cure of the kingdom* (London, 1649), first published in January. An alternative version of *An Alarum* included more material defending Poole from attacks by members of her former congregation. The best study of Poole is Wiseman, *Conspiracy and Virtue*, 143–75; see also Manfred Brod, 'A Radical Network in the English Revolution: John Pordage and his Circle, 1646–54', *English Historical Review* 119 (2004), 1230–53; Nevitt, *Women and the Pamphlet Culture*, 73–79.

157 Wiseman, *Conspiracy and Virtue*, 144, 160–65.

158 Mary E. Fissell, *Vernacular Bodies. The Politics of Reproduction in Early Modern England* (Oxford: Oxford University Press, 2004), 116–18, 124–25; Wiseman, *Conspiracy and Virtue*, 102–18.

159 Mary Cary, *A Word in Season to the Kingdom of England* (London, 1647). This work was published by the radical bookseller Giles Calvert.

160 Cary, *The Resurrection of the Witnesses, and Englands Fall from (the mystical Babylon) Rome clearly demonstrated to be accomplished* (London, 1648 and 2nd edition, 1653).

161 Mary Cary, *The Little Horn's Doom and Downfall, with a New and More Exact Mappe or Description of New Jerusalem's Glory* (London, 1651), 6–7, 113, 307, sig A3v–4r, A1r–A4v.

162 Anna Trapnel, *The Cry of a Stone*, edited Hilary Hinds (Arizona Center for Medieval and Renaissance Studies, Tempe, Arizona, 2000), title page. The original tract was published in January 1654. For the broader political context: Austin Woolrych, *Commonwealth to Protectorate* (Oxford: Clarendon Press, 1982), 387–89.

163 Trapnel, *Cry of a Stone*, Hinds, ed., 15.

164 Henry Jessey, *Exceeding Riches of Grace Advanced* (London, 1647) sig a1v.

165 Anna Trapnel, *A Legacy for Saints Being Several Experiences of the dealings of God with Anna Trapnel* (London, 1654). For a full account of Trapnel see Ann Hughes, '"Not Gideon of Old": Anna Trapnel and Oliver Cromwell', *Cromwelliana* Series II (2005), 77–96; on betrayal see *Cry of a Stone*, Hinds, ed., xxxii.

166 Trapnel, *Cry of a Stone*, Hinds, ed., 54–55.

167 B.S. Capp, *The Fifth Monarchy Men. A Study on Seventeenth-century Millenarianism* (London: Faber and Faber, 1972), 101; James Holstun, *Ehud's Dagger. Class Struggle in the English Revolution* (London: Verso, 2000); see also Woolrych, *Commonwealth to Protectorate*, 214–15, 388–89; Anna Trapnel, *Report and Plea, or a Narrative of her Journey into Cornwall* (London, 1654), 15–29.

168 Trapnel, *Report and Plea*, 38, 49, 53, 55. Information from the Bridewell records is through the kindness of Professor Paul Griffiths.

169 Trapnel, *Cry of a Stone*, Hinds, ed., 16, 38. The visions of Sarah Wight who moved in similar circles to Trapnel in the 1640s had also been recorded by a 'relator': *Exceeding Riches of Grace Advanced*.

170 *A Legacy for Saints*, title page, sig A2r–v. The preface, in the name of the church of God meeting in Great All Hallows, where Simpson was teacher, was signed by John Proud, elder and Caleb Ingold, deacon (A4r).

171 Trapnel, *A Legacy for Saints*, 23.

172 Ibid., 42.

173 Trapnel, *Cry of a Stone*, Hinds, ed., 16.

174 Diane Purkiss, 'Producing the voice, consuming the body: seventeenth century women prophets' in Susan Wiseman and Isabel Grundy, eds, *Women, Writing, History* (London: Batsford, 1992), 139–58, 144; Trapnel, *Cry of a Stone*, Hinds, ed., xlv.

175 Trapnel, *A Legacy for Saints*, 27.

176 Trapnel, *Report and Plea*, 23–26, 28.

177 Ibid., 17.

178 Nevitt, *Women and the Pamphlet Culture*, 9 (Evans), 10 (Hobbes), 15n (Jessey and Wight).

179 Holstun, *Ehud's Dagger*, 257–304, especially 262.

180 *Calendar of State Papers Domestic 1653–1654*, 393, 7 February.

181 *Mercurius Politicus*, 13–20 April 1654, 3430; *The Weekly Intelligencer of the Commonwealth*, 18–25 April 1654, 229–30; *Certain Passages of Every dayes Intelligence*, 14–21 April 1654, 111; all had very similar accounts.

182 *The Moderate Intelligencer*, 19–26 April 1654, 1383.

183 Trapnel, *A Legacy for Saints*, 59–61.

184 Trapnel, *A Lively Voice for the King of Saints and Nations* (London, 1658), 75–76.

185 For important recent studies of the Quakers see Kate Peters, *Print Culture and the Early Quakers* (Cambridge: Cambridge University Press, 2005) and Catie Gill, *Women in the Seventeenth-Century Quaker Community* (Aldershot: Ashgate, 2005).

186 Hilary Hinds, 'Embodied rhetoric: Quaker public discourse in the 1650s', in Jennifer Richards and Alison Thorne, eds, *Rhetoric, Women and Politics in early modern England* (London: Routledge, 2007), 191–211 at 195, quoting *The Lambs Defence Against Lyes* (1656).

187 Stephen Roberts, 'The Quakers in Evesham 1655–60: A study in religion, politics and culture', *Midland History* 16 (1991), 63–85, at 73–74.

188 Peters, *Print Culture*, 125–29; Patricia Crawford, 'Women's published writings 1600–1700', in Mary Prior, ed., *Women in English Society* (London: Routledge, 1985), 211–34, at 213.

189 Hester Biddle, *A Warning from the Lord God of life and power, unto thee O city of London* (London, 1660), 5,7, 10–11.

190 *To the Priests and People of England* (London, 1655), 3, 6; Peters, *Print Culture*, 140–43.

191 Nevitt, *Women and the Pamphlet Culture*, 160–71; Steven A. Kent, '"Handmaids and Daughters of the Lord": Quaker women, Quaker families and Somerset's anti-tithe petition in 1659', *Quaker History* 97 (2008), 32–61.

192 Peters, *Print Culture*, 135, 124, 148.

193 Wiseman, *Conspiracy and Virtue*, 166; Peters, *Print Culture*, 234–35.

194 E.B. Underhill, ed., *Records of Churches of Christ Gathered at Fenstanton, Warboys and Hexham* (Hanserd Knollys Society, 1854), 186, 193, 211.

195 William Kiffin, *A Brief Remonstrance* (London, 1645), 1.

196 B.R. White, ed., *Association Records of the Particular Baptists of England* (Baptist Historical Society, 1973), Part I, 28.

197 White, ed., *Association Records*, Part II, 55. The text is 'But every woman that prayeth or prophesieth with her head uncovered dishonoureth her head: for that is even all one as if she were shaven'. Like their midlands brethren, the West Country Baptists cited 1 Corinthians 14 (on prophesying) and 1 Timothy 2, especially verse 11, 'Let the woman learn in silence with all subjection.'

198 *Association Records*, Part I, 30–31, 29; Part II, 58–59, 67.

199 Underhill, ed. *Records of Churches of Christ*, 218, 233, 242.

200 Ibid., 163, 172–75.

201 John Rogers, *Ohel or Beth-shemesh. A Tabernacle for the Sun* (London, 1653), 463, 354, 404–6, 465–76; for Avery see Wiseman, *Conspiracy and Virtue*, 200–4.

202 Hayden, ed., *Records of a Church of Christ*, 130–32.

203 Huntington Library Ellesmere MS EL8543; Collinges, *The Excellent Woman*, 36; Wiseman, *Conspiracy and Virtue*, chapter 7.

204 Hayden, ed., *Records of a Church of Christ*, 155.

205 Gill, *Women in the Seventeenth-Century Quaker Community*, 146–48; Mack, *Visionary Women*.

3 Manhood and civil war

1 Hilda Smith, *All Men and Both Sexes: Gender, Politics, and the False Universal in England, 1640–1832* (University Park: Pennsylvania State University Press, 2002), 113.

2 Stefan Dudink, Karen Hagemann and Anna Clark, eds, *Representing Masculinity: Male Citizenship in Modern Western Culture* (New York: Palgrave Macmillan, 2007), introduction, ix.

3 Diane Purkiss, *Literature, Gender and Politics during the English Civil War* (Cambridge: Cambridge University Press, 2005), 231; Jerome de Groot, *Royalist Identities* (Basingstoke: Palgrave Macmillan, 2004); Susan Wiseman, '"Adam the father of all flesh": Porno-political rhetoric and political theory in and after the English Civil War', in James Holstun, ed., *Pamphlet Wars* (London: Frank Cass, 1992), 134–57.

4 I am grateful to Rachel Weil in particular for discussions on this point.

5 Gina Hausknecht, 'The gender of civic virtue' in Catherine Gimeli Martin, ed., *Milton and Gender* (Cambridge: Cambridge University Press, 2004), 19–33, at 19; Bruce Smith, *Shakespeare and Masculinity* (Oxford: Oxford University Press, 1999), 4–5, 99, 103–4.

6 Diane Purkiss, *Literature, Gender and Politics*, 34–37.

7 For excellent accounts see Keith Thomas, *The Ends of Life* (Oxford: Oxford University Press, 2009), 45–60; William Hunt, 'Civic Chivalry and the English Civil War' in

Anthony Grafton and Ann Blair, eds, *The Transmission of Culture in Early Modern Europe* (Philadelphia: University of Pennsylvania Press, 1990), 204–37, at 204–5.

8 William Bridge, *A Sermon Preached unto the Voluntiers of the City of Norwich* (London, 1643), 6, 8–11, 18, 20.

9 Diane Purkiss, 'Dismembering and Remembering: the English Civil War and Male Identity', in Claude J. Summers and Ted-Larry Pebworth, eds, *The English Civil War in the Literary Imagination* (Columbia: University of Missouri Press, 1999), 220–41.

10 See Ann Hughes, 'Men, the "public" and the "private" in the English Revolution' in Peter Lake and Steve Pincus, eds, *The Politics of the Public Sphere in Early Modern England* (Manchester: Manchester University Press, 2007), 191–212.

11 Victoria Kahn, *Wayward Contracts: the crisis of political obligation in England 1640–1674* (Princeton, NJ: Princeton University Press, 2004), 8–19, 107, 280–83.

12 Marcus Nevitt, *Women and the Pamphlet Culture of Revolutionary England* (Aldershot: Ashgate, 2006), 31–32, 39.

13 Edmund Symmons, *Militarie Sermon* (1644) quoted in de Groot, *Royalist Identities*, 92.

14 Brome quoted in de Groot, *Royalist Identities*, 111.

15 *Mercurius Britanicus*, 15–22 July 1644.

16 George Lawrence, *The Debauched Cavaleer or the English Midianite* (London, 1642), 3: the name itself was honourable, but had now become a reproach. Ian Roy, 'Royalist reputations: the Cavalier ideal and the reality' in Jason McElligott and David L. Smith, eds, *Royalists and Royalism during the English Civil Wars* (Cambridge: Cambridge University Press, 2007), 89–111, at 90; for the argument that parliamentarianism was essentially English, while royalism had a broader appeal encompassing the Cornish and Welsh as well as Irish and Scots, see Mark Stoyle, *Soldiers and Strangers. An Ethnic History of the English Civil War* (New Haven, CT: Yale University Press, 2005).

17 John Milton, *Eikonoklastes* (*Complete Prose Works*, III, 344), quoted in Rosanna Cox, 'Neo-Roman Terms of Slavery in *Samson Agonistes*', *Milton Quarterly* 44 (2010), 1–22; George Wither, *Republica Anglican or the Historie of the Parliament in their Late Proceedings* (London, 1650), 39–40.

18 Barbara Donagan, *War in England 1642–1649* (Oxford: Oxford University Press, 2008), is a brilliant account of these matters.

19 *Twenty Lookes over all the Roundheads that ever lived in the world* (London, 1643), A4v; John Taylor, *The Devil Turn'd Round-Head or Pluto become a Brownist* (1642), no pagination.

20 *Cornucopia, or Roome for a Ram-head* (London, 1642) sig A2v.

21 De Groot, *Royalist Identities*, 101–5; Roy, 'Royalist reputations'.

22 *The Soundheads Description of the Roundhead* (London, 1642), 7 (a parliamentarian response to attacks on Roundheads).

23 1 Corinthians 11.14 quoted in *An Exact Description of a Roundhead* (London, 1642).

24 Christopher Breward, 'Fashioning the modern self: clothing, cavaliers and identity in van Dyck's London' in Karen Hearn, ed., *Van Dyck and Britain* (London: Tate Publishing, 2009), 24–35 at 33–35; *A Description of the Roundhead and Rattlehead* (London, 1642), quoted in de Groot, *Royalist Identities*, 105.

25 Lawrence, *Debauched Cavaleer*, 4. For the Midianites see Judges, chapters 6–7.

26 *A Description of the Roundhead and Rattlehead*, 1; John Hadfred, *A wonderfull and strange miracle* (London, 1642), 3–5.

27 Taylor, *Devil Turn'd Roundhead*; John Taylor, *The Resolution of the Roundheads to pull down Cheapside Crosse* (London, 1641), 1.

28 Roy, 'Royalist reputations', 105–6.

29 Edward Walsingham, *Britannicae Virtutis Imago or the Effigies of True Fortitude* (Oxford, 1644), especially 3, 15, 17, 19, 23–26.

30 Purkiss, *Literature, Gender and Politics*, 53–59, 70; Christine Faure, 'Rights or Virtues: Women and the Republic' in Martin van Gelderen and Quentin Skinner, eds, *The*

Values of Republicanism in Early Modern Europe (Cambridge: Cambridge University Press, 2002), 125–37; Susan Wiseman, *Conspiracy and Virtue. Women, Writing and Politics in Seventeenth Century England* (Oxford: Oxford University Press, 2006), 40–44.

31 John Taylor, *The Conversion of a Mis-led, Ill-bred Rebellious Roundhead* (London, 1643), 5.

32 *The Poetry of Anna Matilda ... to which are added Recollections ... written by General Sir William Waller* (London, 1788), 134–35.

33 David Norbrook, 'Lucy Hutchinson versus Edmund Waller: An Unpublished Reply to Waller's *A Pangyrick to my Lord Protector*', *The Seventeenth Century* XI (1996), 61–86, at 80. Cf Laura Lunger Knoppers, *Constructing Cromwell. Ceremony, Portrait and Print, 1645–1661* (Cambridge: Cambridge University Press, 2000), 105–6.

34 Annabel Patterson, 'No meer amatorious novel?' in David Loewenstein and James Grantham Turner, eds, *Politics, Poetics, and Hermeneutics in Milton's Prose* (Cambridge: Cambridge University Press, 1990), 85–101; John Milton, *Defensio Secunda* (1654) and *The Doctrine and Discipline of Divorce* (1643), quoted from *Complete Prose Works of John Milton*, IV, Part 1, 625; II, 247, 347. See also chapter two above, p. 51.

35 Hughes, 'Men, the "public" and the "private"'.

36 *The Memoirs of Anne, Lady Halkett, and Ann, Lady Fanshawe*, edited John Loftis (Oxford: Clarendon Press, 1979), 115–16.

37 Mike Braddick, 'The celebrity radical', *BBC History Magazine* October 2007; John Lilburne, *The Resolved Mans Resolution* (London, 1647), 8, 23. For a fuller account of Leveller portrayals of their households, see Ann Hughes, 'Gender and Politics in Leveller Literature' in Susan D. Amussen and Mark A. Kishlansky, eds, *Political Culture and Cultural Politics in Early Modern England* (Manchester: Manchester University Press, 1995), 162–88.

38 John Lilburne, *As You Were* (Vianen, May 1652), 33.

39 John Lilburne, *The Upright Man's Vindication* (London, 1653), 4–8, 25–26.

40 John Lilburne, *L. Colonel John Lilburne Revived* (London, 1653), 8; *L. Colonel John Lilburne His Apologetical Narration* (London, 1652), 42–43; John Lilburne, *As You Were*, 9.

41 Anthony Fletcher, *Gender, Sex and Subordination in England 1500–1800* (New Haven, CT: Yale University Press, 1995), 96.

42 Carla Pestana, 'English Character and the Fiasco of the Western Design', *Early American Studies* 3 (Spring 2005), 1–31.

43 Jack Binns, ed., *Memoirs and Memorials of Sir Hugh Cholmley of Whitby 1600–1657*, Yorkshire Archaeological Society, 153 (published in 2000, for 1997 and 1998), 61, 105. See p. 53 above.

44 See, for example, British Library Additional MS 31,984 fos 42r–v, 78r.

45 British Library Additional MS 37,344 f. 296r.

46 Ibid. f. 296v.

47 Ibid.

48 See Kahn, *Wayward Contracts*, 138–40, for the discussion of Hobbes's *Behemoth*.

49 For the Countess see *Lords' Journals* 28 December 1646 (British History online).

50 Alastair Bellany and Andrew McRae, eds, *Early Stuart Libels: an edition of poetry from manuscript sources*, *Early Modern Literary Studies*, Text Series I (2005) http://purl.oclc.org/emls/texts/libels/, nos H3 and R6.

51 *Mercurius Aulicus*, 6–13 August 1643, 425.

52 Ian Gentles, 'The Iconography of Revolution, England 1642–49', in Gentles, John Morrill and Blair Worden, eds, *Soldiers, Writers and Statesmen of the English Revolution* (Cambridge: Cambridge University Press, 1998), 91–113, at 101; Ian Roy, 'Royalist Reputations', 95.

53 David Underdown, *Revel, Riot and Rebellion* (Oxford: Oxford University Press, 1985), 180; Ian Atherton, 'An Account of Herefordshire in the First Civil War', *Midland History* 21 (1996), 136–55, at 141–42, 146.

54 Alastair Bellany, *The Politics of Court Scandal in Early Modern England: News Culture and the Overbury Affair 1603–1660* (Cambridge: Cambridge University Press, 2002),

272–73; Mark Robson, 'Swansongs: Reading voice in the poetry of Lady Hester Pulter', *English Manuscript Studies*, 9 (2000), 238–56, at 247.

55 Henry Neville, *The Ladies Parliament* (1647), sig C1v.

56 Richard Overton, *The Commoners' Complaint* (London, 1647), title page.

57 Overton, *Commoners' Complaint*, 13–14.

58 Alexandra Shepard, *Meanings of Manhood in Early Modern England* (Oxford: Oxford University Press, 2003), 6.

59 Overton, *Commoners' Complaint*, 17–20.

60 Kiffin, *Walwins Wiles* (1649) quoted in Wiseman, *Conspiracy and Virtue*, 158.

61 William Walwyn, *The Fountain of Slaunder Discovered* (London, 1649), 7–8.

62 The work was published in February 1651 as *Defensio pro populo Anglicano*; this translation is from *Complete Prose Works*, IV, Part I, 326–27. For a recent account of Milton's Defences see Joad Raymond, 'John Milton, European: The Rhetoric of Milton's Defences' in Nicholas McDowell and Nigel Smith, eds, *The Oxford Handbook of Milton* (Oxford: Oxford University Press, 2009), 272–90.

63 *CPW*, IV, Part I, 327. See Su Fang Ng, *Literature and the Politics of Family in Seventeenth Century England* (Cambridge: Cambridge University Press, 2007), 66–73.

64 *The Law of Freedom in a Platform*, from *The Complete Works of Gerrard Winstanley*, edited Thomas N. Corns, Ann Hughes and David Loewenstein (2 vols, Oxford: Oxford University Press, 2009), II, 312–13.

65 *Complete Works of Gerrard Winstanley*, II, 313–15. For Hobbes, see Ng, *Literature and the Politics of Family*, chapter 3; Victoria Kahn, *Wayward Contracts*, 164–70.

66 Andrew Sharp, ed., *The English Levellers* (Cambridge: Cambridge University Press, 1998), 111–12.

67 See introduction, p. 19.

68 Purkiss, *Literature, Gender and Politics*, 2, 53.

69 Hughes, 'English Revolution'; John Walter, 'The English people and the English revolution revisited', *History Workshop Journal* 61 (2006), 170–82, at 174 and 176.

70 S.R. Gardiner, *Constitutional Documents of the Puritan Revolution 1625–1660* (Oxford: Clarendon Press, 1962), 155–56; *Commons Journal*, II, 387–90.

71 Ordinance of 5 February 1644 for taking the Covenant: C.H. Firth and R.S. Rait, eds, *Acts and Ordinances of the Interregnum* (3 vols, London, 1911), I, 376–78.

72 Guildhall Library MS 4415/1 f. 118r.

73 Walter, 'English People', 179. See also Patricia Crawford, '"The poorest she": women and citizenship in early modern England' in Michael Mendle, ed., *The Putney Debates of 1647. The Army, the Levellers and the English State* (Cambridge: Cambridge University Press, 2001), 197–218, at 205–6 for women taking the Protestation and the Covenant.

74 Anthony Fletcher, *The Outbreak of the English Civil War* (London: Arnold, 1981), chapter 6; David Zaret, *Origins of Democratic Culture: printing, petitions and the public sphere in early-modern England* (Princeton, NJ: Princeton University Press, 2000).

75 *An Humble Declaration of the Apprentices and other Young Men of the City of London* (London, 1642), 3; *To the King's Most Excellent Majestie, in the Parliament now Assembled* (London, 1641); cf *To the Honorable the Knights, Citizens and Burgesses in the Commons House of Parliament now Assembled, the Humble Petition of 1500 poore labouring men, known by the name of Porters, and the lowest Members of the Citie of London* (London, 1641), where the petitioners, describing themselves as 'the lowest and meanest Members of this City', declared 'we have nothing to lose but our lives, and those we will willingly expose to the utmost peril'.

76 *To the Supreme Authority of this Nation, the Commons of England … the Humble Petition of divers Young Men and Apprentices of the City of London* (London, 1649); *An Outcry of the Youngmen and Apprentices of London* (London, 1649), 5–6.

77 *To the Supreme Authority of this Nation*.

78 Mihoko Suzuki, *Subordinate Subjects. Gender, the Political Nation and Literary Form in England 1588–1688* (Aldershot: Ashgate, 2003), 21–24, 135–45. See also p. 61 above.

79 *Records of the Churches of Christ Gathered at Fenstanton, Warboys and Hexham*, edited E.B. Underhill (Hanserd Knollys Society, 9, 1854), 283–84. Of the fifty, twenty-eight were men and twenty-two women.

80 See chapter two above.

81 B.R. White, ed., *Association Records of the Particular Baptists of England* (Baptist Historical Society, 1973), Part 2 'The West Country and Ireland', 59.

82 Details taken from a search of *Oxford Dictionary of National Biography*, Oxford University Press, 2004 (www.oxforddnb.com/view/article/21142, accessed 12 January 2010).

83 Edmund Chillenden, *Preaching without Ordination* (London, 1647).

84 Anna Clark, 'The Rhetoric of Masculine Citizenship: Concepts and Representations in Modern Western Political Culture' in Dudink, Hagemann and Clark, eds, *Representing Masculinity*, 3–22; Robert A. Nye, 'Western Masculinities in War and Peace', *American Historical Review* 112 (2007), 417–38, covers the period after the French revolution.

85 Henry Foster, *A True and Exact Relation of the Marching of the Two Regiments of the Trained-Bands of the City of London* (London, 1643) sig B3v, B4v.

86 *The Souldiers Catechisme* (London, 1644), 6–7, 11.

87 *Souldiers Catechisme*, 18–19; Edmund Chillenden, *Nathans Parable. Sin's Discovery with its Filthy Secret Lurking in the brest of Men* (London, 1653); *The Clarke Papers* V, Frances Henderson, ed. (Camden Society Fifth Series, 27, 2005), 107. This was in 1653.

88 Norah Carlin, 'Liberty and Fraternities in the English Revolution: The politics of London Artisans' Protests', *International Review of Social History* 39 (1994), 223–54.

89 Nathaniel Burt, *For every individual member of the honorable House of Commons* (London, 1649); Burt, *A New-yeers Gift for England* (London, 1653), 12 and unpaginated postscript. I became aware of Burt through Carlin's article.

90 *A Declaration, or, Representation* in William Haller and Godfrey Davies, eds, *The Leveller Tracts* (Gloucester, MA: Peter Smith, 1964), 55.

91 Sharp, ed., *The English Levellers*, 103.

92 The classic debate on the franchise focused on C.B. Macpherson, *The Political Theory of Possessive Individualism* (Oxford: Oxford University Press, 1962); see, for example, Keith Thomas, 'The Levellers and the Franchise' in Gerald Aylmer, ed., *The Interregnum. The Quest for Settlement* (London: Macmillan, 1972), 57–78. For other accounts of Putney: M.A. Kishlansky, 'The Army and the Levellers: the Roads to Putney', *Historical Journal* 22 (1979), 795–824; Ian Gentles, *The New Model Army* (Oxford, 1994), chapters 6–7; S.D. Glover, 'The Putney Debates: popular versus elitist republicanism', *Past and Present* 164 (1999), 47–80; Mendle, ed., *The Putney Debates*; Elliott Vernon and Philip Baker, 'What was the first Agreement of the People', *Historical Journal* 53 (2010), 39–59.

93 Sharp, ed., *The English Levellers*, 109, 113, 122, 129.

94 Ibid., 120, 122. See also the introduction, and for Sexby's later rejection of the father-ruler analogy see chapter four below.

95 Sharp, ed., *The English Levellers*, 106, 118.

96 Ibid., 170, May 1649. See also the remarks of Maximilian Petty at Putney: 'I conceive the reason why we would exclude apprentices, or servants, or those that take alms, is because they depend upon the will of other men and should be afraid to displease them': ibid., 130.

97 Macpherson, *Political Theory of Possessive Individualism*, argued that wage-labourers would be excluded on these grounds; a recent account suggests a broader conception of political rights: Rachel Foxley, 'John Lilburne and the Citizenship of Free-born Englishmen', *Historical Journal* 47 (2004), 849–74.

98 Hughes, 'Gender and politics in Leveller literature'.

99 William Larner, *A Vindication of Every Free-mans Libertie* (London, 1646), title page; William Walwyn, *The Fountain of Slaunder Discovered* (London, 1649), title page, and 11.

100 *A true relation of all the remarkable Passages and Illegall Proceedings of some Sathannicall or Doeg-like Accusers of their Brethren, Against William Larner, A Freeman of England* (London, 1646), 8, 10–11, 16; Larner, *A Vindication*, 3.

101 Phyllis Mack, *Visionary Women: Ecstatic Prophecy in Seventeenth-Century England* (Berkeley: University of California Press, 1992), 68–73, at 72; for a more sympathetic account see James Holstun, *Ehud's Dagger. Class Struggle in the English Revolution* (London: Verso, 2000).
102 *Complete Works*, II, 352–53.
103 Ibid., 357.
104 For Winstanley's life, *Complete Works*, I, 2–20; for the letter to Eleanor Douglas, II, 425.
105 *Complete Works*, II, 290.
106 Ibid., 354, 327, 378.
107 Ibid., 320, 328–29.
108 Ibid., 326, 371.
109 *Mercurius Britanicus*, 14–21 July 1645. I owe this reference to Ann McGruer.
110 Lucy Hutchinson, *Memoirs of the Life of Colonel Hutchinson*, edited N.H. Keeble (London: Everyman, 1995), 67.
111 *The King's Cabinet Opened* (London, 1645), 6–7. There are many discussions of the significance of the revelations in the king's captured correspondence: see Purkiss, *Literature, Gender and Politics*, 67; Frances E. Dolan, *Whores of Babylon. Catholicism, Gender and Seventeenth-Century Print Culture* (Notre Dame, IN: University of Notre Dame Press, 1999, 2005 pbk), 126–28; Derek Hirst, 'Reading the Royal Romance: or, Intimacy in a King's Cabinet', *Seventeenth Century* 18 (2004), 211–29; Michael McKeon, *The Secret History of Domesticity. Public, Private and the Division of Knowledge* (Baltimore, MD: Johns Hopkins University Press, 2005), 482–86.
112 *King's Cabinet*, 38–39, 43.
113 Ibid., sig A3r, A4r.
114 Lois Potter, *Secret Rites and Secret Writing. Royalist Literature 1641–1660* (Cambridge: Cambridge University Press, 1989), 183–88.
115 Philip A. Knachel, ed., *Eikon Basilike. The Portraiture of His Sacred Majesty in his Solitudes and Sufferings* (Ithaca, NY: Cornell University Press, 1966), xiv–xv, 129–30, 31. The most recent discussion of its form and impact, and of Milton's response, is Kevin Sharpe, *Image Wars. Promoting Kings and Commonwealths in England 1603–1660* (London: Yale University Press, 2010), 391–401.
116 Quoted in Laura Lunger Knoppers, 'Noll's Nose or Body Politics in Cromwellian England' in Amy Boesky and Mary Thomas Crane, eds, *Form and Reform in Renaissance England: Essays in Honor of Barbara Kiefer Lewalski* (Newark: University of Delaware Press, 2000), 21–44 at 35.
117 John Milton, *Eikonoklastes. In Answer to a Book Intitled Eikon Basilike* (London, 1649), from *Complete Prose Works*, III, 366, 419–21; for a recent discussion see Purkiss, *Literature, Gender and Politics*, 80–84.
118 Nevitt, *Women and the Pamphlet Culture*, 56–61.
119 John Cook, *Monarchy no Creature of God's Making* (Waterford, 1651), 2, 35, 101. Cook is quoted in G.E. Aylmer, 'Collective Mentalities in Mid Seventeenth Century England: III Varieties of Radicalism', *Transactions of the Royal Historical Society*, 5th series 38 (1988), 1–25, at 13. This pamphlet outlined the arguments Cook planned for the trial but had not been able to deliver when Charles refused to enter a plea at the high court.
120 *Complete Prose Works*, IV, Part I, 428, 380.
121 'The Diary of Isabella, wife of Sir Roger Twysden', *Archaeologia Cantiana* 51 (1939), 130.
122 *Obsequies on That unexemplar champion of chivalry and perfect pattern of true prowess, Arthur, Lord Capell* (1649).
123 *Mercurius Pragmaticus*, 6–13 March 1649.
124 *The several speeches of Duke Hamilton, Earl of Cambridge, Henry Earl of Holland, and Arthur Lord Capel, Upon the Scaffold* (London, 1649), a long account of the speeches also published in Dutch; *The Manner of the Beheading of Duke Hambleton, the Earle of Holland, and the Lord Capell* (London, 1649).

125 Marika Keblusek, 'Wine for Comfort: Drinking and the Royalist Exile Experience' in Adam Smyth, ed., *A Pleasing Sinne: Drink and Conviviality in Seventeenth-Century England* (Woodbridge: D.S. Brewer, 2004), 55–68, at 59 and 67; Angela McShane Jones, 'Roaring Royalists and Ranting Brewers: the Politicisation of Drink and Drunkenness in Political Broadside Ballads from 1640–1689' in Smyth, ed., 60–87.
126 Knoppers, *Constructing Cromwell*, 34–35, 71–72, 124, 129. For an account that sees Cromwell's image as more 'regal and imperial', see Sharpe, *Image Wars*, 505–20.
127 Sharpe, *Image Wars*, 514; Potter, *Secret Rites and Secret Writing*, 194–95; Purkiss, *Literature, Gender and Politics*, 142–44; Knoppers, *Constructing Cromwell*, 48–49.
128 Knoppers, 'Noll's Nose', 21–44; Knoppers, *Constructing Cromwell*; David Underdown, *A Freeborn People. Politics and the Nation in the Seventeenth Century* (Oxford: Oxford University Press, 1996), 101.
129 Samuel Sheppard, *The Famous Tragedie of King Charles I Basely Butchered* (1649), 33, 41; Knoppers, *Constructing Cromwell*.
130 David Farr, *John Lambert, Parliamentary Soldier and Cromwellian Major General, 1619–1685* (Woodbridge, Suffolk: Boydell Press, 2003), 97–103, 154–55; Hutchinson, *Memoirs of the Life of Colonel Hutchinson*, 251–52, 257. In similar fashion, the fact that the republican zealot Henry Marten lived with a woman who was not his wife gave some colour to the sexual satires which sought to discredit his political positions by establishing him as a promiscuous whore-master: Wiseman, '"Adam the father of all flesh"'.
131 *The recantation and confession of John Lambert* (London, 1660); *A brief account of the meetings, proceedings and exit of the Committee of Safety* (London, 1660), 7, 24. There are many other references to Cromwell and the Lamberts in 1660 royalist propaganda: *Cromwell's Conspiracy. A tragic-comedy, relating to our latter times* (London, 1660) updated *The Famous Tragedie*.

4 Bodies, families, sex: using gender, imagining politics

1 See Kevin Sharpe, *Image Wars. Promoting Kings and Commonwealths in England 1603–1660* (London: Yale University Press, 2010), 330–33.
2 Cowley, *The Puritan and the Papist*, quoted in Jerome de Groot, *Royalist Identities* (Basingstoke: Palgrave Macmillan, 2004), 118.
3 *Mercurius Aulicus*, 3–10 September 1643, 487.
4 *Mercurius Britanicus*, 12–19 September 1643, 26–28.
5 *Vox Populi, or the people's rage against the Clergy* (London, 1646), 10; *An Hue-and-Cry after Vox Populi, or An Answer to Vox Diaboli* (Norwich, 1646), 25. As with much slander there is some connection with 'reality' for the membership of the Norwich Independent church was largely female: Dr Williams Library Harmer MS 76/1 (Norwich Church Book), f. 13r for membership in November 1645.
6 Su Fang Ng, *Literature and the Politics of Family in Seventeenth Century England* (Cambridge: Cambridge University Press, 2007), 7; Rachel Weil, 'The family in the exclusion crisis: Locke versus Filmer revisited' in Alan Houston and Steve Pincus, eds, *A Nation Transformed. England after the Restoration* (Cambridge: Cambridge University Press, 2001), 100–24.
7 Susan Wiseman, '"Adam, the father of all flesh": Porno-political rhetoric and political theory in and after the English Civil War', in James Holstun, ed., *Pamphlet Wars* (London: Frank Cass, 1992), 134–57, 142, 153.
8 *A Discovery of Six Women Preachers in Middlesex, Kent, Cambridge, and Salisbury* (London, 1641). This pamphlet was a mixture of obvious satire and apparently factual accounts. *The Sisters of the Scabards Holiday* (London, 1641). This material is discussed in Sarah Toulalan, *Imagining Sex: pornography and bodies in seventeenth-century England* (Oxford: Oxford University Press, 2007); Tamsin Williams, '"Magnetic Figures": Polemical Prints of the English Revolution', in Lucy Gent and Nigel Llewellyn, eds, *Renaissance Bodies: the Human Figure in English Culture c. 1540–1660* (London: Reaktion Books, 1990), 86–111.

9 *The Resolution of the Women of London to the Parliament* (London, 1642).

10 *The Midwives Just Petition* (London, 1643); *The Virgins Complaint for the Losse of their Sweet-Hearts by these present Wars* (London, 1642), actually 31 January 1643; *The Humble Petition of Many Thousands of Wives and Matrons of the City of London … for the Cessation and Finall Conclusion of these Civill Wars* (London, 1643); *The Widows Lamentation for the Absence of their deare Children and Suitors* (London, 1643).

11 Wiseman, '"Adam, the father of all flesh"', 145–48.

12 *The Maid's petition* (London, 1647); *A Remonstrance of the Shee-Citizens of London* (London, 1647). Thomas Patient was a real Baptist leader.

13 *A Case for the City-Spectacles* (London, 1648), 4.

14 *The Parliament of Women* (London, 1646). An earlier version was published in 1640 and condemned as 'lascivious, idle and unprofitable' in the Grand Remonstrance: Gaby Mahlberg, *Henry Neville and English Republican Culture in the Seventeenth Century* (Manchester: Manchester University Press, 2009), 90–91.

15 *An Exact Diurnall of the Parliament of Ladyes* (London, 1647); although often attributed to Neville it is clearly not his work: Mahlberg, *Henry Neville and English Republican Culture*, 93–94.

16 Henry Neville, *The Parliament of Ladies* (1647), especially 12–13; Neville, *The Ladies Parliament* (1647); Neville, *The Ladies, a second time assembled in parliament* (London, 1647), 9, 12; Wiseman, '"Adam, the father of all flesh"', 145–48; Purkiss, *Literature, Gender and Politics*, 59–60, 67; Sharon Achinstein, 'Women on Top in the pamphlet literature of the English Revolution', first published 1994, reprinted in Lorna Hutson, ed., *Feminism and Renaissance Studies* (Oxford: Oxford University Press, 2000), 339–72; Mahlberg, *Henry Neville and English Republican Culture*, 96–101.

17 Henry Neville, *Newes from the New Exchange* (London, 1650), 1–2.

18 *Now or Never, or a New Parliament of Women* (London, 1656).

19 See, for example, the popularity of the body politic metaphor with preachers of Assize sermons: Arnold Hunt, *The Art of Hearing* (Cambridge: Cambridge University Press, 2010), 309–11.

20 Sharpe, *Image Wars*, 392.

21 Mary E. Fissell, *Vernacular Bodies. The Politics of Reproduction in Early Modern England* (Oxford: Oxford University Press, 2004), 157–62.

22 Cowley quoted in Purkiss, *Literature, Gender and Politics*, 50; see also de Groot, *Royalist Identities*, 117–19, 121–22. For the peace petitioning see p. 57 above.

23 Purkiss, *Literature, Gender and Politics*, 61–62, using the work of Neil Hertz.

24 Purkiss, *Literature, Gender and Politics*, 178–80.

25 John Taylor, *Conversion … of a Mis-led, ill-bred Rebellious Roundhead* (London, 1643), 2, 8.

26 Thomas Edwards, *Gangraena* (London, 1646), 64–65.

27 Fissell, *Vernacular Bodies*, 157–62; Purkiss, *Literature, Gender and Politics*, 178–80.

28 [Mercurius Melancholicus] *Mistress Parliament brought to bed of a monstrous childe of reformation* (1648), title page, 4–7.

29 *The Famous Tragedie of the Life and Death of Mrs Rump* (London, 1660), 2 (and passim).

30 Mark Jenner, 'The Roasting of the Rump: Scatology and the Body Politic in Restoration England', *Past and Present* 177 (2002), 84–120, especially 100, 102.

31 Michael Braddick, *God's Fury, England's Fire* (London: Penguin, 2008), 202–3 (for the baptism example), 504–6 (for examples from 1647); David Cressy, 'Lamentable, strange and wonderful: headless monsters in the English Revolution' in Laura L. Knoppers and Joan B. Landes, eds, *Monstrous Bodies/Political Monstrosities in Early Modern Europe* (Ithaca, NY: Cornell University Press, 2004), 40–63; *A Declaration of a strange and wonderful monster* (London, 1646); *The Ranters Monster* (London, 1652), another Horton production.

32 R. Andrewes, *A Declaration of the Barbarous and Cruell Practices* (London, 1642), sig A2r.

33 *A Nest of Serpents Discovered, or a knot of old heretiques revived* (London, 1641); *A New Sect of Religion Descryed, called Adamites* (London, 1641); *The Ranters Religion* (1650); David

Cressy, *Travesties and Transgressions in Tudor and Stuart England* (Oxford: Oxford University Press, 2000), 261–62, 273–79; Williams, '"Magnetic Figures"'; Toulalan, *Imagining Sex*, 243–70.

34 Fissell, *Vernacular Bodies*, 8, 53–65, 118–25, 143–55, 185–88.
35 For Chidley see chapter two, p. 59.
36 Susan Wiseman, *Conspiracy and Virtue. Women, Writing and Politics in Seventeenth Century England* (Oxford: Oxford University Press, 2006), 40–44; Marcus Nevitt, 'Shakespeare for royalists' in Jason McElligott and David L. Smith, eds, *Royalists and Royalism during the Interregnum* (Manchester: Manchester University Press, 2010), 171–93.
37 Christina Larner, *Enemies of God* (Oxford: Blackwell, 1983), 195.
38 David Underdown, *A Freeborn People. Politics and the Nation in the Seventeenth Century* (Oxford: Oxford University Press, 1996), 102.
39 John Walter, '"Abolishing Superstition with Sedition?": the politics of popular iconoclasm in England 1640–1642', *Past and Present* 183 (2004), 79–124.
40 For Winstanley see, for example, *A Vindication* (1650) in *The Complete Works of Gerrard Winstanley*, edited Thomas N. Corns, Ann Hughes and David Loewenstein (2 vols, Oxford: Oxford University Press, 2009), 236–38; for Pordage: Manfred Brod, 'A Radical Network in the English Revolution: John Pordage and his Circle, 1646–54', *English Historical Review* 119 (2004), 1230–53.
41 *The Souldiers Catechisme* (London, 1644), 18–19.
42 *Perfect Occurrences*, 2nd week, ending 16 January 1646 E 506 (1); 22nd week, ending 29 May 1646. E 339 (5).
43 Sharon Achinstein, '"A law in this matter to himself": Contextualizing Milton's Divorce Tracts' in Nicholas McDowell and Nigel Smith, eds, *The Oxford Handbook of Milton* (Oxford: Oxford University Press, 2009), 174–85; Robert Baillie on the debates, quoted at 182; *A Directory of Worship for the Publique Worship of God* (London, 1645), 24–25.
44 Achinstein, '"A law in this matter to himself"'; Milton quoted in Ann Hughes, 'Milton, *Areopagitica*, and the Parliamentary Cause', 200–217, at 203; Diane Purkiss, 'Whose Liberty? The Rhetoric of Milton's Divorce Tracts', 186–99 – both in McDowell and Smith, eds, *Handbook of Milton*.
45 Thomas Edwards, *The Second Part of Gangraena* (London, 1646), 11.
46 *The New Letanie* (March 1647).
47 *Mercurius Politicus*, 25 August–1 September 1653, 2691–95; Fissell, *Vernacular Bodies*, 173–77.
48 Christopher Durston, '"Unhallowed wedlocks": the regulation of marriage during the English Revolution', *Historical Journal* 31 (1988), 45–59; Edward Holberton, '"Soe Hunny from the Lyon came": the 1657 wedding masques for the Protector's daughters', *Seventeenth Century* 20 (2005), 97–112.
49 Ann Kussmaul, 'Time and Space, Hoofs and Grain: The Seasonality of Marriage in England', *Journal of Interdisciplinary History* 15 (1985), 755–79, at 766.
50 Keith Thomas, 'The Puritans and Adultery: the Act of 1650 reconsidered' in D. Pennington and K. Thomas, eds, *Puritans and Revolutionaries* (Oxford: Oxford University Press, 1978), 257–82; C.H. Firth and R.S. Rait, *Acts and Ordinances of the Interregnum* (3 vols, London, 1911), II, 387–89.
51 G.R. Quaife, *Wanton Wenches and Wayward Wives* (London: Croom Helm, 1979), 197.
52 Stephen Roberts, 'Fornication and Bastardy in mid-seventeenth century Devon: How was the act of 1650 enforced?' in John Rule, ed., *Outside the Law* (Exeter Papers in Economic History, 1982), 1–20.
53 Bernard Capp, 'Republican reformation: family, community and the state in Interregnum Middlesex, 1649–60' in Helen Berry and Elizabeth Foyster, eds, *The Family in Early Modern England* (Cambridge: Cambridge University Press, 2007), 40–66, at 49–55. Another woman confessed and four people escaped before trial.
54 Nottinghamshire County Record Office, DD/HU/1 (Lucy Hutchinson commonplace book), 239–40. I owe this material to the kindness of Jason Peacey. See also Jerome de

Groot, 'John Denham and Lucy Hutchinson's Commonplace Book', *Studies in English Literature 1500–1900* 48(1) (2008), 147–63. De Groot associates this ballad with a pamphlet about one Anne Greene who was hung but revived, but this second Anne Greene was convicted in Oxford not London, and for infanticide, not adultery: *Newes from the Dead* (Oxford, 1651).

55 *A Dialogue between Mistres Macquerella, a Suburb Bawd, Ms Scolopenda, a noted Curtezan, and Mr Pimpinello an Usher etc* (London, 1650); see also Fissell, *Vernacular Bodies*, 170–73.

56 Capp, 'Republican reformation', 65; Janet Todd, ed., *The Works of Aphra Behn* (London: Pickering and Chatto, 1996), VI, 358, 415.

57 Richard Overton, *The Commoners' Complaint* (London, 1647), 20–21.

58 Henry Parker, *Observations upon some of his Majesties Late Answers and Expresses* (2nd edition, 1642), here quoted from *Tracts on Liberty in the Puritan Revolution*, edited William Haller (New York: Octagon Books, 1965), II, 185. This is a widely quoted passage: see, for example, Victoria Kahn, 'Margaret Cavendish and the Romance of Contract', *Renaissance Quarterly* 50 (1997), 526–66, at 532; Wiseman, '"Adam, the Father of all Flesh"', 142.

59 Margaret Sommerville, *Sex and Subjection. Attitudes to Women in Early Modern Society* (London: Edward Arnold, 1995), 231–32, 238.

60 Mahlberg, *Henry Neville and English Republican Culture*, 84, 108.

61 David Norbrook, 'Lucy Hutchinson's "Elegies" and the situation of the republican woman writer', *English Literary Renaissance* 27 (1997), 468–521; Purkiss, *Literature, Gender and Politics*, 59–64.

62 Ng, *Literature and the Politics of the Family*, 7.

63 John Hall, *The Grounds and Reasons of Monarchy Considered in a review of the Scotch Story, gathered out of their best Authors and Records* (1650), 22–23, 42–43, 48. Like Milton, Hall included 'obedience to his wife' among the crimes of Charles I: 125.

64 Edward Sexby, *Killing no Murder* (London, 1659), 4, 2; for interesting discussions of Sexby see Holstun, *Ehud's Dagger*, chapter 8; Ng, *Literature and the Politics of the Family*, 109–11.

65 Richard Tuck, *Philosophy and Government 1572–1651* (Cambridge: Cambridge University Press, 1993), 255–57.

66 Milton quoted in Victoria Kahn, *Wayward Contracts: the crisis of political obligation in England 1640–1674* (Princeton, NJ: Princeton University Press, 2004), 198.

67 Ann Baynes Coiro, '"A ball of strife": Caroline poetry and royal marriage', in Thomas Corns, ed., *The Royal Image: Representations of Charles I* (Cambridge: Cambridge University Press, 1999), 26–46.

68 Sharpe, *Image Wars*, 398.

69 Derek Hirst, 'Reading the Royal Romance: or, Intimacy in a King's Cabinet', *The Seventeenth Century* 18 (2003), 211–29; *A Satyr Occasioned by the Author's Survey of a Scandalous Pamphlet Intituled the Kings Cabinet Opened* (Oxford, 1645), 1–3.

70 *Coll Henry Marten's Letters to his Lady of Delight* (1662) quoted in Wiseman, '"Adam, the father of all flesh"', 144.

71 Kahn, *Wayward Contracts*, 195.

72 Kahn, *Wayward Contracts*, 188–93; Ng, *Literature and the Politics of the Family*, 175–79.

73 Lucy Hutchinson, *Order and Disorder*, edited David Norbrook (Oxford: Blackwell, 2001), introduction, xlvii; S.R. Gardiner, *Constitutional Documents of the Puritan Revolution 1625–1660* (Oxford: Clarendon Press, 1962), 385.

74 *The excellencie of a free state*, quoted in Geoff Baldwin, 'The "public" as a rhetorical community in early modern England' in Alexandra Shepard and Phil Withington, eds, *Communities in Early Modern England* (Manchester: Manchester University Press, 2000), 199–215, at 208.

75 Lawrence E. Klein, 'Gender and the Public/Private Distinction in the Eighteenth Century: Some Questions About Evidence and Analytic Procedure', *Eighteenth Century Studies* 29 (1995), 97–109; Amanda Vickery, 'Golden Age to Separate Spheres? A

review of the categories and chronology of English women's history', *Historical Journal* 36 (1993), 383–414; Susan Wiseman, '"Public", "private", "politics": Elizabeth Poole, the Duke of Monmouth, "political thought" and "literary evidence"', *Women's Writing* 14 (2007), 338–62.

76 These remarks are drawn from Ann Hughes, 'Men, the "public" and the "private" in the English Revolution' in Peter Lake and Steve Pincus, eds, *The Politics of the Public Sphere in Early Modern England* (Manchester: Manchester University Press, 2007), 191–212.

5 Conclusion

1 Cf Susan Wiseman, *Conspiracy and Virtue. Women, Writing and Politics in Seventeenth Century England* (Oxford: Oxford University Press, 2006), 171.

2 Victoria Kahn, *Wayward Contracts: the crisis of political obligation in England 1640–1674* (Princeton, NJ: Princeton University Press, 2004), 99, 165.

3 Gordon Schochet, 'The significant sounds of silence: the absence of women from the political thought of Sir Robert Filmer and John Locke (or "why can't a woman be more like a man?")' in Hilda Smith, ed., *Women Writers and the Early Modern British Political Tradition* (Cambridge: Cambridge University Press, 1998), 220–42, at 229.

4 Hilda Smith, *All Men and Both Sexes: Gender, Politics, and the False Universal in England, 1640–1832* (University Park: Pennsylvania State University Press, 2002), 114–15.

5 I owe this point to the researches of Professor Rong Xiang of Wuhan University. The legal handbook, William Sheppard, *The Offices and Duties of Contsables* (London, 1641), 16, insisted that constables should be men and that even when a widow headed a house normally liable for service, she was not to be chosen.

6 Carole Pateman, *The Disorder of Women: Democracy, feminism and political theory* (Stanford, CT: Stanford University Press, 1989).

7 On these competing tendencies see James Grantham Turner, ed., *Sexuality and Gender in Early Modern Europe* (Cambridge: Cambridge University Press, 1993), 7.

8 Mary Astell, *Reflections upon Marriage* in Patricia Springborg, ed., *Astell, Political Writings* (Cambridge: Cambridge University Press, 1996), 46–47; Karen O'Brien, *Women and Enlightenment in Eighteenth-Century Britain* (Cambridge: Cambridge University Press, 2009); Ruth Perry, *The Celebrated Mary Astell: an early English Feminist* (Chicago: Chicago University Press, 1986).

9 Mark Jenner, 'The Roasting of the Rump: Scatology and the Body Politic in Restoration England', *Past and Present* 177 (2002), 84–120. See also chapter four.

10 Janet Todd, ed., *The Works of Aphra Behn* (London: Pickering and Chatto, 1996), VI, 358–59. Behn's play took its plot from John Tatham's *The Rump*, performed just before the Restoration. For the card collection: *The Knavery of the Rump* (1679); the epithet was taken from Thomas Flatman's satire on leading republicans, *Don Juan Lamberto, or a Comical History of our Late Times* (1660, and subsequent editions). See the life of Lambert by C.H. Firth in *The Dictionary of National Biography* (Oxford: Oxford University Press, 1921–2, first published 1885–1901).

11 These issues are brilliantly analysed in Rachel Weil, *Political Passions: gender, the family and political argument in England, 1680–1714* (Manchester: Manchester University Press, 1999).

12 Susan Wiseman, '"Adam, the father of all flesh": Porno-political rhetoric and political theory in and after the English Civil War', in James Holstun, ed., *Pamphlet Wars* (London: Frank Cass, 1992), 134–57, 152–53; Gaby Mahlberg, *Henry Neville and English Republican Culture in the Seventeenth Century* (Manchester: Manchester University Press, 2009), 84, 109, 117–20.

13 Rachel Weil, 'The family in the exclusion crisis: Locke versus Filmer revisited' in Alan Houston and Steve Pincus, eds, *A Nation Transformed: England after the Restoration* (Cambridge: Cambridge University Press, 2001), 100–24.

14 Rachel Weil, 'Sometimes a Scepter is only a Scepter: Pornography and Politics in Restoration England' in Lynn Hunt, ed., *The Invention of Pornography* (New York: Zone Books, 1993), 124–53; James Grantham Turner, 'Pepys and the private parts of monarchy' in Gerald Maclean, ed., *Culture and Society in the Stuart Restoration* (Cambridge: Cambridge University Press, 1995), 95–110, at 108; Nancy Klein Maguire, 'The duchess of Portsmouth: English royal consort and French politician, 1670–1685' in Malcolm Smuts, ed., *The Stuart Court and Europe* (Cambridge: Cambridge University Press, 1996), 247–73.

15 Anna Bryson, *From Courtesy to Civility. Changing Codes of Conduct in Early Modern England* (Oxford: Oxford University Press, 1999), 257–58, 271–75.

16 Melinda Zook, 'Contextualizing Aphra Behn: plays, politics and party, 1679–89' in Hilda Smith, ed., *Women Writers and the Early Modern British Political Tradition* (Cambridge: Cambridge University Press, 1998), 75–94, at 86.

17 Michael McKeon, *The Secret History of Domesticity. Public, Private and the Division of Knowledge* (Baltimore, MD: Johns Hopkins University Press, 2005), xix, 12–13, 111–12, 494; Kahn, *Wayward Contracts*, 107.

18 Susan Wiseman, '"Public", "private", "politics": Elizabeth Poole, the Duke of Monmouth, "political thought" and "literary evidence"', *Women's Writing* 14 (2007), 338–62, 352–57; McKeon, *Secret History*, 519–23.

19 Faramerz Dabhoiwala, 'Lust and Liberty', *Past and Present* 207 (2010), 89–179.

20 McKeon, *Secret History*, 519–22.

21 Anna Clark, 'Wilkes, Sexuality and Liberty: How Scandal Transforms Politics' in her *Scandal. The Sexual Politics of the British Constitution* (Princeton, NJ: Princeton University Press, 2004), 19–52. I owe this reference to Rachel Weil.

22 Amanda Capern, *The Historical Study of Women. England 1500–1700* (Basingstoke: Palgrave Macmillan, 2008), 315–16.

23 Turner, 'Introduction' in his ed., *Sexuality and Gender in Early Modern Europe*, 7. Margaret J.M. Ezell, 'The laughing tortoise: speculations on manuscript sources and women's book history', *English Literary Renaissance* 38 (2008), 331–55, 339; Wiseman, *Conspiracy and Virtue*, 168.

24 See p. 121.

25 Margaret Fell, *An evident demonstration to God's elect* (1660), 4; cf Fell, *A Call to the Universall Seed of God* (1665).

26 Sarah Apetrei, *Women, Feminism and Religion in Early Enlightenment England* (Cambridge: Cambridge University Press, 2010).

27 Mary Fissell, *Vernacular Bodies. The politics of reproduction in early modern England* (Oxford: Oxford University Press, 2004); Dror Wahrman, *The Making of the Modern Self* (New Haven, CT: Yale University Press, 2004), 34–35, 39, 220–25, 238–42.

28 For some insights on these matters see Michael Braddick, *God's Fury, England's Fire* (London: Penguin, 2008), 587–93; Ann Hughes, 'Gender and Politics in Leveller Literature' in Susan D. Amussen and Mark A. Kishlansky, eds, *Political Culture and Cultural Politics in Early Modern England* (Manchester: Manchester University Press, 1995), 162–88; Wiseman, '"Public", "private", "politics"', 356–58; Wahrman, *Making of the Modern Self*.

INDEX